THE GREATEST MYSTERIES ...EVER!

HISTORY'S BIGGEST PUZZLES

AND THE PEOPLE WHO MADE THEM

METRO BOOKS
New York

An Imprint of Sterling Publishing Co., Inc.
1166 Avenue of the Americas
New York, NY 10036

ISBN 978-1-4351-6466-6

For information about custom editions, special sales, and premium and corporate
purchases, please contact Sterling Special Sales at 800-805-5489
or specialsales@sterlingpublishing.com.

Manufactured in China

2 4 6 8 10 9 7 5 3 1

www.sterlingpublishing.com

Editorial & Design by Tall Tree

[THE GREATEST MYSTERIES ...EVER!

HISTORY'S BIGGEST PUZZLES
AND THE PEOPLE WHO MADE THEM

BILL PRICE

METRO BOOKS
New York

CONTENTS

INTRODUCTION

For as long as we have been telling each other stories, people have been captivated and enthralled by a good mystery. In fiction, such stories always come to a neat resolution, when the murderer is unmasked or the hidden treasure is discovered, but we all know that life is rarely so straightforward. Even though we are told often enough that we live in the information age, in which a vast resource of knowledge is available at our fingertips, we are fooling ourselves if we think we know all there is to know. In reality, the world is full of gray areas and enigmas, of unsolved mysteries and unresolved stories, which can fascinate, intrigue, and occasionally annoy us in equal measure.

GRAY AREAS

This book delves into these gray areas to examine the imponderable and sometimes unlikely stories of actual events and real people. Some of the stories are deadly serious, some a little less so, while one or two are out there on the far side of barking mad. There are cases of determined individuals who have struggled against the odds in an attempt to unravel the truth, while in others people have not been held back by the principle of Occam's Razor, which states that the simplest answer is usually the right one, and have come up with all manner of convoluted theories. Sometimes the persistence of the researcher has paid off and a solution to the mystery has been found. More often, the answer to the riddle is either tantalizingly just out of reach or it defies any sensible or rational approach.

MYSTERY TRAINS

The mysteries have been arranged chronologically, but a thematic approach could have worked equally well. There are "Unexplained Events," including strange occurrences, such as the massive explosion in the Tunguska region of Siberia, which have no apparent cause or defy a rational interpretation. Then there are those mysteries with an "Unknown Purpose," in which people have expended a great deal of effort to do something, like build Stonehenge or carve the statues of Easter Island, without leaving us any clues as to what they were trying to achieve.

Some mysteries would perhaps best fit under the heading "Fact or Fiction?" For these, we'll look at people, like King Arthur, and places, like Atlantis, which may have really existed or could have been completely made up, as well as examining the plausibility of contested objects, including the Shroud of Turin, and the existence of mysterious animals like the yeti and the Loch Ness monster. The strange circumstances of several "Missing Persons" including Lord Lucan and Jimmy Hoffa will be investigated alongside several "Unknown People," with questionable identities, as in the story of Kaspar Hauser. One of the most intriguing categories is "Unsolved Crimes," which is made up of those famous cases that have baffled investigators over the years and, in some instances, still resist resolution.

Throughout the course of the book, I have tried to maintain a healthy dose of skepticism over the more outlandish and bizarre claims made by those who prefer

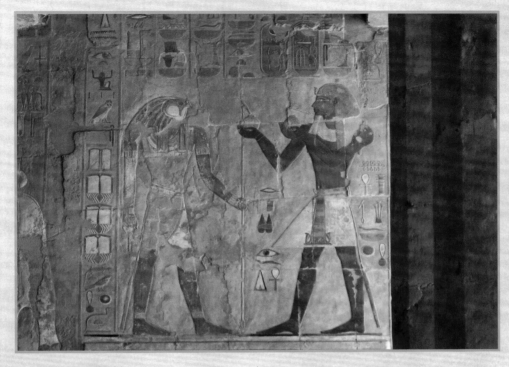

MYSTERIOUS MISSION
A wall painting showing Hatshepsut's trade mission from Egypt to the mysterious land of Punt (see page 32).

not to let the facts get in the way of a good story. By taking this approach, what emerges is that several have more clear-cut explanations than is sometimes made out, while, in one or two cases, supposedly inexplicable events are not nearly as mysterious as they are claimed to be. These manufactured mysteries, as they may be called, usually have more to do with the imaginations of people promoting them than they do with the facts on the ground and, with a little digging, can often easily be exposed for what they really are—the pitches of charlatans and snake-oil salesmen eager to cash in on the public appetite for all things unknown.

NO FINAL ANSWERS
Apart from obvious cases of exaggeration or outright fraud, I'm not about to pretend that I have all the answers to these unexplained events and unsolved crimes. And, in the end, it is exactly this sense of mystery, of the unknown and the unknowable, which attracts us to these unfinished stories in the first place. My intention, rather, is to sift through the evidence and to present the case. Most of the time, there isn't one right answer anyway. So, if you feel inclined, take a look for yourself and make up your own mind. You may be left with more questions than answers, but that is the risk you run by reading a book about mysteries. After all, who wants to live in a world where everything is transparent and where nothing remains uncertain? That would be a very dull place indeed.

WHEN DID THE FIRST AUSTRALIANS ARRIVE?

ca. 50,000 BCE

Clue: The Kimberley rock art appears to be thousands of years old

Main players: Early humans, the first Aboriginal Australians

Verdict: Humans arrived in Australia considerably earlier than previously thought

Even by Australian standards, the Kimberley region is remote. It is located at the top end of Western Australia, separated from the islands of the Indonesia by the Timor Sea. The landscape here is rough and rugged and the climate, like much of the rest of the country, is hot and as dry as a bone, except in the wet season, when torrential rain makes the area all but inaccessible. The Kimberley boasts an abundance of Australia's dangerous animals: spiders, snakes, and crocodiles. But, despite the inhospitable nature of the region, it is also thought to be one of the earliest inhabited parts of the continent. As a result, archaeological research conducted there has the potential to shed light on one of the most contentious issues in the study of early humans: when and how did Australia first become colonized and who were these first Australians?

BRADSHAW ROCK ART

Evidence for early human life in the Kimberley comes in the form of rock paintings, known as Bradshaw art, after the settler who first described them in the nineteenth century. Dating petroglyphs, as rock paintings are known by scientists, is notoriously difficult. Where it has been possible, Bradshaw paintings have been shown to be many thousands of years old, held by some to predate the arrival of the Aboriginal people who live in the region today. Such claims have proved controversial, as they have been used to undermine the ongoing struggle by aboriginal peoples to claim ownership of land (previously taken away from them by British settlers), both in the Kimberley region and in other parts of Australia.

The study of Bradshaw art has shown the difficulties faced by anybody

Tens of thousands of pieces of early rock art in Australia, scattered over an area the size of Spain, are almost completely unknown outside the country.

have braved the criticism, have greatly expanded our knowledge of when and how humans first arrived in Australia.

MUNGO MAN
The fossilized skeleton of the earliest known Australian was found in 1974, near Lake Mungo in western New South Wales. The dating of Mungo Man, as he has become known, proved to be typically controversial. After a lot of argument, he was dated at between forty thousand and sixty thousand years old, at the time pushing the date for the first colonization

attempting to investigate the early settlement of Australia. Studies quickly become minefields of prejudice and political correctness. Perhaps this is why such an abundance of early rock art— tens of thousands have been found across an area the size of Spain—is rarely discussed in Australia and is almost completely unknown outside the country. But this has not stopped everybody. Those of a more determined nature, who

of the continent back by almost thirty thousand years. This is still not accepted by everybody, but there is some agreement on how people first arrived. With no other possible route available, other than a monumental oceanic voyage, it is generally assumed that people crossed the Timor Sea in boats and rafts. At the time this would have been a much easier expedition than the 300-mile (480-km) sea crossing it is today. Up until the end

MUNGO MAN

The fossilized skeleton found near Lake Mungo is at least forty thousand years old.

of the last ice age, about ten thousand years ago, sea levels were considerably lower, meaning that Australia, New Guinea, and Tasmania were connected by land to the Sahul landmass. This was still separated from Sunda, the southeast Asian landmass, by the Timor Sea, but the distance was at times as short as 60 miles (100 km). As temperatures increased and glaciers melted, the sea level rose and any signs left by these first people were covered over. So, if the archaeological objects still exist, it is under 300 feet (90 m) of water.

THE ABORIGINAL GENOME

Physical evidence is, then, unlikely to surface, but there are other ways of investigating the question. A study in 2011 by the University of Copenhagen sheds light on the Aboriginal genome, using DNA taken from a sample of hair collected a hundred years ago from an Aboriginal man in Western Australia. Analysis of the genome has shown that the first Australians separated from other humans about seventy thousand years ago and arrived in Australia twenty thousand years later.

This gives support to the dating of Mungo Man and suggests that, once people had arrived, they spread across the continent relatively quickly. The genome also indicates that Aboriginal people living in Australia today are directly descended from the first arrivals, making these some of the oldest societies to have continuously occupied the same territory in the world outside of Africa.

DREAMTIME

The many different languages spoken across Aboriginal Australia is a further sign of the age of these societies. More than 250 language groups have been identified, with numerous dialects existing within each group, which suggests that Aboriginal people have been present on the continent for many thousands of years because of the length of time required for so many languages to have developed. Further indications of the age of Aboriginal societies can be found in some traditional stories, which tell of mythic ancestors who are said to have created both the Aboriginal people and the places in which they live. This is known as the Dreaming or Dreamtime, a mythical era not associated with any specific historical period. According to the stories, people were simply brought into existence and, from that point on, have always lived in the same place.

There are obvious differences between these mythological creation stories and the results obtained through research in the fields of archaeology, genetics, and linguistics. But, at the same time, parallels can be drawn between the two in that they point toward the conclusion of Aboriginal people having lived on the Australian continent for a very long time indeed.

In recent years, advances in science have increased our understanding of the first human habitation of Australia to the extent that it is now possible to say with a reasonable degree of certainty that those living on the continent today are descended from the first people to colonize it some fifty thousand years ago. The Bradshaw paintings of the Kimberley could relate back to this period of first settlement, which would mean they represent some of the earliest examples of rock art in the world, making them every bit as important as the Neolithic cave paintings of Western Europe. If this is the case, then, rather than undermining Aboriginal rights,

DESCENDANT
Modern-day Aboriginal Australians are the direct descendants of the first people who arrived in Australia some fifty thousand years ago.

as some people have suggested, they actually provide further confirmation, along with the science, of their claims to have always lived on their land.

> *"By sequencing the genome, the researchers have demonstrated that Aboriginal Australians descend directly from an early human expansion into Asia that took place some 70,000 years ago, at least 24,000 years before the population movements that gave rise to present-day Europeans and Asians. The results imply that modern day Aboriginal Australians are in fact the direct descendants of the first people who arrived in Australia as early as fifty thousand years ago."*
>
> —Sciencedaily.com, September 22, 2011

WHAT CAUSED NEANDERTHAL MAN TO BECOME EXTINCT?

ca. 28,000 BCE

Clue: Modern DNA testing has produced surprising results

Main players: *Homo neanderthalensis* and *Homo sapiens* species

Verdict: Perhaps they didn't disappear after all, but are still around in some form

By the time modern humans arrived in Europe, about forty thousand years ago, the continent had already been home to another closely related species of hominid for a very long time. The Neanderthals had gotten there several hundred thousand years before we did at a point when we had not yet even evolved into a separate species in our ancestral home of Africa.

Archaeological evidence suggests that the two species shared this living space, while generally keeping themselves to themselves, for about ten thousand years, until the Neanderthals died out. The last sign we have of them comes from evidence of their occupancy of caves on the Rock of Gibraltar, on the coast of southern Spain, from about twenty-eight thousand years ago. This site has been described as the last refuge of a doomed species, who, once they had gone, left us as the sole occupants of the region and the last surviving species of our genus. Many questions remain about the Neanderthals, but central to our understanding of them are the questions of how and why their extinction occurred.

"Of course, if the Neanderthals passed on their genes to modern humans they did not become entirely extinct, since some of their DNA lives on within us. Nevertheless, as a population with their own distinctive bodily characteristics they have vanished, and there are many scenarios constructed around what may have happened to them. Explanations have ranged widely from suggestions of imported diseases to which they had little natural immunity through to economic competition from, or even conflict with, early modern humans."

—**Chris Stringer,** *The Origin of Our Species*

GIBRALTAR
The location of the last known refuge of the Neanderthals in Europe.

CAVEMEN

The Neanderthals have rarely had good press. Since they were first described in the mid-nineteenth century, after a skeleton was found in the Neander valley, near Düsseldorf in Germany, they have been presented as the archetypal cavemen: slow-witted, communicating with one other using guttural grunts, and generally just not quite as "human" as we are. Artists' impressions accompanying accounts of the Neanderthal male show him as being stooped over, usually carrying a club, dressed in animal skins, and with a tangled mass of hair and an unkempt beard. Even the name is now associated with coarse and boorish behavior. To accuse somebody of acting like a Neanderthal is to suggest they are behaving in a fashion that might have been acceptable in the Stone Age, but certainly isn't now.

Looking at them more scientifically, archaeological research has shown this portrait of the Neanderthals to be entirely inaccurate. They lived in small family groups, based around couples of of men and women. They took care of others who were sick or injured, and buried their dead in a manner similar to humans. They were accomplished hunters and craftsmen, communicated with an early form of language, and could travel across open water. Evidence for this comes from Neanderthal finds on Mediterranean islands that have never been connected to the mainland by land bridges. They were either phenomenal swimmers or had figured out how to make boats or rafts. There is even some indication that they produced art. A rock painting of a seal found in a cave in Spain has been dated to about forty-two thousand years ago, before modern humans had arrived in the region. Either the date is wrong—that is always a possibility—or the painting was made by a Neanderthal. Much as we might like to think of ourselves as being unique, the simple truth is that the Neanderthals were very similar to us indeed.

HEAVILY BUILT

The similarities aside, humans and Neanderthals were by no means identical. Looking at their bodies, the differences were most apparent in the skull. Neanderthals had foreheads that sloped backward, with prominent brow ridges and much less of a protruding chin than we have. They were shorter and more heavily built, making them better

NEANDERTHAL MAN
A reconstruction of a Neanderthal man by the Neanderthal Museum in Mettman, Germany.

> If a Neanderthal man was given a decent haircut, a shower, and was dressed in a pair of jeans and a shirt, he would hardly stand out walking down the street today.

adapted to the cold climate of Europe, which is hardly surprising considering that our slender, less muscular physique evolved in the heat of the African savannah. But, in spite of these differences, if a Neanderthal man was given a decent haircut and a shower and was dressed in a pair of jeans and a shirt, he would hardly stand out walking down the street today. Saying that, he would look like the sort of fellow not to be messed with—not very tall, but built like a tank.

SOCIAL CIRCLES

The archaeological record also provides evidence of some cultural differences between humans and Neanderthals. Neanderthals appear to have been less socially inclined than we are; they tended to live in smaller groups than we do and did not have much contact with others from outside of their immediate circle. Our Neanderthal man with the haircut might not stand out on a city street, but he probably wouldn't feel very comfortable being surrounded by so many strangers either.

COMMON ANCESTOR

Even though the archaeological record is not yet complete enough to say for sure, it would appear that Neanderthals separated from the evolutionary line that would lead to modern humans about four hundred thousand years ago. The common ancestor is thought to be *Homo heidelbergensis*, itself an ancestor of *Homo erectus*, the first hominid to walk with an upright posture. A group of *Homo heidelbergensis* traveled out of Africa into Europe, so the theory goes, and became isolated from the parent population during a glacial period. Under such radically different climatic conditions, the European group developed into the Neanderthals. Meanwhile, back in Africa, modern humans developed from *Homo heidelbergensis* around a hundred and fifty thousand years ago, and then, perhaps seventy thousand years ago, also began to migrate out of Africa. By this time, the Neanderthals were quite widely dispersed through the Middle East and Central Asia, as well as in Europe, and it is in these areas that the two species most likely first encountered one another.

MODERN HUMANS

There are some indications of interaction between Neanderthals and modern humans, but, for the most part, the two appear to have kept to themselves. Over the course of thousands of years, the spread of Neanderthals contracted until only the final isolated population remained in those caves in Gibraltar. One possible cause of this decline is the arrival of modern humans. Either through direct confrontation, competition for the same resources, the spread of disease, or through a combination of all of these factors, we may have pushed the Neanderthals out of their territory. The historical record of our expansion in other parts of the world in more recent times would tend to support this scenario. Whenever people have colonized a new region, they have brought havoc with them. Forests get

STONE TOOLS

A significant difference between modern humans and Neanderthals can be seen in the range of stone tools used by the two species. Neanderthal stone tools changed very little over hundreds of millennia and as a result can be used to distinguish between those sites used by Neanderthals and modern humans. The lack of adaptation shown by Neanderthals has been seen by some archaeologists as evidence that they were not capable of the kind of inventive and problem-solving behavior shown by the humans.

GORHAM'S CAVE
Tools believed to have once belonged to Neanderthals living in their last refuge of Gorham's Cave, Gibraltar.

THE CHANGING CLIMATE

The range of the Neanderthals reached a high point around one hundred thousand years ago, when it is possible they had spread as far east as China. After that, there is a steady decline, which accelerates markedly after about fifty thousand years ago. This corresponds with a period of climatic instability, including some intense cold snaps which are thought to have come on very quickly. The rapidly changing environment, in which forests were replaced by vast, frozen regions and grasslands, would have led to a change in the type of prey available to Neanderthal hunters. As the stone tools they used remained largely the same, perhaps they were not able to adapt quickly enough to the new circumstances forced upon them.

In his book *The Humans Who Went Extinct*, Clive Finlayson puts forward the theory that Neanderthal hunting strategies could not cope with these sudden changes brought on by climate change. As a result, their population numbers were greatly reduced and those left were forced to take refuge in areas where the changes had been less severe, such as in the south of Spain.

The climate began to warm up again by forty thousand years ago, allowing modern humans to expand into the territory formerly occupied by the Neanderthals before they could spread back out to their previous range. So, according to this theory at least, the extinction of the Neanderthals was not

cleared, the wildlife is decimated, and any indigenous people encountered are either wiped out completely or their society is so disrupted that their way of life becomes untenable. It is not hard to imagine a similar set of circumstances undermining Neanderthal society and driving them toward extinction.
The problem with this theory is that it is solely based on an assumption of how modern humans behave; it is not backed up by any known evidence.

After intense cold snaps, the climate began to warm up again by forty thousand years ago, allowing modern humans to expand into the territory formerly occupied by the Neanderthals.

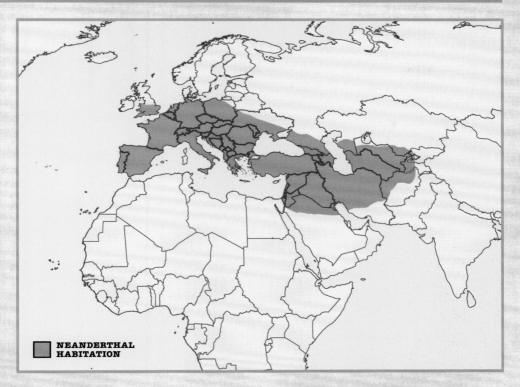

NEANDERTHAL HABITATION

the fault of modern man; it was merely a question of chance. As Finlayson puts it, the Neanderthals were simply in the wrong place at the wrong time.

PART OF US

A third and largely unconsidered possibility has become apparent since 2010, when the full sequence of Neanderthal DNA (genetic information) was published. As well as highlighting just how closely human beings and Neanderthals were related to each other, the results revealed that all modern humans, with the exception of people from Africa, have directly inherited between 1 and 4 percent of their genes from Neanderthals, demonstrating that interbreeding between us and Neanderthals not only occurred after

NEANDERTHAL RANGE
By 100,000 BCE, the Neanderthals had spread throughout much of Europe, the Middle East, and Central Asia.

we had migrated out of Africa, but that it produced viable offspring. This opens up the intriguing question: should modern humans, Neanderthals, and our common ancestor *Homo heidelbergensis*, be regarded as separate species at all? It also points to the possibility that Neanderthals did not become extinct; rather, when modern humans began to move into their territory, they were simply absorbed into those populations. If this turns out to be the case, then the Neanderthals did not completely die out after all. They remain with us because they are part of us. They are in our DNA.

DID THE LOST CONTINENT OF ATLANTIS REALLY EXIST?

ca. 9000 BCE

Clue: The writings of one of ancient Greece's greatest philosophers

Main players: Plato and others

Verdict: A fascinating and ongoing mystery or complete nonsense, depending on how you look at it

The story of Atlantis, of how a continent in the Atlantic Ocean sank beneath the sea, is a familiar one. It has been widely dismissed in the academic world as being a fantasy concocted by pseudo-historians to promote one crazy theory or another. These are the people who contend that the people of Atlantis were supreme beings, members of an advanced civilization responsible for all the achievements of the ancient world, from the pyramids of Egypt and the New World, to Stonehenge.

So, is there any substance in the story, or are they simply the ravings of the sort of people who think that crop circles are messages from aliens from outer space rather than the work of a couple of guys with a pole and some rope who don't have anything better to do after the bars have closed? After all, the story was first told by the ancient Greek philosopher Plato, who, along with Socrates and Aristotle, is one of the founding fathers of Western philosophy and, as such, is not a man to be disregarded so lightly.

WHAT PLATO WROTE

Late in life, Plato (429–347 BCE) began an ambitious project that appears to have been an attempt to sum up his thoughts on various matters, including the nature of statehood and what would constitute an ideal way of living. These were conveyed as a dialogue, and presented as a discussion held by others. In this case the speakers include fellow thinkers Socrates, Timaeus, and Critias, and the discussion is presented as taking place in 421 BCE (when Plato would have seven years old). The proposed work was divided into three parts—*Timaeus, Critias*, and *Hermocrates*—but Plato appears to have abandoned the project without completing *Critias* and, as far as we can tell, before starting *Hermocrates*, so it is hard to know what his overall intention was for the work.

Atlantis has been widely dismissed in the academic world as being a fantasy concocted by pseudo-historians to promote one crazy theory or another.

PLATO
A bust of the great
Athenian philosopher
who first described
Atlantis.

Athens, but the Atlanteans have let the power go to their heads, becoming over-confident and wayward, leading to their defeat by the more down-to-earth and better organized Athenians. After the Atlanteans have been defeated, a series of natural disasters occurs. In Plato's words:

"Afterward there came a time of extraordinary earthquakes and floods. There came a day when your warships were swallowed up by the earth and the island of Atlantis also sank beneath the sea and disappeared. So now the ocean beyond the Pillars of Hercules can not be traversed, the way blocked by mud just below the surface of the sea, left behind when the island settled down."

In *Timaeus*, Plato tells the story of Atlantis in the form of a response given by Critias to Socrates, who has been talking about the nature of the ideal state. It is, Plato says, a long forgotten episode in Athenian history in which a war was fought between Athens and Atlantis, an island state "beyond the Pillars of Hercules." These are the two promontories on either side of the Straits of Gibraltar, meaning that Atlantis is to be found out in the Atlantic Ocean. It is much bigger and more powerful than

BENEATH THE WAVES

Although Athens was damaged in the earthquakes and floods that followed the war, it survived, whereas Atlantis was destroyed, sinking below the waves of the Atlantic Ocean. The dialogue then moves on to other areas of discussion, before

state, but one that has fallen from grace and been destroyed, a fate, he is implying, that will also happen to Athens if it does not mend its ways.

PURE FANTASY?

It is impossible to know now if Plato based his story of Atlantis on any documentary evidence or if he invented it himself just to suit the purpose of the point he was making. Herodotus (ca. 484–425 BCE), the so-called "father of history," makes no mention of it at all in *The Histories*, written a generation before Plato, which suggests that it was not a particularly well-known story in Athens. Some later classical writers have treated the story as being one of historical fact, but most, in common with modern classical scholars, saw it as a device used by Plato in order to suit his own purposes.

Plato has Critias return to his subject in the section of the work named for him. There follows a long, rambling and, in truth, tedious account of Atlantis and Atlantean society. The work stops at this point. It is hard to know whether Plato took a break to gather his thoughts or if he gave up on it; whatever the reason, he didn't finish it. What has become clear, though, is that Plato is really discussing Athens and has used the example of Atlantis to show what happens to a state if it becomes bloated and corrupt. Atlantis, in Plato's account, is not an ideal

"The records tell how your city stopped a great power, coming in from the Atlantic Ocean, that had attacked all Europe and Asia. In those days the ocean could be traversed, for there was an island in it in front of the strait you call the Pillars of Hercules. This island was larger than Libya and Asia put together, and from it voyagers of those times could reach other islands, from which the whole of a continent on the opposite side of that ocean could be reached."

—**Plato,** *Timaeus*

American lawyer Ignatius Donnelly suggested that Atlantis had been destroyed in the same Great Flood as the one Noah had to deal with in the Old Testament.

Since classical antiquity, numerous people have written about Atlantis in one form or another. The Elizabethan philosopher Sir Francis Bacon (1561–1626) wrote a novel called *The New Atlantis*, about a utopian society on an island off the North American coast, while the otherwise serious Swedish scientist Olaus Rudbeck (1679–1702) went to enormous lengths

LANDMARK BOOK
Ignatius Donnelly in his influential book of 1882 described Atlantis as the origin of all ancient civilizations.

in an effort to prove that Sweden was in fact Atlantis. But it would not be until Ignatius Donnelly (1831–1901) published *Atlantis: The Antediluvian World* in 1882 that the idea of Atlantis as we know it today really began to take root in the public imagination.

IGNATIUS DONNELLY
Donnelly was an American lawyer and politician of Irish descent who set out his theory that Atlantis had been destroyed in the same Great Flood as the one Noah had to deal with in the Old Testament. He went on to describe how Atlantis had been the origin of all ancient civilizations and the homeland of the Aryan race, who, after the flood had forced them to move, settled in Ireland and established a new homeland of red-haired supermen.

To a few of his contemporaries, Donnelly's ideas proved influential. The Austrian philosopher and mystic

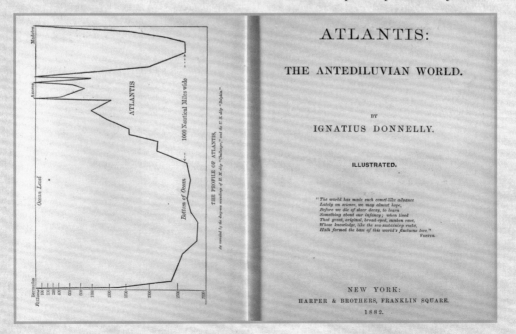

Rudolph Steiner was a follower, as was the American psychic healer Edgar Cayce. More recently, the works of the writers J. V. Luce and Graham Hancock can be seen as modern evolutions of Donnelly's theories, which, while not taken seriously in the academic world, have a large popular following.

VOLCANIC ERUPTION

If some press reports and internet sites are to be believed, then Atlantis has been discovered many times. As well as Sweden and Ireland, it has been positively identified in the Azores, Cuba, the Bahamas, and a mudbank off the Spanish coast. A few years ago, Google Earth changed a satellite photograph of the seabed west of the Canary Islands that had originally depicted a series of straight lines not unlike the regular grid pattern of city streets. Google said they were correcting a fault that had developed during the transference of a digital image, an explanation not swallowed by everybody. There are those who see it as yet another example of a wide-ranging conspiracy to keep the truth from the people.

As well as press and internet speculation, there have been a few attempts by serious archaeologists to engage with the issue. The best known of these is the theory that associates the destruction of Atlantis with an enormous volcanic eruption on the Aegean island of Thera. The theory suggests that it occurred around 1600 BCE and caused

a tsunami that contributed to the collapse of the Minoan civilization on Crete as well as destroying Thera. What was left of the island after the eruption is now known as Santorini and the scale of the volcanic blast can be gauged by the size of the caldera, or crater, it left after blowing out the heart of the original island. It is almost 8 miles (13 km) long and 4 miles (6.4 km) wide, with cliff faces on three sides that are 1,000 feet (300 m) high. Archaeological excavations

We will never know for sure if Plato's account of Atlantis had a basis in fact, or whether he simply invented the story. In a sense, it doesn't much matter either way because he was using it to illustrate a point he was making.

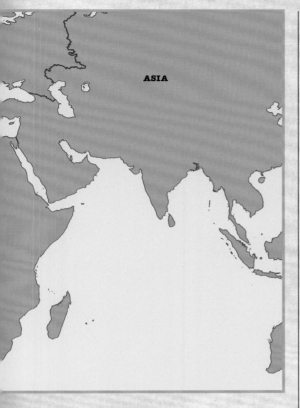

ASIA

PLATO'S ATLANTIS
According to Plato, Atlantis lay beyond the Pillars of Hercules, placing it in the Atlantic Ocean.

continue at the site of Akrotiri, a Minoan town completely covered in volcanic ash, where complete houses and some truly beautiful murals have been uncovered.

The parallels between Plato's account of the destruction of Atlantis and what the archaeological evidence shows us about the fate of the Minoans on Thera are clear. The attraction of the theory is that it is based on actual evidence rather than wild speculation. However, the differences are also obvious. Compared to what Plato tells us about Atlantis,

Thera is the wrong size and in the wrong place, and the eruption on the island occurred at the wrong time, something like 7,500 years after Atlantis is said to have disappeared. To ignore such discrepancies, or to explain them away, places the Theran theory in the same company as all the crazy theories for which the facts have been manipulated to fit in with a pre-formed idea rather than allowed to stand for themselves.

It seems that we will never know for sure if Plato's account of Atlantis had a basis in fact, or whether he simply invented the story. In a sense, it doesn't much matter either way because he was using it to illustrate a point he was making about the fate that befalls corrupt cities, and may not have been trying to tell the truth at all.

THE MINOANS
The Minoan civilization, which emerged on Crete between 3000 and 1450 BCE, was the first great civilization to emerge in Europe. As a result of an extensive network of trade, the Minoans built cities and ports, dominated by magnificent palaces. A huge volcanic eruption on Thera (now Santorini) in around 1600 BCE destroyed Minoan palaces and towns, and contributed to the collapse of the Minoan civilization. The ancient Greeks remembered Minoa as a lost and golden land and Minoans, including the half-bull, half-man monster, the Minotaur, featured in a number of Greek legends.

WHO WERE THE "HOBBITS" OF FLORES?

362 CE

Clue: Folk tales told about "little people" on the island of Flores

Main players: *Homo floresiensis* and us

Verdict: Nothing is straightforward in human evolution

The stories of mischievous little people told by the Nage, the indigenous people of the beautiful Indonesian island of Flores, which means "flowers" in Portuguese, were not given any more credibility than the many other similar stories from around the world. That is, not until 2004, when archaeologists discovered the skeletons of people in a cave on the island who stood not much more than 3 feet (1 m) tall when fully grown. According to the team who made the discovery, these people were anatomically different from modern humans in more respects than just height alone; they had tiny brains, about the size of an apple, together with enormous feet and a wrist joint that, when compared to ours, was much more primitive. These differences, they said, were significant enough for the specimens to be described as a species of hominid new to science, which they named *Homo floresiensis*.

The hobbits of Flores weren't just small, they had tiny brains, enormous feet, and primitive wrist joints.

If there is one thing archaeologists enjoy more than anything else, it is a quarrel dressed up as a serious scientific debate. The claims made about the finds on Flores provided them with the perfect opportunity for a good old-fashioned argument. By the time the argument really got going, the press had gotten hold of the story and *Homo floresiensis* had been nicknamed as the hobbit of Flores, presumably on account of their small size rather than because of any adventures they may have shared with Bilbo and Frodo in Middle-earth.

HOBBIT OR HUMAN?

Classifying the hobbits as a new species really threw a fox into the henhouse as far as theories of human evolution were concerned. Up until then, the spread of humans around the world was seen as being quite straightforward. Waves of migration were thought to have occurred on three separate occasions: *Homo erectus* left Africa about 1.5 million years ago, followed by *Homo heidelbergensis* about four hundred thousand years ago, and finally, by our ancestors about seventy thousand years ago. Our ancestors are thought to have displaced their

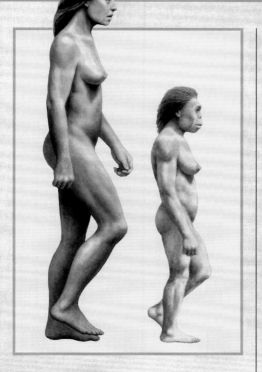

HOBBIT HEIGHT
The hobbits of Flores (right) were significantly smaller than modern humans, standing not much more than 3 feet (1 m) tall when fully grown.

The team who made the find proposed that the hobbits were descended from *Homo erectus*—not an unreasonable suggestion given that the first known example of *Homo erectus* had been found in the late nineteenth century on the island of Java, a few hundred miles to the west of Flores. The obvious problem with this was the difference in size. *Homo erectus* were considerably taller and more robust than modern humans, never mind the diminutive hobbits. This difference was explained as being the result of the biological phenomenon of "insular dwarfism," whereby a population of a species isolated on an island evolves to become smaller as a response to the limited resources available. This seemed to be supported by the discovery of bones from an extinct species of pygmy (miniature) elephant in the same location. Stone tools were also found in the cave, including ones thought to have been used to kill and butcher the pygmy elephants. These were similar to tools found elsewhere on Flores, which have been dated as being one million years old, lending support to the *Homo erectus* theory. But this poses another problem: how could the hobbits, with such small brains and primitive wrists, make and use these tools?

Critics of the theory have picked up on this point, but their main bone of contention has been with the

predecessors as they spread out. The problem arising with the hobbits, in relation to this conventional view, is that they were anatomically different from all three, so their presence on Flores could not be explained by this theory.

"hobbit n. in the stories of J. R. R. Tolkien (1892–1973): a member of a fictional race related to humans, characterized by their small size and hairy feet."

—Definition from the *Shorter Oxford English Dictionary*

classification of the hobbits as being a new species. They proposed that the hobbits were actually humans who—through disease or disorder—had suffered stunted growth. One suggestion was the disorder microcephaly, a condition in which the brain does not develop to its usual size. The problem with this and other proposals is that they only account for the differences in height and brain size and don't explain all the other physical differences. Comparisons between the skulls of hobbits and those of modern humans who had suffered from similar diseases revealed significant differences, tending to confirm that the hobbits were not suffering from any of them.

DNA MYSTERY

There is a way for the mystery of the hobbits of Flores to be solved. DNA (genetic material) analysis could determine who the hobbits were once and for all, settling the debate over whether they are a new species or were modern humans suffering from a disease. Unfortunately, DNA degrades much more quickly in hot climates than it does in colder ones. Even though DNA has been recovered from older samples than the hobbits, such as from the bones of Neanderthals, no method has yet been devised that can extract DNA from the bones found on Flores. Until a technique has been developed to overcome these difficulties, we will have to make do with the competing theories.

There is the possibility that the hobbits of Flores survived after modern humans arrived on the island. Could they even have survived into modern times?

Despite evidence to the contrary, some scientists refused to accept that the hobbits represented a new species of hominid. It would appear that some of these objections have been made out of professional jealousy, perhaps because the individuals concerned didn't make the discovery themselves, while others were finding fault because they were not willing to accept a challenge to their own opinions on human evolution. To do this would force them to reevaluate, and perhaps even reject, work they had been involved with for many years, and few people much like admitting they are wrong.

DESCENDANTS OF LUCY?

In recent years, an alternative theory about the origin of the hobbits has emerged, based on the evidence as it is rather than on what some people would like it to be. This suggests that they were actually the descendants of some of the first hominids to evolve, possibly *Australopithecus afarensis* or *Homo habelis*. Both lived in Africa between two and three million years ago; the best known of these is Lucy, the skeleton of an *A. afarensis* found in Ethiopia in 1974 and known as the "grandmother of humanity." Lucy had a small brain, primitive wrists, and was less than 3 feet (1 m) tall, so the comparison with the hobbits is obvious. No evidence for any hominids older than *Homo erectus* has ever been found outside of Africa, so, if this theory proves to be correct, it will prompt a fundamental rethinking of human evolution.

TRUE STORIES?

A further intriguing mystery surrounds the hobbits of Flores. Current evidence suggests that they died out about twelve thousand years ago, either before modern humans arrived on the island or as a direct result of their arrival. But there is also the possibility, which scientists have not dismissed out of hand, that they survived for a while longer. In this scenario, hobbits and modern humans would have lived on the island at the same time and so must have interacted with each other to some extent.

The stories told by the Nage relate how the little people persisted into modern times, perhaps until as recently as the nineteenth century and, while there is no evidence to back this up, it would be unwise to dismiss what they say out of hand either. The storytellers, after all, have been right before.

HOBBIT HEAD

A comparison between an adult hobbit skull (shown on the left) and that of a modern human.

WHY WAS STONEHENGE BUILT AND BY WHOM?

ca. 2500 BCE

Clue: The giant stones are aligned with the solstices

Main players: Ancient Britons

Verdict: Lots of theories but no real idea

Salisbury Plain in England's southwest can be a bleak place in midwinter. This may explain why far fewer people gather at Stonehenge to mark the setting sun on the winter solstice than they do six months later for sunrise on the longest day of the year, even though the people who originally built it aligned the stones with both.

On the summer solstice these days, a procession of druids in full druid costume enter the stone circle and perform rituals as the sun comes up while a crowd of onlookers get in touch with their spiritual side. In the 1970s and '80s, a much noisier free festival took place at the site. What any of this has to do with Stonehenge itself is difficult to know. The people who built it forty-five hundred years ago haven't left us any indication of what they had in mind. That they had a purpose is clear from the monumental amount of work it must have taken to build the stone circle. Nobody goes to all that effort without a very good reason and, while archaeology has been getting to grips with the identity of these people and how they went about erecting the stones, we still don't really have the faintest idea why they did it.

NEOLITHIC SHIFT

The megalithic monuments built in Britain and along the Atlantic coast of mainland Europe date to the Neolithic, or New Stone Age, a period of great change in the way humans lived. In Britain, this period began around 4000 BCE, and included the adoption of what has been termed by some archaeologists as the "Neolithic package." Exactly how and why this great change happened is an enduring question in archaeology, not least because the Neolithic period involved the single biggest shift in human society that has ever occurred: the move from hunting and gathering to farming. It led to a more settled way of life within a more stratified society, the use of more advanced tools, and the first use of pottery.

One theory, first proposed by the French archaeologist Jacques Cauvin, suggests that the Neolithic transition was

Whoever built Stonehenge must have been highly skilled in working stone, with good organizational abilities to achieve what they did.

driven by changes in the way people thought about their place in the world. Put simply, hunter-gatherers live in the present, providing for themselves from what is available around them. Their belief systems draw on local features such as the landscape, animals, and plants. Neolithic farmers, on the other hand, would have been more concerned with what the future might bring—a change in the weather could wreck their harvest. This uncertainty was reflected in their religions; offerings would be made in an effort to appease the gods and bring order to a chaotic world.

The people who built Stonehenge were farmers who lived in small, settled communities. It is, of course, impossible to know exactly what they thought or how they responded to the world around

STONEHENGE

The site was in use for some sixteen hundred years and may have formed part of a complex of monuments.

them, but, at the same time, it is not unreasonable to suggest that their religious life would have been in line with that of other farming communities.

The fact that they expended such huge amounts of energy and resources to build Stonehenge, which surely can only have had a ritual purpose, shows they must have had a highly developed religious sense, presumably based on the worship of the dead and the ancestors. The placement of the stones also suggests an advanced awareness of the cosmos (universe), in which great importance was attached to the movements of the sun and to the changing of the seasons, which are, of course, vital components of the agricultural way of life.

THE PHASES OF STONEHENGE

Stonehenge, like Rome, wasn't built in a day. In fact, there were three phases of construction stretching out over the sixteen-hundred-year period that the site was in use. In the first phase, at around

3100 BCE, a circular ditch was dug, with the earth and chalk extracted from it used to form a bank. On the inside of the bank a series of fifty-six pits were dug at regular intervals. The purpose of these pits is unclear, but they may have been used to erect either wooden posts or stone megaliths. One theory suggests they were the original position of the bluestones, which were then moved to their present position within the main circle at a later date.

Nothing now remains of the second phase of work, which occurred over the course of the following five hundred years. This saw the erection of wooden structures, most of which were then replaced by stone during the third and final phase of construction. This began in about 2600 BCE and continued in stages for the next few hundred years. The massive sarsen stones of the outer circle, each weighing 25 tons (22.7 tonnes), were brought to the site from the Marlborough Downs, 20 miles (32 km)

BLUESTONES

These stones, which weigh between four and five tons, originally came from the Preseli Hills in Pembrokeshire, 150 miles (240 km) away, and were presumably either dragged on some form of sledge or taken most of the way around the coast by boat and dragged the remainder of the way. Whichever method was used, it would have been an enormous undertaking, showing just how important the site was to successive generations of people.

away. They were cut to shape on site, with tongue and groove joints so that the ends connected together and each was slightly curved so that, when placed into position on top of the sarsens, they formed a ring. The impression given by this form of construction is of it being carried out by a highly skilled workforce.

Even larger sarsens of up to 50 tons (45 tonnes) were erected inside the circle to form five trilithons—two upright stones joined by a lintel—and these were arranged in a horseshoe pattern. The bluestones were also arranged within the circle in a similar pattern and a number of other stones erected, including one in the middle of the circle. This phase of building does not appear to have been fully finished, with one section of the outer circle left open, perhaps because the builders had run out of stones of sufficient size. Minor modifications were carried out while the site remained in use over the course of the next thousand years, until about 1500 BCE, after which it seems the site fell into disuse.

A RITUAL LANDSCAPE

Over the years, hundreds of theories have been put forward to explain what these Neolithic farmers were up to at Stonehenge. One of these theories was proposed by Professor Mike Parker Pearson, who led a series of excavations at the site, and is one of the world's leading authorities on the subject.

His theory places Stonehenge within an interconnected complex of Neolithic monuments in the surrounding area known as a ritual landscape. Other parts of this landscape include contemporary features such as Durrington Walls, the remains of a wooden version of Stonehenge a few miles to the west,

STONE MONUMENT
The sarsen stones form the outer ring, with a horseshoe of trilithons at the center.

where a Neolithic village of about a hundred houses has also been excavated. Both Durrington Walls and Stonehenge are sited near the River Avon and were connected to it by avenues lined with earthworks. Parker Pearson envisages bodies being transported from the domain of the living, represented by the wood of Durrington Walls, to the domain of the dead, the stone of Stonehenge, via the river, which, he suggests, was considered to be a transitional zone between life and death.

Numerous burials have been found both in and around Stonehenge, including, most famously, the Amesbury Archer, the skeleton of a Bronze Age man found buried with numerous grave goods near the site. There is evidence of more than two hundred cremation burials in the outer earthworks, lending support to the theory that the site was a place of burial.

One aspect of Stonehenge not addressed by Parker Pearson's theory is the fact that the stones are positioned to follow the path of the sun. It could be that the site had more than one purpose, much as a cathedral or temple has today.

Perhaps the best way of considering Stonehenge and the surrounding ritual landscape is to think of them as places where a community came together to honor the dead and to celebrate festivals at specific times of the year. These ceremonies may be long forgotten, but, in many respects, what they were doing is not so very different from how we behave today. They recognized their place in the world and sought to influence the future by asking their gods to interfere in worldly affairs in their favor.

WHERE WAS THE LOST LAND OF PUNT?

ca. 1500 BCE

Clue: Tantalizing reliefs in Queen Hatshepsut's mortuary temple

Main players: Ancient Egyptians and the people of Punt

Verdict: Several possible (but no definite) locations

If there is one thing you can say about the ancient Egyptians, it is that they liked to build monuments. Pyramids, temples, tombs, obelisks, and statues litter the landscape of the modern country. And, as well as building them, they liked to cover their monuments in some form of decoration: inscriptions, reliefs, and, where they survive, innumerable paintings and designs.

Taken together with the written documents, on papyri (Egyptian paper scrolls) and clay tablets, we have been left with a remarkable insight into a culture that lasted for more than three thousand years, from about 3000 BCE right up until the Roman period. As well as documenting themselves, the Egyptians have also left us with a mine of information about the people who occupied the territories around them. Most of these are well known, but one remains a mystery. There are a number of references to trading missions to a place the Egyptians called the Land of Punt. It was regarded by them as a place of great beauty, where the living was easy, or at least, a great deal easier than it was in Egypt. What they don't tell us is where this land actually was.

A HARMONIOUS LAND

The Egyptians are the only people to have referred to the Land of Punt, suggesting that either it wasn't well connected with the outside world or that everybody else referred to it by a different name. In Egypt, Punt is mentioned throughout the entire history of the civilization and, almost always, descriptions of it are positive, usually relating to its abundance of resources and the good trading relations between the two countries. Unlike almost every other country known to the Egyptians, who were always fighting somebody, there are no reports of wars or invasions between the two countries. Punt appears to have been regarded as being wholly peaceful and harmonious, as well as being the source of many highly desirable trade goods.

The Land of Punt was regarded by the ancient Egyptians as a place of great beauty and the source of many desirable trade goods. What we don't know is where it actually was.

TRADING MISSION

By far the most extensive of the reports concerning Punt comes from the mortuary temple of Queen Hatshepsut in Deir el-Bahri, on the west bank of the Nile in Upper Egypt, near the Valley of the Kings. On the second level of the three terraces that make up the building, extensive reliefs depict a trading mission to Punt. These reliefs are the only ones known that show the people and landscape of a country other than Egypt, giving an indication of the importance attached to Punt by the otherwise self-obsessed Egyptians.

Hatshepsut became Pharaoh on the death of her husband, Thutmose II, and reigned in her own right for twenty-two years, roughly from 1479 BCE to 1458 BCE. As a Pharaoh of the eighteenth dynasty, she was a direct ancestor of

QUEEN HATSHEPSUT'S TEMPLE
A wall painting from Hatshepsut's mortuary temple depicting trade between an Egyptian and a Puntite.

Tutankhamun, who came to the throne about a hundred years later. The crowning of a female Pharaoh was unusual in Egypt, but not without precedent, and Hatshepsut's reign coincided with a period of prosperity and stability. This is reflected in the amount of building commissioned during her lifetime, including the mortuary temple, in which she attempted to ensure she would not be forgotten after her death.

The number of reliefs in the mortuary temple depicting Punt clearly show that Hatshepsut regarded the trading mission as one of her greatest achievements as Pharaoh. Perhaps the reliefs depict the

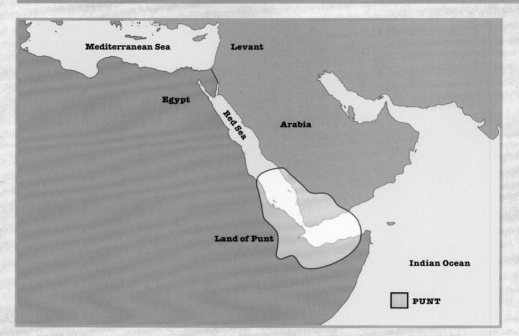

Mediterranean Sea

Levant

Egypt

Red Sea

Arabia

Land of Punt

Indian Ocean

PUNT

reestablishment of trading links after a long period of inactivity. Hatshepsut sent five ships to Punt, where they traded for, among other things, gold, ivory, wild animals, and various aromatic resins, particularly myrrh. The reliefs show the king of Punt, named as Parahu, and his wife Ati, who is shown in a not entirely flattering way. She is a rather large lady who requires a donkey to get around. In scenes of village life, the people of Punt are depicted as being tall and good-looking, and the men, in contrast to the Egyptians, have short beards and long hair. They live in conical houses, which are raised off the ground on stilts, and they keep short-horned cattle. There are numerous depictions of wild animals, including giraffes, rhinos, hippos, and leopards, and these, together with scenes showing fish associated with the Red Sea, imply that Punt was located on the Red Sea coast of Africa, in the region of

LOST LAND
The location of Punt most likely lay on the Red Sea coast of either Africa or the Arabian Peninsula.

what is now Eritrea, Djibouti, and Somalia. This is supported by the trade goods acquired by the Egyptian mission, all of which would have been available in this part of Africa.

ARABIAN PENINSULA
The reliefs in Hatshepsut's temple may not provide sufficient evidence to say exactly where Punt was, but they certainly point to an African location somewhere to the south of Egypt. But not everybody accepts this interpretation. The French Egyptologist Dmitri Meeks argues that if all the sources of information on Punt are taken into consideration, rather than solely relying on the reliefs, then the theory of placing

Punt in Africa comes under serious doubt. He thinks that the more probable location is on the Red Sea coast of the Arabian Peninsula, specifically the southern end of it, in what is now Yemen. In texts relating to Punt from several different periods of Egyptian history, the location is suggested to be east of Egypt, reached overland through the Sinai and Negev deserts as well as by ship across the Red Sea.

The list of trading goods given by the Egyptians also, in some respects, points to the Arabian Peninsula. The Egyptians were particularly keen to acquire aromatic resins, which they used in religious rituals, as well as myrrh, which is found in both Africa and Arabia. They also traded for other varieties, such as the resin from the pistachio tree, which are only found in the Middle East. The presence of African wildlife in Hatshepsut's temple reliefs could, according to Meeks, be the result of trade by the Puntites, who acted as middle men trading animals taken from elsewhere. Of course, this could equally well explain the presence of Arabian resins in Africa, so, without any supporting evidence, it is difficult to know for certain.

The upshot of the various debates is that Punt could be in several locations in either Africa or Arabia. The Egyptians tell us that they traveled to Punt in large ships, which they depict as sailing on the Red Sea, which doesn't actually narrow

DINKA PEOPLE

An alternative theory places Punt farther inland in Africa, along the the upper Nile in what is now South Sudan. Intriguing evidence that supports this theory is that the Dinka people, who live in the region today, are notably tall and, during the wet season, still build conical houses on stilts. The obvious problem with this identification, apart from the thirty-five-hundred-year time gap, is that the fish depicted in the reliefs are saltwater species of the Red Sea rather than the freshwater ones found in the Nile.

down the choices. One possible explanation is that the Egyptians regarded Punt as a fabled land of plenty rather than as a specific place, so, at different periods and depending on the trade items they were receiving, referred to more than one place by the same name. In this line of reasoning, Punt was, in effect, an idea rather than a specific place, so trying to say exactly where it was becomes pointless. Whatever the truth of the matter, for the moment the true identity of the Land of Punt remains out of our reach. But, as our knowledge of ancient Egypt increases, perhaps one day it will emerge from the mists of time.

The people of Punt are depicted as being tall and good-looking, and the men, in contrast to the Egyptians, have short beards and long hair. They live in conical houses raised off the ground on stilts.

WAS THE BOY KING TUTANKHAMUN MURDERED?

ca. 1360 BCE

Clue: Did damage to the skull point to foul play?

Main players: Tutankhamun, Ay, and Horemheb

Verdict: Probably not

The discovery of Tutankhamun's tomb by the British archaeologist Howard Carter in 1922 propelled one of the most obscure Pharaohs of ancient Egypt into the limelight and onto the front pages of the newspapers. Unlike the known tombs of every other Pharaoh, which had all been robbed in antiquity, Tutankhamun's tomb was found almost entirely intact. The artifacts recovered, including his solid-gold funeral mask, have toured the world in exhibitions and now reside in the Egyptian Museum in Cairo. The embalmed mummy initially received rather less attention; it was damaged when the bandages around it were unwrapped by Carter's team, who were more interested in recovering the amulets and jewels found within the bandages and on the body than in the corpse itself.

By the time an autopsy was carried out, so much damage had been done that a cause of death could not be established. X-rays of Tutankhamun's body were taken in 1968, which showed a dark spot at the base of his skull and two loose bone fragments within the cranium. This was interpreted by some at the time as evidence that he had been murdered by a blow to the head with a blunt instrument, leading to all sorts of lurid speculation about who could have been responsible. The finger was pointed at those who stood to gain the most from his death, notably his chief advisor in the royal court, a man named Ay, who succeeded him as Pharaoh, and

> *"Now when His Majesty was crowned king, the temples and estates of the gods and goddesses from Elephantine as far as the marshes of Lower Egypt had fallen into ruin. Their shrines had fallen down, turned into piles of rubble and overgrown with weeds. Their sanctuaries were as if they had never existed at all. Their temples had become footpaths. The world was in chaos and the gods had turned their backs on the land."*
>
> **—From Tutankhamun's Restoration Stela**

HAWK GOD
Various treasures were found in Tutankhamun's tomb, including a gold-plated statuette of the hawk god Horus.

Egypt. It was a time of great social change and religious turmoil, in which the entire pantheon of Egyptian gods was replaced by a single god, the Aten, represented by the symbol of a sun disc. This reformation was initiated by Akhenaten, the so-called heretic Pharaoh, who moved the capital of his country away from the old religious capital of Thebes and established the new city of Amarna in the desert, where he could rule the country free from the interference of the Priests of Amun, the holy men of the old religion. Recent DNA evidence supports the long-held view that Akhenaten was Tutankhamun's father, while his mother has, in the typically incestuous way of Egyptian Pharaohs, been identified as one of Akhenaten's sisters. This inbreeding more than likely accounts for the congenital problems that have been described in Tutankhamun's corpse, including a partially cleft palate and, according to some researchers, a club foot. Tutankhamun himself would marry his half-sister, Ankhesenamen, a union that predictably resulted in the births of two stillborn daughters. Their mummified bodies were found in Tutankhamun's tomb and were described by Howard Carter as the saddest things he had ever seen.

Horemheb, the head of the army, who became Pharaoh in turn after Ay.

But does the evidence really stack up against either of these two? And, in the light of further research, including a CT scan, which uses X-rays and a computer to see inside the body, and analysis of DNA, the material carrying genetic information, what more can we say about the manner of Tutankhamun's death?

BACKGROUND

Tutankhamun may not have lived a very long life, dying at the age of about eighteen or nineteen, but he lived through an extraordinary period in the three-thousand-year history of ancient

IN MEMORY

The only substantial inscription concerning Tutankhamun is known as the Restoration Stela. It gives an account of how Egypt had been falling into ruin before the worship of Amun was restored and the country began to flourish again. A crude attempt had been made to replace Tutankhamun's cartouche — an ornamental oblong or oval enclosing the name and title of an Egyptian monarch — with that of Horemheb, although Tutankhamun's name can still be made out. Presumably, it was defaced after Tutankhamun's death in an attempt to wipe out his memory. In Egyptian belief, for a person to live on in the afterlife, they have to be remembered in the present, which is why the Pharaohs built so many monuments to themselves and covered them in inscriptions of their names and great deeds. So, by removing his name from inscriptions, he was not only being erased from history, but also killed off in the afterlife. A similar fate had already befallen Akhenaten and everybody else associated with the Amarna period, one of the reasons why so little was known about Tutankhamun before the discovery of his tomb.

Akhenaten was succeeded on his death by Smenkhkare, a Pharaoh about whom almost nothing is known other than he reigned in Amarna for four years until being succeeded in turn, in about 1340 BCE, by Tutankhamun, who became the twelfth Pharaoh in the eighteenth dynasty of the New Kingdom of Egypt. He was only eight or nine years old at the time and, it is generally accepted, was advised by members of his royal court, prominent among whom were Horemheb and Ay. In the third year of his reign, the court was moved back to Thebes and the worship of the Aten, along with the city of Amarna, was abandoned. The old religion was restored to its former place and the Priests of Amun returned to their positions. This break with the past was confirmed by a change in the name of the Pharaoh, from the original Tutankhaten, which means, "the living image of Aten," to Tutankhamun, "the living image of Amun."

DEATH OF TUTANKHAMUN

Tutankhamun died during his tenth year on the throne and was buried in the Valley of the Kings, the traditional burial place of Pharaohs of the New Kingdom. The tomb and its contents give the impression of the funeral being a hastily arranged affair. Compared to those of other Pharaohs, it is small and in a poor position, being cut into the rock in the floor of the valley, which was prone to flash flooding. The wall paintings in the tomb are also quite crude by the standards of the day and some of the walls have been left undecorated, while some of the grave goods appear to have been recycled from other tombs.

Tutankhamun was buried in a hurry, without much care and attention, leading to the suspicion that someone wanted to get rid of him as quickly as possible.

TUTANKHAMUN'S TOMB

Howard Carter (kneeling) examines a burial shrine in the tomb with two of his colleagues.

Even the stone sarcophagus in which his body was placed had been intended for somebody else. The inscriptions on it were changed to include Tutankhamun's name and the lid appears to have been made for a completely different base. It also had a big crack in it, which had been hurriedly and rather badly repaired. Overall, then, he was buried in a hurry and without a great deal of care and attention, leading to the suspicion that Ay, the person responsible for the funeral, wanted to get rid of him as quickly as possible.

THE EVIDENCE

When a young man dies unexpectedly, as appears to have been the case with Tutankhamun, there can only be two conclusions: he died either as the result of an accident or he was killed. In Tutankhamun's case, this is complicated by the fact that we don't know for certain that he did die suddenly; it is speculation based on the state of his tomb.

Another scenario is that the tomb he was actually buried in was not initially intended to be his final resting place, but was used as a temporary measure while another tomb, larger and more fitting of his status, was being prepared. It has been suggested that the tomb in which Ay was buried four years after Tutankhamun could originally have been intended for him, but the move never took place because Ay, on becoming Pharaoh, decided to keep the larger tomb for himself.

The X-ray evidence of a blow to the back of the head does not really add up either. For a start, even if this is what killed him, there is nothing to say it was caused intentionally by somebody else. And, in truth, the evidence of a bang on the head has largely been discredited now anyway. The dark spot shown on the X-ray is much more likely to have been a consequence of the original embalming process, in which Tutankhamun's brain was removed through his nose and the empty space in the cranium filled with resin. The dark spot is simply the residue of this resin, while the bone fragments in the skull were most likely either dislodged in the embalming process or as a result of the first autopsy.

The CT scan and DNA analysis, while not conclusive, have thrown up

FUNERAL MASK
The solid gold mask, now in the Egyptian Museum in Cairo, was found on Tutankhamun's mummy.

several more likely causes of death. Tutankhamun was shown to have broken his leg not long before he died and appeared to be missing part of his rib cage and sternum (breastbone). The cause of the missing ribs and sternum cannot be definitively established; they may have been removed at some stage after his death. If this was the case, it is not known why, unless Howard Carter's team damaged the body when they removed the

jewelry from around Tutankhamun's neck and decided not to mention it. As well as these injuries and the congenital diseases previously mentioned, he was also suffering from a severe form of malaria which, on its own, could have proved fatal.

THE VERDICT

If all the evidence we have is taken together, then the most likely cause of Tutankhamun's death is some sort of accident in which he broke his leg and possibly his ribs as well. This may have been enough to kill him on its own, but, even if not, then taken together with the weakened state of his body as a consequence of the congenital diseases and malaria, the added strain of such a serious accident was too much for him.

In the light of all the uncertainty, the only sensible verdict is one of an unexplained death. Murder is not the most likely cause, but it cannot be ruled out either. Who's to say, for instance, that

RUN OVER BY A HIPPO

There has been plenty of speculation about the type of accident Tutankhamun was involved in. Most people come down in favor of either a hunting accident or a fall from his chariot, presumably because these are more interesting ways of having an accident than suggesting he might have fallen down the stairs. In one account, a scenario has been constructed in which he fell from his chariot while hunting and was then run over by a hippo. While not impossible, this is perhaps stretching the available evidence a little further than it will go.

EGYPTIAN PAINTING

A mural from the tomb of Tutankhamun showing the pharoah with his wife Ankhesenamen.

Tutankhamun wasn't pushed out of his chariot into the path of an oncoming hippo rather than falling out of it of his own accord? And, even if he was murdered, there is no firm evidence of the involvement of those cast in the role of main suspects, Ay and Horemheb. They both had motives because they benefited from his death, but it is just as easy to speculate that the pair of them were devoted to their Pharaoh and were devastated by his death at such a young age. Much as we might like to have a definitive answer, at the distance of almost thirty-five hundred years, it just isn't possible to say for sure.

The most likely cause of Tutankhamun's death is some sort of accident in which he broke his leg and possibly his ribs as well. Murder is not the most likely cause, but it cannot be ruled out either.

WILL THE ARK OF THE COVENANT EVER BE FOUND?

ca. 1000 BCE

Clue: A mysterious Ethiopian chapel that no one can enter

Main players: Moses and the Israelites

Verdict: Indiana Jones found it, but nobody else has

In the movie *Raiders of the Lost Ark*, Indiana Jones sets out to discover the location of the Ark of the Covenant before the Nazis can get their evil hands on it. In the ensuing romp, Indy survives numerous close shaves with death, has a few good fist fights, and rescues his female companion on more than one occasion, before he finally outsmarts the Nazis and saves the free world. And he achieves all this without losing his hat even once.

As a general rule, it is probably best not to pay too much attention to Hollywood movies as far as historical accuracy is concerned, and this is definitely no exception. But what it does demonstrate is our continuing fascination with the whereabouts of the Ark, which has been lost since 586 BCE, after the Temple of Solomon, where it was housed, was destroyed by the Babylonians during the siege of Jerusalem.

BOOK OF EXODUS

A rather more thoughtful and sober account of the Ark than found in *Raiders of the Lost Ark* is given in the book of Exodus, which relates how Moses leads the children of Israel out of slavery in Egypt and into the Promised Land.

While on the way there, Moses spends forty days and forty nights on Mount Sinai, where God gives him the Ten Commandments written on two tablets of stone. God also provides Moses with a detailed set of instructions about what to do with the Ten Commandments, including how to build a portable ark to carry them in and exactly what materials to use in its construction. It is to be made of acacia wood and lined with gold, with four rings attached to its side so that it could be carried on poles. The lid is to be made of gold, with two cherubim, wings outstretched, on top of it. God goes on to tell Moses, "I will make myself known to

---

The Ark, carrying the Ten Commandments, was to be made of acacia wood and lined with gold, with two cherubim wings outstretched on top of the gold lid.

ARK of the Covenant.
Fig. 5.

you there and I will speak to you from above the cover, from between the cherubim, which are above the Ark of Testimony" (Exodus 25: 22).

By the time Moses comes down from the mountain, the Israelites have grown impatient with his absence and have begun to worship an idol of a golden calf. In a fit of anger, Moses smashes the tablets, but, fortunately for all concerned, God replaces them with a fresh set.

THE PROMISED LAND

The chastened Israelites carry out the instructions to the letter. They spend the next forty years wandering in the desert in repentance, with the Ark being carried before them. When they stop for the night, it is placed in a sacred tent, the

THE ARK

An eighteenth-century illustration based on the details given in the book of Exodus.

Tabernacle, the dwelling place of God among the people of Israel.

Eventually the Ark leads the Israelites out of the desert and into Canaan, where its mystical power is used by them in a series of battles to defeat the Canaanites, most famously in bringing down the walls of Jericho, and thereby enabling the Israelites to find their home in the Promised Land.

THE LOST ARK

King Solomon, the son of David, brought the Ark to Jerusalem in, as far as we can tell, the early tenth century BCE. It was placed in the inner sanctum of his temple

DRUM OF ANCESTORS

One story tells that the Ark traveled much farther south and is held by the Lemba people of South Africa and Zimbabwe. According to their oral tradition, at some point the Ark had to be remade from remnants of the old one and then kept in a secret place. In the 1940s it was found and moved to a museum in Harare. The object, it must be said, looks nothing like the one described in Exodus and has been carbon dated to the fourteenth century. It's known to the Lemba as the Ngoma Lungundu, which means "the drum of the ancestors," which tends to suggest that it is more likely a sacred drum rather than the Ark of the Covenant.

on Mount Zion, now usually called the Temple Mount, where it would remain for four hundred years, until the city was sacked by the Babylonians under the command of King Nebuchadnezzar. The temple was completely destroyed and the Jews sent into exile in Babylon, but the fate of the Ark is far from clear.

The most likely outcome is that the Ark was either destroyed along with the temple or that Nebuchadnezzar took it to Babylon. There are also many different stories of how it was taken out of the temple by the Jews and hidden before the city fell to the Babylonians. The location of this hiding place has been the subject of intense speculation ever since. One version of the story states that it was hidden in a cave directly below the Tabernacle; in another, it was taken to Mount Nebo, in modern-day Jordan, together with other sacred items from the temple, and buried in a cave. Whatever the truth, about the only thing we can say now with any degree of certainty, more than twenty-five hundred years after the event, is that we have no reliable evidence of what happened to it.

SON OF SOLOMON

In a different version of the story, the Ark is said to have been taken to Ethiopia by Menelik I, the son of Solomon and the Queen of Sheba, who became the first Jewish emperor of Ethiopia. Solomon had replicas of the Ark made to give to his sons and, with divine assistance, Menelik exchanged the replica he had been given for the real one in the Tabernacle.

The earliest known source for this version of events is the *Kebra Nagast*, or *The Book of the Glory of the Kings of Ethiopia*, which dates to the late thirteenth century. It is a compilation of writings from many different sources, including Jewish sacred works and Ethiopian legends, some of which are clearly very much older. Modern scholars believe the book was brought together as a means of legitimizing the rule of the Ethiopian emperor Yekuno Amlak, who came to the throne in 1270, by deposing his predecessor and who claimed to be a direct descendant of Solomon. The presence of the Ark in Ethiopia provided the emperor and his successors with further legitimacy because of its links with Menelik I, a situation that continued right up until 1974, when the last emperor of the dynasty, Haile Selassie, was deposed in a military coup.

According to the Ethiopian Orthodox Church, the Ark still remains in the country and is housed in a specially built chapel next to the Church of Our Mary of Zion in the city of Axum. It plays an important role in the Orthodox Church, with replicas, known as tabots, held in every Ethiopian church and used as centerpieces in religious festivals and processions. The Ark itself is considered to possess such great spiritual power that it is dangerous for it to be seen by anybody other than a specially appointed priest, who, on attaining the position, becomes its guardian for life, which he will spend entirely within the chapel.

SOLOMON
King Solomon, shown here with the Queen of Sheba, brought the Ark to Jerusalem.

In Ethiopia, the Ark is considered to possess such great spiritual power that it is dangerous for it be seen by anyone other than a priest.

As nobody else can see the Ark, it is not possible to verify the story of its presence in Ethiopia, even if it is an article of faith to the Christians of that country.

AN ENIGMA
In his book on the subject, Stuart Munro-Hall reluctantly comes to the conclusion that there is no chance of a wooden box built in the Sinai desert in the time of Moses surviving into modern times in Ethiopia or in southern Africa, or anywhere else for that matter. There may well be an ark within the church in Axum, but Munro-Hall is of the opinion that it is a replica. It continues to be revered by Ethiopian Christians as a symbolic representation of a connection between them and their God and so it doesn't much matter if it was made more than three thousand years ago or was put together last week by a carpenter.

The Ark of the Covenant, missing for twenty-five hundred years, remains an enigma. The only way it could have survived is if it had been hidden before Nebuchadnezzar sacked Jerusalem. The Temple Mount is known to have tunnels, some of which most likely date back to the relevant period. If the Ark were ever to be found, these tunnels represent the most likely location. The current political situation in Israel has prevented any archaeological investigation of Temple Mount in the modern era. Should this situation ever change, who knows what may turn up.

WHERE ARE THE LOST TRIBES OF ISRAEL?

ca. 720 BCE

Clue: They were last seen in Assyria

Main players: Israelites, Assyrians, and all sorts of other people

Verdict: Still lost

The Israelites who followed Moses out of Egypt were, according to the Hebrew Bible and Old Testament, made up of twelve tribes. Each of these tribes was headed by one of the twelve sons of Hebrew elder Jacob, who, after a vision in which he wrestled with God, became known as Israel. Once the Israelites had settled in the Promised Land, all but one of the tribes were assigned land, with members of the tribe of Levi serving as priests to the other tribes. To maintain the number twelve, which had a religious significance to the Israelites, the tribe of Joseph was split into two and these twelve tribes formed the Kingdom of Israel, which roughly corresponds to Israel and the Palestinian territories of today.

The unity of the kingdom lasted until the tenth century BCE, when, after the death of Solomon (king of Israel), most of the ten tribes in the north of the country refused to accept his successor, splitting the kingdom into Israel in the north and Judah in the south. In about 732 BCE, Israel was invaded by the Assyrians under their king Tiglarth-Pilesar, who annexed part of the country and began the process of deporting the Israelites out of the region. The Assyrian king Sargon the Great completed the job, invading the remnants of Israel in 721 BCE and exiling the remaining people, who, together with those who had already been deported, became known as the Ten Lost Tribes of Israel.

HISTORY AND MYTHOLOGY

It is generally accepted today, at least by those who accept the biblical story in the first place, that the entire population of Israel was not expelled. Scholars have suggested that the leaders and their families, together with some other prominent people, were driven out of Israel, amounting to about 20 percent of the population and perhaps forty thousand individuals. According to the book of Kings in the Old Testament, they were moved to Assyria itself and to other parts of the Assyrian Empire.

> **When Israel was invaded by the Assyrians, the people who were forced to flee the country became known as the Ten Lost Tribes of Israel.**

And that is the last we hear of them. Presumably, within a few generations they would have become assimilated with the local people and, in doing so, disappeared from history.

At this point, the creation of myths involving the lost tribes goes into

MOSES
When leading the Israelites out of Egypt to the Promised Land, Moses smashes the tablets bearing the Ten Commandments.

overdrive. In one version, it is claimed that the lost tribes will be reunited in Israel during the Messianic Age, a time of peace and prosperity that, according to some, will follow the coming of a new Messiah. In numerous other versions, a diverse range of people claim to have identified one of the lost tribes. Usually, the people making the claims do so on behalf of themselves in order to substantiate their belief that, as much as they might appear to be just another bunch of average men and women, in reality they are in fact God's chosen people. Over the years, such claims have been made on behalf of the British, the Irish, and the Americans, which, if we are being honest, must surely be a severe case of wishful thinking.

AROUND THE WORLD
A more likely place to look, it might be thought, is among the dispersed communities of Jews around the world, many of whom identify themselves with the lost tribes. Jewish communities have persisted in some unlikely places, including in China, Burma, southern India, and Iran, and have often been the subject of persecution. In such circumstances, a belief in their descent from one of the lost tribes becomes a

> *"Thus saith the Lord God: Behold, I will take the children of Israel from among the nations, whither they are gone, and will gather them on every side, and bring them into their own land; and I will make them one nation in the land, upon the mountains of Israel, and one king shall be king to them all; and they shall be no more two nations, neither shall they be divided into two kingdoms any more at all …"*
>
> **—Ezekiel 37: 21–23**

WISE KING
King Solomon is believed to have ruled over Israel in the tenth century BCE.

defense mechanism in that it gives them a sense of a collective identity and reinforces their community bonds.

But perhaps the most surprising group to claim descent from the lost tribes are the Pashtuns from the border regions of Afghanistan and Pakistan. Despite being devoutly Islamic, their oral tradition includes stories of their descent from Jewish ancestors, specifically one of the lost tribes. They also have some religious practices, such as the observance of the Sabbath as a day of rest, with clear parallels with the Jewish faith, which has been cited by some academics as giving the possibility of their Jewish ancestry more credibility than some. Suggesting such a thing to the Taliban (radical Islamic fundamentalists), who are predominantly ethnic Pashtuns, would presumably be unwise.

THE LEMBA PEOPLE

Another group with a similar oral tradition and with religious practices bearing some resemblance to Jewish traditions are the Lemba people of southern Africa, whom we have already encountered in the previous entry. They claim to be descended from Jewish people who migrated to southern Africa from a place they call Sena. This could be either Sana'a, the capital of Yemen, or the abandoned town of Sena in the north of the same country, both of which had substantial Jewish populations up until a few centuries ago. Genetic tests carried out on Lemba men add some scientific weight to the oral tradition. A similar percentage of these men have been found to carry the same unique genetic marker found in Jewish communities in Israel and America. The highest incidence of this marker occurs in the Bhunda clan, who have traditionally provided the leaders of the Lemba, where it is at levels

It is not known whether the Lemba people of southern Africa are one of the Lost Tribes of Israel. Genetic tests, however, show that their stories of their Jewish ancestry have some basis in fact.

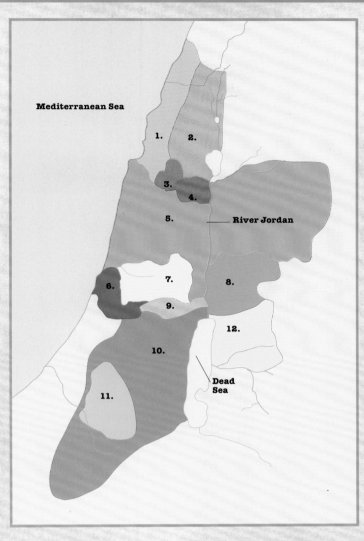

Mediterranean Sea

1. 2.

3.
4.

5.   River Jordan

6.   7.   8.

9.

12.

10.

Dead
Sea

11.

TRIBES
The twelve tribes
of the Kingdom
of Israel:

1. Asher
2. Naphtali
3. Zebulun
4. Issachar
5. Manasseh
6. Dan
7. Ephraim
8. Gad
9. Benjamin
10. Judah
11. Simeon
12. Reuben

to show that people are of Jewish ancestry is, then, a different thing from claiming they are part of the Lost Tribes of Israel.

THE REALITY
Jewish history is a long and constant story of exiles and migrations, both forced and voluntary, making any attempts to untangle the web of where people with Jewish ancestry originally came from difficult. Those who have claimed to be part of a lost tribe have usually done so for their own reasons. While it is not impossible that there are communities remaining today who are ancestors of the lost tribes, proving it after almost three thousand years would be next to impossible. In reality, the lost tribes will most probably always remain exactly that: lost.

comparable with the kohanim, the Jewish priests who are said to be directly descended from Aaron, the brother of Moses. No other non-Jewish group has been found with anything like this level of the marker and, while this does not prove that the Lemba are one of the Lost Tribes of Israel, it clearly shows that their stories of Jewish ancestry have some basis in fact. Using DNA analysis

DID THE HANGING GARDENS OF BABYLON EXIST?

ca. 600 BCE

Clue: A Babylonian queen yearns for a green garden

Main players: King Nebuchadnezzar and his homesick wife

Verdict: If the Greek writer Strabo says the gardens existed, then that's good enough for me

The Seven Wonders of the World was a list compiled by the ancient Greeks as a sort of early travel guide for people in the classical world, not unlike those books published today with titles like *Things to Do Before You Die*. Of these wonders, only one remains largely intact—the Great Pyramid of Giza is very obviously still standing in Egypt. Five of the others are well-known to us today, even if they are in ruins or no longer exist at all. The Statue of Zeus at Olympia, the Temple of Artemis at Ephesus, the Mausoleum of Halicarnassus, the Colossus of Rhodes, the Pharos Lighthouse at Alexandria— the locations of all of these have been firmly established and, where the ruins still remain, they have been investigated by archaeologists. That leaves only one, the Hanging Gardens of Babylon, about which we know almost nothing beyond what can be inferred from the name. We don't know exactly where the gardens were, what they looked like, or even if they actually existed at all.

EARLY CLUES

The earliest descriptions we have of the Hanging Gardens are from the classical period, in which Greek and Roman writers, such as Strabo, who was working early in the first century CE, quoted from sources that are now lost. These accounts attribute the creation of the gardens to Nebuchadnezzar, the king of the Neo-Babylonian Empire from 605 BCE to 562 BCE, who, as we have seen, destroyed the Temple of Solomon and sent the Jews into exile. It was a period of great prosperity and the expansion of empire—achievements marked by Nebuchadnezzar with a program of building works in Babylon.

The Hanging Gardens of Babylon were listed by the ancient Greeks as one of the Seven Wonders of the World. We don't know where they were, what they looked like, or even if they existed at all.

GREAT CITY
A lion adorning the Ishtar Gate of Babylon, also built by Nebuchadnezzar.

The Hanging Gardens could have been part of these works, built, so the story goes, by the king in an attempt to ease the homesickness felt by his wife Amyitis. She had grown up in the mountains of what is now Iran and, after she had come down to the hot and arid plain of Mesopotamia, missed the landscape and plants of her youth.

As romantic as the story is, there is no way of knowing if it is based on anything other than attempts to fill in the missing pieces of the story with some colorful anecdotes. No mention of either the Hanging Gardens or of a queen called Amyitis have been found in the Babylonian texts, which were excavated from the ruins of the city and date to the period of Nebuchadnezzar.

The Greek historian Herodotus, writing in the fifth century BCE, also has nothing to say on the subject, but does give a lengthy description of the walls of Babylon, considered by some to be another wonder of the ancient world. Modern archaeology has not been able to confirm the story either, although the inaccessibility of the site of Babylon in Iraq has meant that, in recent years, opportunities for further excavations have been limited.

The location of the ancient city of Babylon is well known, lying about 60 miles (100 km) to the south of

"The hanging garden consists of vaulted terraces, raised one above another and resting upon cube-shaped pillars. These are hollow and filled with earth to allow trees of the largest size to be planted. The pillars, the vaults, and the terraces are constructed of baked brick and asphalt. The ascent to the highest story is by stairs, and at their side are water engines, by means of which persons, appointed expressly for the purpose, are continually employed in raising water from the Euphrates into the garden. For the river, which is a stadium in breadth, flows through the middle of the city, and the garden is on the banks of the river."

—**Strabo,** *Geographica*

VAULTED TERRACES

Another depiction of the Hanging Gardens of Babylon, with trees and plants hanging from vaulted terraces supported by pillars.

Baghdad, on the other side of the Euphrates River from the modern town of Hillah. Ancient sources describe the Euphrates running through the middle of the city in Nebuchadnezzar's time, while today it runs on a different course to the west of the ruins. Unfortunately for any archaeologists hoping to uncover the remains of the king's palace, and any gardens he might have built, the change in the river's course could have resulted in the ruins now being underwater.

PLEASURE GARDENS

We may not have any solid evidence for Nebuchadnezzar's gardens in Babylon, but there are plenty of signs that gardens were an integral part of royal palaces in other parts of Mesopotamia. It is not hard to imagine a king withdrawing from the complexities of his court and the searing heat of the day to relax in a pleasure garden, where running water and the plants themselves would create a comfortable environment and an atmosphere of tranquility.

The Assyrian King Sennacherib (704–681 BCE) is known to have built a garden in his palace at Nineveh, the ruins of which are near the northern Iraqi city of Mosul. The interior of the palace was lined with stone reliefs, many of which are now in the British Museum, and in one of these a later Assyrian king is shown standing in his garden. He is surrounded by trellises from which luxurious vines hang down around him, an indication that, as wondrous as the Hanging Gardens of Babylon may have been, they could easily have been a much simpler structure than later accounts have made them out to be.

WRONG KING

Some academics have suggested that the classical writers had gotten the Assyrian and Babylonian kings confused in their accounts of Babylon and were actually describing Sennacherib's hanging garden rather than the one they attributed to Nebuchadnezzar. There are certainly similarities between these classical descriptions and what we know of Sennacherib's garden. It was laid out in terraces up the side of a hill and was watered by means of a mechanical system, in which water from the river was transported up to the top and then trickled back down through the garden.

Whatever the truth of the matter, the garden at Nineveh gives us an indication that wealthy Mesopotamian kings included such features in their palaces. As well as being a soothing place to relax, a garden could have been regarded as being the height of fashionable living at the time. If this was the case, then surely Nebuchadnezzar would have included a garden when he built a new palace for himself in Babylon, so it is possible that, one of these days, it will be discovered under the waters of the Euphrates.

HANGING GARDENS

The Hanging Gardens were supposedly built by the Babylonian king Nebuchadnezzar for his homesick wife Amyitis.

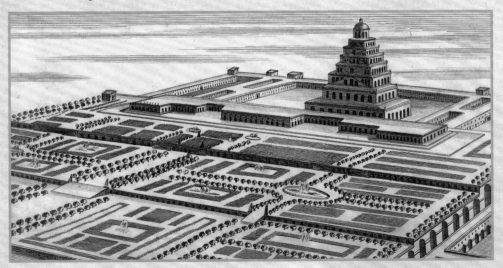

WHO MADE THE ANTIKYTHERA MECHANISM?

ca. 100 BCE

Clue: Its cogs and gears measure the positions of the planets

Main players: Various ancient Greeks

Verdict: Whoever made it built an astronomical calculating machine fifteen hundred years before anyone else did

Numerous articles appeared in the press about the Antikythera mechanism in 2006, describing it as one of the most extraordinary and mysterious objects made in antiquity. The headlines were along the lines of "two-thousand-year-old computer discovered," which, while not entirely inaccurate, was not exactly correct either. Presumably not much else was happening in the world that week, because the discovery of the mechanism was not quite up-to-the-minute breaking news. It was found in 1900 and its purpose has been extensively debated ever since. The theory generally accepted today, that it was used to calculate the positions of the sun, moon, and planets, was first put forward in the 1950s, so that hardly counts as a current event either. The accuracy of the newspaper headlines also rather depends on what is being implied by describing the mechanism as a computer. It would not, for instance, be a great deal of use for checking your email or updating your profile on Facebook. But what it was capable of doing, had it not spent the previous two thousand years underwater, is still remarkable enough considering it was made in the first century BCE. It might not be able to connect to the

> "This device is just extraordinary, the only thing of its kind. The design is beautiful, the astronomy is exactly right. The way the mechanics are designed just makes your jaw drop. Whoever has done this has done it extremely well. It does raise the question: What else were they making at the time? In terms of historic and scarcity value, I have to regard this mechanism as being more valuable than the Mona Lisa."
>
> —Professor Michael Edmunds, quoted in *The Scotsman*, November 30, 2006

THE MECHANISM
Even in its corroded state, the gears of the Antikythera mechanism can be made out.

internet, but no other device even approaching this level of complexity is known to have been built until the fifteenth century, when mechanical clocks were first constructed. So, now we know what it was capable of doing, the questions left to answer about it involve figuring out what it was used for and who built it.

THE DISCOVERY

The mechanism was recovered from the wreck of a Roman ship found in 200 feet (60 m) of water just off the coast of the tiny Aegean island of Antikythera. Greek sponge divers who were returning home to another Greek island from their diving grounds off the coast of Africa were forced to stop at the island due to bad weather. Diving off the coast, they stumbled across what they described as bodies lying on the seabed. These turned out to be Greek statues in both marble and bronze; these were salvaged the following year and sent to the National Archaeological Museum in Athens, where some of them are on display today.

The ship appears to have been transporting a cargo of artwork from provinces of Greece, where it had either been bought or looted, to Rome, and the archaeological importance of the find was immediately recognized. Few bronze statues from classical Greece remain

The mechanism was an astronomical calculating machine, which could be described, without any exaggeration, as being a manual analog computer.

intact, as almost all were melted down so that the metal could be reused for other purposes. The only statues to survive were ones that had been lost, like those on the Antikythera wreck. When these were first recovered, many had broken into fragments and had to be reassembled in the museum. In some cases, complete statues were put back together, a feat made possible because bronze survives

SPLIT OPEN

The mechanism was an encrusted block of bronze and wood and made little impression on the staff of the museum in Athens. After a few months, it is said to have split open on its own due to the corrosion of the bronze in the middle of the block, exposing a number of cogs and gears together with some Greek lettering and what appeared to be dials, scales, and pointers. A more likely story is that somebody in the museum applied a hammer to the block to see what would happen and, when it split, decided it would be best not to mention what they had done. Whatever the truth of the matter, the importance of what had been uncovered was clear and proper conservation measures were taken on the remaining heavily corroded pieces of bronze.

reasonably well in seawater. On immersion, a crust begins to form on the exposed surface that protects the metal beneath, but, once it is brought to the surface, the bronze quickly begins to corrode, so conservation measures need to begin as soon as possible.

FIERCE DEBATE

The mechanism was recovered with the statues and, initially at least, received little attention. However, it wasn't long before a fierce and at times vitriolic debate broke out among Greek archaeologists concerning what the mechanism might be. According to the more senior archaeologists at the museum, it was some kind of ancient astrolabe, a relatively straightforward device used to measure the position of the sun and stars and that does not rely on cogs and gears to work. Even though the mechanism looked nothing like any known astrolabe, and despite the protests of some junior staff members, who understood that it was a much more complicated mechanism, few further investigations were carried out.

CALCULATING MACHINE

It remained in relative obscurity until the 1950s, when a British scientist, Derek de Solla Price, took X-rays of the pieces in an attempt to determine its real purpose and to build a working model. He showed that it was composed of more than thirty gears, including some which allowed it to run backward as well as forward. It was operated by turning a crank handle as

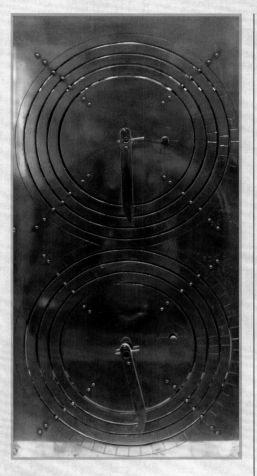

THE DIALS
Detail of a model of the mechanism showing what its dials would have looked like.

a means of entering a particular date, which caused the cogs and gears to turn, thereby rotating the pointers to show the position of the sun, moon, and the planets on a number of different dials. In essence, it was an astronomical calculating machine, which could be described, without any exaggeration, as being a manual analog computer.

The state of our knowledge remained at this level for another sixty years, until a number of scientists revisited Price's work. This is what prompted the newspaper articles in 2006 and, in doing so, brought the mechanism out of obscurity once and for all. For the most part, Price had been correct in his deductions about the workings of the mechanism. The only thing he got wrong was the nature of the gearing, which turned out to be epicyclic, a system that mirrors the movements of the planets around the sun. More of the Greek lettering has also been deciphered in recent years, again confirming Price's suspicions that some of the inscriptions provide an instruction manual for using the mechanism.

In a further twist, one of the dials has been shown to predict the timing of the four-year cycle of ancient Greek games, including those held at Olympia. The timing of these games was of great cultural significance to the Greeks, even if showing them on an astronomical device could have had little practical purpose. It is almost as if whoever built the mechanism was intentionally going beyond what was necessary in order to show what they were capable of achieving.

WHO MADE IT AND WHY?
Nothing comparable to the Antikythera mechanism has ever been found, so it is almost impossible to say with any degree of certainty where it was made. Also, unfortunately for us, whoever made it doesn't appear to have signed it or left us any other clues to their identity. References to the use of simple gears exist from antiquity, including in the work of Archimedes, now best known

for the story of how he jumped out of the bath and ran down the street naked shouting, "Eureka," after the idea of measuring volume through the displacement of water had suddenly come to him. He was working in Syracuse in Sicily in the third century BCE, more than one hundred years before the mechanism is thought to have been constructed, so it could not have been made by him.

ARCHIMEDES
The use of simple gears was referred to by Archimedes. Whoever made the mechanism may have been influenced by his work.

The person who made the mechanism must have had a high level of engineering skill and a detailed knowledge of astronomy.

CORINTH IN AROUND 100 BCE
The inscriptions on it are in a style of Greek in use in the city-state of Corinth in about 100 BCE, giving us both an approximate date for its construction and a possible clue to where it was made. At that time, Syracuse was a Corinthian colony, so it would not be unreasonable to conclude that it was made in the city,

perhaps in a workshop carrying on the type of innovative engineering experiments begun by Archimedes.

FARTHER EAST

An alternative theory is that the mechanism was made farther to the east, in one of the places where the ship on which it was discovered had visited before it sank. The cargo and coins found in the wreck indicate that the ship probably set out from Pergamon, an ancient Greek city on the coast of modern Turkey. It appears to have sailed first to the island of Rhodes, then on to Alexandria, before setting out on its final, ill-fated voyage, presumably with the intention of taking the loot it had collected back to Rome.

Both Rhodes and Alexandria were centers of learning in the Greek world, so it could have been made in either one, perhaps by somebody originally from Corinth. Scholars generally favor Rhodes over Alexandria because a number of Greek astronomers are known to have worked there at about the right time and, as well as having a high level of engineering skill, the person who made the mechanism must also have had a detailed knowledge of astronomy.

ITEM OF CURIOSITY

The intricate nature of the mechanism means that, whoever made it, they went to a great deal of time and trouble, so we can only assume they had a specific use for it in mind. It would not have been much good as a navigational aid because it was made of bronze and, if it had been taken to sea for any length of time, the metal would have quickly corroded, rendering it useless. One theory suggests it was made to give public demonstrations of astronomy and engineering, a common enough occurrence in Greece at that time. But the mechanism is only about the size of a shoebox so it would not have been easy for anybody to see it from any sort of distance.

Another problem is that some of the dials are on the back, which, again, would not have been very helpful for public demonstrations. But, other than this, it is difficult to know what else it could have been used for unless it was simply intended to elicit amazement and admiration.

ENGINEERING SKILL

After the fall of the Roman Empire, a great deal of the knowledge accumulated by the Greeks was lost, including work by Archimedes on the use of gears, so we may never know if the mechanism was used for anything in particular. Much of what has survived was copied by Arab scholars in the Byzantine Empire and was then reintroduced into Europe in the fifteenth and sixteenth centuries during the Renaissance. This may have been the source of the knowledge used in Europe to develop the first mechanical clocks and, if this was the case, it would provide a direct link between the Antikythera mechanism and the use of clockwork devices fifteen hundred years later. At present, no evidence exists to lend support to this theory, so, for the moment at least, the mechanism stands on its own as a unique example of engineering and scholarship from antiquity, and one which, until its discovery, we were not even aware the ancient Greeks were capable of achieving.

WHY WERE THE DEAD SEA SCROLLS HIDDEN IN CAVES?

ca. 150 BCE–70 CE

Clue: The scrolls were written in either Hebrew or Aramaic

Main players: Jews and Romans

Verdict: Probably written by a Jewish sect

If a religious community decided to live an austere life in order to get closer to their God, then choosing a spot near the Dead Sea would certainly help them in their efforts. It is the lowest-lying land on the surface of the earth and the terrain around it is mostly desert. The climate is hardly any better; it is hot and arid, making it inhospitable to all forms of life except for those specially adapted to live in such a place.

At Qumran, an archaeological site near the northwest shore of the sea, it appears a Jewish sect lived here, amid these harsh conditions and, while they were there, they also made copies of important religious texts. But, beyond the fact that people chose to live here, what makes it truly remarkable is that these texts have survived. They were hidden in caves in the steep sides of a valley near the site and, since their discovery, have become known as the Dead Sea Scrolls.

The first of the scrolls was found by a Bedouin shepherd who was out tending his flock near Qumran.

In the years since this discovery, all sorts of stories have circulated about the scrolls, brought about mainly by the incredibly slow rate of publication of the contents. Conspiracy theories, mostly concerning the implications of the scrolls for the Christian faith, have concentrated on what the people in possession of the scrolls have been trying to hide. In particular, they have claimed that the scrolls included lost or suppressed biblical works that told a very different story than the Bible's New Testament. As the contents have gradually been made public, over a period of fifty years, it has become apparent that all these theories have been baseless speculation. The real mystery surrounding the scrolls is not so much what they contain, which is remarkable enough, but who wrote them and why they decided to hide them in caves.

THE SCROLLS

The first of the scrolls was found in 1947 by a Bedouin shepherd who was out tending his flock near Qumran and accidentally fell into one of the caves. Over the following ten years, more than nine hundred were discovered in eleven different caves, the majority being written on parchment in either Hebrew or Aramaic. Almost all date from between 150 BCE and 70 CE, a crucial period in the development of both the Jewish and Christian faiths, and the content is mostly religious in nature. About 40 percent of the scrolls contain books of the Hebrew Bible. All the books are included, at least to some extent, with the exception of the book of Esther, and the scrolls constitute the earliest known copies of these texts in existence, predating the next earliest by about one thousand years.

A second group of scrolls, comprising 30 percent of the total, are religious texts that did not make it into the Bible. These are known as the Apocrypha and Pseudepigraphs and include the book of Enoch and the book of Jubilees. The rest of the scrolls are grouped together as the Sectarian manuscripts. The contents of these relate to the sect who wrote out the texts and include religious commentaries, the rules of the sect, and calendars. These were important documents because disputes about the dates and timings of religious ceremonies were often the cause of sects splitting from the mainstream Jewish religious community, known as the Second Temple.

The importance of the scrolls lies in both their age and in what they can tell us about the development of the Hebrew Bible and Judaism in the first century BCE and the first century CE. In the early years of research, the focus was primarily on how the scrolls related to Christianity, but, as most were written in the century before the birth of Christ, scholarly attention is now mostly concentrated on Jewish religious life at that time. However, they are still important to the study of Christianity as the Hebrew Bible forms the basis of the Old Testament.

PSALMS SCROLL

One of the best preserved of the Dead Sea Scrolls, comprising Psalms written in Hebrew.

QUMRAN

The scrolls also shed light on the Jewish background of the New Testament and provide an insight into the general state of religious life in Judea in the years immediately before and after the birth of Christ. It was a period of religious ferment, in which many sects, such as the one thought to have been responsible for writing the scrolls, were formed by those dissatisfied with the Second Temple. The first Christians were not involved in writing the scrolls, but they were part of the overall religious movements of the period.

The scrolls contain no direct references to the identity of the sect who wrote them. There is a great deal of information about the rules of the sect, but not enough to clarify who they were. Since the caves are close to the settlement at Qumran, most academics have concluded that this was where they

CAVE 4
This cave in the cliff face at Qumran contained almost 90 percent of the scrolls ever found.

were written. It was, the theory suggests, a seminary (training school) in the desert, not unlike later Christian monasteries, where religious texts were copied out as an act of devotion.

This interpretation is by no means accepted by everybody. Some have proposed that it was not a religious establishment at all, but an inn for travelers, the house of an estate, a factory for making pottery, or that the scrolls were written somewhere else and brought to the area to be hidden.

SIEGE OF JERUSALEM

So, if the scrolls were not written at Qumran, then where were they written? One theory proposes that they were removed from the libraries in Jerusalem and hidden in the desert during the Roman siege of the city after the Great Jewish Revolt of 66 CE. This began as a religious argument between Jews and Greeks, before escalating into a protest against taxation and all-out rebellion. In 70 CE, the revolt was crushed by the Romans, Jerusalem was ransacked, and the Second Temple was destroyed.

This provides a very good reason why important documents would be removed from the city. Some of the caves, however, are within a stone's throw of the buildings at Qumran, so they would have been a very poor choice of hiding place if the location was supposed to be secret. It would seem more likely that the people living at Qumran hid the scrolls in the caves, with most probably written on site. Whatever the truth of the matter, archaeological evidence also shows that Qumran was attacked and destroyed by the Romans in about 68 CE and, if anybody survived this assault, then they never came back to retrieve the scrolls.

THE IDENTITY OF THE SECT

In the absence of definitive proof from the scrolls themselves, and at the distance of two thousand years, it is not possible to say for certain exactly who wrote the scrolls. The contemporary historian Josephus (ca. 37–100 CE), provides details of a number of sects in Judea

Recent archaeological excavations at Qumran have found a number of ink wells, providing support for the theory that the scrolls were written on site.

THE ESSENES

A Jewish sect formed in the second century BCE, possibly by priests who had broken away from the Second Temple, the Essenes abstained from worldly pleasures and lived in voluntary poverty. One of their ritual practices involved daily immersion in water to achieve purity. At Qumran, a number of ritual baths have been found. Ritual immersion was by no means unique to them, but it provides a further strand of evidence, which suggest that the Essenes could have been responsible for the scrolls.

during the period when the scrolls were being written. A comparison between what Josephus wrote and the sectarian rules given in some of the scrolls has led some scholars to identify the most likely candidates as being the Essenes.

It is quite possible that a sect about which we know nothing was actually responsible for the scrolls, particularly as this period of Jewish history was one of constant religious turmoil. Nonetheless, the scrolls remain arguably the greatest discovery relating to the history of Judaism and Christianity. The identity of the people who wrote the scrolls is, in some respects, of secondary importance to the manuscripts themselves, but, at the same time, they are an integral part of the story. Work continues on both the scrolls and the site of Qumran, so, who knows, one day we may be able to complete the picture.

WILL THE HOLY GRAIL ALWAYS BE LOST?

ca. first century CE

Clue: It is said to be kept somewhere secret in Europe

Main players: Joseph of Arimathea, King Arthur, some medieval knights, and a bunch of other people

Verdict: The quest continues...

The Holy Grail is the mother of all mysteries. For a start, it is far from clear what it is supposed to be or what it could be used for. It could be a piece of tableware, like the cup or dish used by Christ at the Last Supper, or it could be a mystical and unobtainable object of desire, one containing all that is holy, the pure essence of God. It's hard to know, not least because the people who write about it don't give the impression of having much idea what it is either. In stories in which the grail appears, authors imply it is different things, almost always without explaining what that thing actually is, leaving us with the impression that they don't have the foggiest idea themselves. In fact, as far as I can tell, not having the foggiest idea about it would appear to be a must for going on about it at great length.

Mind you, there is one thing that can be said about the grail with some degree of certainty: it is not easy to find. And the job of finding it, usually referred to as "the Quest," is hardly made any easier if you don't know what the thing you are searching for looks like, never mind where it is. On a more serious note, if the Holy Grail is a physical object, such as the cup or dish used by Christ at the Last Supper, then it bears a close resemblance to the Holy Chalice, mentioned in several books of the New Testament and used by Christ to serve wine to the Apostles. It is described in the Gospel of Matthew:

> *"And he took a cup and when he had given thanks he gave it to them saying, "Drink this, all of you; for this is my blood of the covenant, which is poured out for many for the forgiveness of sins. I tell you, I shall not drink again of the fruit of the vine until I drink it new with you in my Father's kingdom."*

Beyond the Last Supper, no further mention is made of this vessel in the Gospels.

The job of finding the Holy Grail, usually referred to as "the Quest," is not made easy if you don't know what the thing looks like or where it is.

Later traditions say that the vessel was also used to collect the blood of Christ after the Crucifixion. In many Christian denominations, the sacrament of the Eucharist, or Holy Communion, reenacts the breaking of bread and taking of wine as symbols of the body and blood of Christ. Several vessels have turned up over the years that have been identified as the chalice. One of the best known is the Antioch Chalice, found near the Turkish city in the early years of the twentieth century. It is now in the Metropolitan Museum of Art in New York, where it has been studied by experts in the field, who describe the description of it as either the chalice or the grail as being "ambitious."

They say it was made in Antioch in the sixth century CE and was probably intended for use as a lamp rather than a

THE CRUCIFIXION

Joseph of Arimathea collects Christ's blood in the Grail in this fourteenth-century Italian illustration.

chalice. A rather more convincing chalice can be seen in the Cathedral of Valencia in Spain. It is a small cup made of agate stone, said to date from the first century BCE, and has at some stage been mounted on an elaborate gold stand. It apparently was taken to Rome by St. Peter, where it came into the possession of the pope and, by a somewhat roundabout route, ended up in Spain.

LEGEND OF KING ARTHUR

In truth, there is very little we can say with certainty about the physical object, so the literature on the subject mostly concentrates on the grail legend. This dates back to the medieval period, beginning in the late twelfth century with the French poet Chrétien de Troyes, who brings the grail into the stories he tells of King Arthur and the Knights of the Round Table. The source of these stories is by no means clear. One theory suggests that Chrétien brought Christian themes together with the work of Geoffrey of Monmouth (ca. 1100–1155), who told the stories of Arthurian legend as if they were matters of historical fact.

Chrétien may also have borrowed some of his themes from the stories of Celtic mythology, which became well known in France after the Norman Conquest of Britain. The mythology contains a number of stories about the exploits of heroes like King Arthur, such as swords being thrown into and retrieved from water, honor and chivalry between warriors, and the appearance of magical figures like Merlin and the Lady of the Lake.

FURTHER LEGENDS

The origins of the grail legends may be far from clear, but we do know that, once Chrétien got the ball rolling, plenty of

others picked it up and ran with it. Many of the features of the legends added at this time probably had more to do with the imagination of the various authors involved than with any particular source. One of these additions is the association of the grail with Joseph of Arimathea, the man who provided the tomb for the burial of Christ after the Crucifixion, and who, according to the stories of Robert de Boron, became the keeper of the grail and brought it to Britain. This is the origin of the legend of the grail being buried at Glastonbury Abbey, a story that some have taken as fact.

Over the years, numerous other mysterious and secretive associations have been attached to the grail legend in some way. The Knights Templar, for instance, were said to have found the grail on the Temple Mount in Jerusalem during the Crusades and brought it back to Europe, where it was kept in secret.

As if to add fuel to the fire, the Templars were founded in Troyes, France in 1129, so the poet Chrétien de Troyes may well have gotten his material for the Arthurian romances from the Templars after they had returned from the Holy Land.

POPULAR CULTURE
As the concept of the grail is so difficult to pin down, the door has been left open for successive generations of writers to adapt it to the requirements of the times. In recent years, it has become part of countless conspiracy theories concerning various secret factions who have passed knowledge of the grail on through the ages to a select few. One of the best known of

these is *The Holy Blood and the Holy Grail* by Michael Baigent, Richard Leigh, and Henry Lincoln, in which the grail is mixed in with all manner of conspiracy theories involving the Knights Templar, the Cathars, the Freemasons, and the Priory of Sion.

The conclusion reached in the book is that the grail actually refers to the bloodline of Christ rather than simply to a cup or dish. Apparently He did not die on the cross after all, but survived to marry and have children with Mary Magdalene. After the Crucifixion, Mary took the children to France to avoid persecution, where their descendants became the Merovingian kings of the Franks. Depending on whose lawyers are consulted, Dan Brown either did or did not base *The Da Vinci Code* on the theories presented in *The Holy Blood and the Holy Grail* and comes to the conclusion that the grail is buried underneath the pyramid that forms the entrance to the Louvre in Paris, France.

Popular culture is on safer ground when it doesn't present itself as historical truth. In the movie *Indiana Jones and the Last Crusade*, our intrepid archaeologist, fresh from wrestling the Ark of the Covenant away from the Nazis, sets about doing the same for the Holy Grail. There is no messing around with the grail legend here. It is presented as being a cup, albeit one with magical properties, and, in the end, after Indy has gone to all sorts of trouble to find it, he has to let it fall into an abyss to save his life rather than taking it home with him. But, as entertaining as the *Last Crusade* is, without a doubt the best, or at least the silliest, movie to feature the grail is *Monty Python and the Holy Grail*, in which we are introduced to the killer rabbit and the Knights Who Say Ni.

It would probably be giving the Monty Python team far too much credit to suggest that its ending was intended to be a metaphor for the nature of the grail itself, in which it is really all about the search for it and not the discovery. Intended or otherwise, the ending of the movie gets as close to telling us what the grail really is as many far more serious, and much less funny, versions of the story. One way of looking at it is to think of the grail as the answer to what Douglas Adams, in his science fiction comedy *The Hitchhiker's Guide to the Galaxy*, calls the big question of life, the universe, and everything. And, no matter what you do, it always remains just out of reach.

Monty Python's Grail
The movie is not the most accurate version of the grail legend, but it is the silliest.

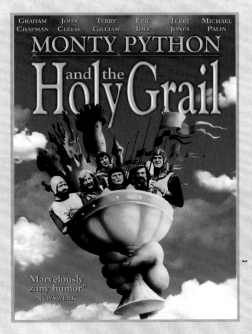

IS THE SHROUD OF TURIN A FAKE?

possibly first century CE

Clue: In the medieval period, more than forty shrouds were doing the rounds of cathedrals

Main players: Sindonologists of all persuasions

Verdict: Your guess is as good as anyone else's

Sindonology is not a word everybody knows. It means the study of the Shroud of Turin, and sindonologists, the people who take this study seriously, have made the shroud the most studied artifact in human history.

For a stretch of linen cloth, about 14 feet (4.2 m) long and 4 feet (1.2 m) wide, to have attained such a status is a remarkable achievement. But, then again, the Shroud of Turin is a remarkable object. The cloth bears the barely perceptible image of the front and back of a man, which shows up much more clearly in a photographic negative. The body depicted bears all the markings consistent with the suffering inflicted on Christ at the Crucifixion as it is described in the Bible.

Those who consider it to be the real thing claim it is the two-thousand-year-old burial cloth of Christ, used to wrap the body after it had been taken down from the Cross and laid out in its tomb, with an image of our Savior miraculously produced on it at the moment of the Resurrection. This view is disputed by those who think it is a fake, a medieval forgery purporting to be something it cannot possibly be.

The shroud was most likely created in the mid-fourteenth century, when there was a brisk trade in relics in all manner of supposedly religious objects.

A BLATANT FORGERY?

The debate appeared to have been settled once and for all in 1988 when a fragment of cloth from the bottom corner of the shroud was removed and sent for carbon dating in three separate laboratories. The findings of all three broadly agreed with each other; it was made between 1260 and 1390. This should have been, you might think, conclusive proof that the shroud was a fake. It was most likely created in the mid-fourteenth century, when a brisk trade in relics was supplying all manner of supposedly religious objects to competing European cities in order to fill their cathedrals with better artifacts than those of their neighbors. Anything associated with the Bible or the saints went for exorbitant sums, while if the relic related directly to Jesus, like a splinter from the Cross or a thorn from the Crown of Thorns, then the sellers could name their own prices.

In such a marketplace, where money was flowing freely and not too many questions were being asked about the authenticity of the objects on sale, it is hardly surprising to find unscrupulous characters taking advantage of the gullibility of their patrons by selling them forgeries. It has been estimated that more than forty shrouds, each claiming to be real, were doing the rounds of cathedral cities in the medieval period, each described as being the one and only Holy Shroud. Most of these were such blatant

TURIN CATHEDRAL

The shroud has been in the Cathedral of Saint John the Baptist since 1576.

forgeries that they would not have fooled anybody who bothered to look at them with any degree of skepticism at all.

HEATED DEBATE

Of the many shrouds, only one has stood up to scrutiny over the years, and it can be found in the Cathedral of Saint John the Baptist in Turin. Even the carbon-dating tests have been disputed, on the grounds that the sample taken for testing was contaminated or that it was from a part of the shroud that had been repaired in the medieval period. The overall effect of the dating process has only really been to increase and widen the debate over the shroud rather than settle it. Far from being out of a job, sindonologists have grown, both in academic circles and on the internet, even if the debates hosted on websites quickly degenerate into an exchange of insults. But, despite all the opinionated nonsense, plenty of unanswered questions surrounding the shroud remain, not least of which is, if it is a fake, how was it made?

DATING THE SHROUD

Modern techniques in such disciplines as forensic and materials science could well provide some of the answers, but so far the tests required have not been allowed by the pope, who technically owns the shroud, or by the people who keep it in Turin. Meanwhile, in a different strand of study, research has continued into the history of the shroud. If it can be shown to have been in existence before the medieval period, then this would at least prove that it was not made during the period when the forgery of relics was commonplace, thereby increasing the chances of it being real.

NEGATIVE SHROUD
The negative image is the best way of making out the details of the shroud.

For those who accept the shroud as real, its history begins in about 30 CE, when, according to the Bible, fine linen cloth was acquired by Joseph of Arimathea to cover the body of Christ. The cloth is all that remains in the tomb after the Resurrection, but no mention is made of any image being on it in any of the Gospels, a point made by, among others, the Protestant reformer John Calvin. He was deeply skeptical about the shroud and all other relics held in veneration by the Catholic Church.

DILEMMA
In a book on the subject, the art historian Thomas de Wesselow argues that the image of Christ on the shroud was what the Apostles saw in the tomb during the Resurrection, rather than the actual risen body. This theory involves a dilemma for those who believe the shroud to be genuine. Most of them are committed Christians and, on the one hand, the theory places the shroud in the tomb at the appropriate moment, while, on the other, it denies the Resurrection as described in the Gospels. De Wesselow also presents evidence obtained from the analysis of pollen found in the shroud, which tends to suggest that it predates the medieval period, together with work

The linen in the shroud has a distinctive herringbone pattern, a weave known to have been in use in the first century CE.

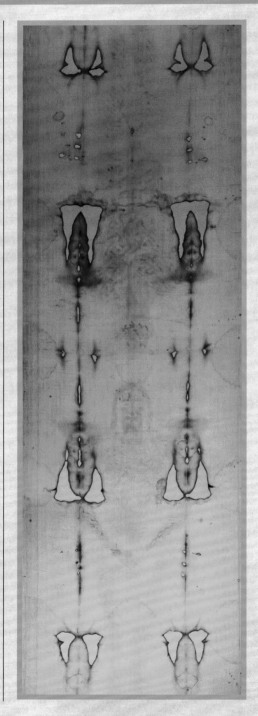

done on the type of textile used. The linen in the shroud has a distinctive herringbone pattern, a weave known to have been in use in the first century CE from other Jewish textiles of the period. Both lines of evidence have been contested, as has almost everything else to do with the shroud, and, even if proved to be correct, does not specifically place it in Christ's tomb. But, if the evidence can be substantiated, it does prove that the shroud is older than the carbon-dating tests have implied.

IMAGE OF EDESSA

The writer Ian Wilson has also developed a theory that suggests the shroud is considerably older than the medieval period. In his opinion, the shroud now in Turin is the same artifact as the Image of Edessa, a relic from the Eastern Orthodox Church that has been lost since the thirteenth century. Scholarly opinion is divided on this theory, with some contending that the relic was destroyed when the Christian city of Edessa, now Sanliurfa in the southeast of Turkey, was captured by the Islamic Ottomans in 1144, who destroyed all the churches and Christian imagery in the city. Others say the relic had been moved to Constantinople before Edessa was captured and it remained there until 1204, when the city was sacked by the knights of the Fourth Crusade, who were supposed to be heading for Jerusalem to recapture the city from the Saracens, but attacked Christian Constantinople instead. Nothing further is known about the whereabouts of the Image of Edessa, indicating that, if it was in Constantinople in the first place, it was either destroyed when the city was sacked or looted.

JOURNEY TO TURIN

The next we hear of the shroud is from 1355, when it is in the possession of the French knight Geoffrey de Charny. This story fits in with the theory of the shroud being looted from Constantinople, as de Charny is thought to have been the descendant of a crusading knight, but can just as easily be made to fit with the time frame suggested by the carbon dating for when it was forged. Whatever the case, by the mid-fifteenth century, the shroud was in the possession of the Duke of Savoy in the South of France, the first occasion when it can be definitely cited as the object now in Turin. In the sixteenth century, the territory controlled by the House of Savoy also included the Piedmont region of Italy and, in 1578, the shroud was transferred from the South of France to the cathedral in Turin, where it remains to this day.

History, then, can only place the shroud in the South of France in the 1450s; any theories that take it back further can only be speculative. Scientific analysis has also yet to prove conclusive. There is still plenty of room for new research, not least in discovering, if it is not the result of a miracle, exactly how the shroud was fabricated, a question that has so far baffled all those who have studied it. Ian Wilson, in his book, *The Shroud*, comes to the eminently sensible conclusion that the best course of action for anyone interested is to consider all the available evidence and then make up their own minds about whether they think it is real or fake. Personally, I think it's a fake. But, then again, what do I know?

DID ALIENS MAKE THE NASCA LINES?

ca. 400–650 CE

Clue: The lines are similar in style to Nasca pottery and textiles

Main players: The ancient Nasca people

Verdict: The lines have got nothing to do with aliens

One of the publishing sensations of the late 1960s and early 1970s was *The Chariots of the Gods?* by the Swiss writer and convicted fraudster Erich von Däniken, in which he set out his theories, mostly borrowed from other people, of extra-terrestrials visiting the earth. One strand of evidence he used to back up his ideas concerned the Nasca lines, a huge collection of markings, or geoglyphs, made in the desert plain between the Andes and the Pacific Ocean in southern Peru. These take a number of different forms: there are straight lines, spirals, and geometric shapes, together with drawings of people, animals, and plants. Perhaps the best known are the drawings of animals, including monkeys, hummingbirds, and condors.

In a nutshell, von Däniken viewed these geoglyphs as having been made to provide landing strips for extra-terrestrial spacecraft in ancient times and these alien astronauts, once they had landed, were worshiped as gods by the ancient Peruvians. It is hard to believe that such crazy theories could be taken even slightly seriously. Were people so gullible back then that they were prepared to accept any old nonsense by way of an explanation, no matter how weird? Or, were people too polite to enquire what use a large drawing of a monkey

> *"Remember the saying, 'Every age has the Stonehenge it desires or deserves?' The lesson learned from Stonehenge, indeed from the deepest study of all the great feats of human engineering we like to call the wonders of the world, is that to know their meaning we must know about the people who built them. To know Nasca means we become acquainted with all the Andean peoples past and present. Unless we do, we are destined to get the Nasca lines we deserve."*
>
> —Anthony F. Aveni, *Nasca: Eighth Wonder of the World*

would have been to aliens coming in to land in their flying saucers? And of course, if we may presume that the Nasca lines had nothing to do with aliens, it begs the question of who really made them and why?

THE NASCA?

The obvious place to start in any investigation of the lines is with the people who were living in the region at the time the lines were made. They are known to us as the Nasca, sometimes spelled as Nazca. Their distinctive culture appears on the plain by about 400 BCE and spreads out along the rivers into the foothills of the Andes. The culture reached its high point in the first four centuries after the birth of Christ and then gradually declined until

NASCA LINES
The arid and rocky plateau where the Nasca made their huge lines. This condor is an example of some of their drawings of animals.

disappearing by about 600 CE. These people were farmers, cultivating the strips of land on either side of the rivers, and are known today particularly for the beautiful pottery and textiles they produced. The designs on surviving examples of these artifacts bear a striking resemblance to the patterns of the lines, so it is not a great leap to suggest that the same people were responsible for both.

The plain is one of the most arid parts of the world and this was reflected in Nasca culture. As well as developing a complex system of water storage and irrigation, they appear to have worshiped the mountains to the east of the plain, from where the rivers, their main source of water, flowed.

NASCA WEAKENED

The Nasca capital city, Cahuachi, is now a major archaeological site and, so far at least, no houses have been uncovered. Archaeologists think it was used entirely as a religious and ceremonial site. As the culture declined, the city was abandoned and gradually covered over with sand. The reasons for the decline are not fully understood at present, but it may be due to a long-term change in the climate, beginning in about 500 CE, when the region became even more arid.

During this period, all the trees lining the banks of the rivers and in small wetland areas appear to have been cut down to make more room for farming.

EXTREME WEATHER

The weather systems in this part of the world can be highly unpredictable and, during extended droughts, some of the rivers can dry up completely. It is also subject to the El Niño effect, a change in weather patterns associated with the reversal of the ocean current in the Pacific, which can cause intense downpours of rain after years of arid conditions, resulting in flash floods sweeping across the plain. The lines may be a kind of offering or prayer to the gods to ward off potential disaster from the extreme conditions.

Von Däniken claimed the lines had been made as landing strips for alien spacecraft in ancient times.

The roots of the trees would have prevented soil from washing away during those occasional flash floods, so, by cutting them down, the Nasca could have exposed their precious soil to erosion, undermining their ability to produce enough food.

By about 600 CE, the territory of the Wari people, who were from the central highlands to the east and were more war-like than the peaceable Nasca, was expanding westward. So it is possible that the Nasca culture, already weakened by long periods of drought and failing harvests, was overwhelmed by the more powerful Wari.

THE LINES

The Nasca plain is made up of a stony desert. On the surface, small pebbles, rich in iron ore, have oxidized to a dark reddish-brown and these rest on a much lighter-colored sandy soil. The people who made the lines simply moved the dark pebbles to expose the sand beneath and then used the pebbles to create edges to the lines. Recent studies have shown that the earth in the lines is more compacted than it is over the rest of the plain, leading to the conclusion that the Nasca maintained their lines by regularly walking along them.

Some people have speculated that walking the lines was a form of ritual prayer, perhaps a means of asking their gods to keep providing them with water from the mountains. Pottery shards have also been found along the lines, which may have been ritually smashed as offerings to the gods.

For people living in such a precarious spot, where their lives were dependent on an unreliable water supply, these kinds of acts in the form of prayers and offerings may have been as much as they could do to ward off the disaster that would follow if the rivers ran dry for an extended period.

SOCIAL PURPOSE

A common mistaken belief about the lines is that they are only visible from the air. The Nasca plain is in a basin, with higher ground rising on three of its sides, from where the lines are clearly visible. Most of the designs were formed from a single continuous line, which doesn't cross over itself, allowing people who were walking the lines not to be interrupted. Presumably, people would come together on vantage points on the higher ground to watch processions along the lines.

So, as well as having a sacred purpose, there was, like many religious festivals around the world, a social side to the gatherings as well. But, as the Nasca culture disappeared about fourteen hundred years ago, it is impossible to know for certain if this was how the lines were used.

At least the theory presented above, unproven as it may be, is based, quite literally, on the evidence on the ground, which surely makes more sense than looking to the skies for aliens and spaceships.

MONKEY
A drawing of a monkey is just one of the hundreds of individual figures that make up the Nasca lines.

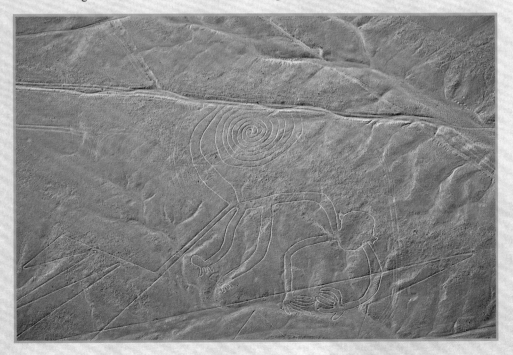

DID KING ARTHUR REALLY EXIST?

ca. 500 CE

Clue: Arthur is linked to a lady in a lake and a magician

Main players: Ancient Britons, Romans, Anglo-Saxons

Verdict: Probably not, but you never know

In a previous entry, we encountered King Arthur and the Knights of the Round Table in relation to the quest for the Holy Grail, an epic of romance and chivalrous behavior written by the French poet Chrétien de Troyes in the late twelfth century. The grail quest was Chrétien's own creation, but many of his other stories followed on from the writings of Geoffrey of Monmouth (ca. 1100–1155), who recounted most of the Arthurian legends we are familiar with today as if they were historical fact. We hear of the sword in the stone and the lady in the lake, as well as of Arthur's court of Camelot, the magician Merlin, and the love affair between Lancelot and Guinevere.

These stories have been retold and added to ever since, including by Sir Thomas Mallory (ca. 1405–1471) in *Le Morte d'Arthur*, one of the first books printed in England by William Caxton. In recent times, Arthur has been given a new lease of life in the movies, even if some of them have been better than others. The question is, was there more than just legend behind these stories? Was Geoffrey of Monmouth correct to treat Arthur as a real historical character, or did he, like many others after him, simply invent a version of the stories to suit his own purposes?

BRITISH WARLORD

After the Romans left Britain, by 410 CE, numerous small warlords filled the now vacant positions of power. As well as fighting between themselves, these warlords faced threats from beyond their borders, from the Picts in what is now Scotland, and from the Irish.

Writing in the mid-sixth century, a little over a hundred years after the event, the British cleric Gildas says that Vortigern, one of the British warlords, invited Saxons to Britain to help in the fight against the Picts and Irish and that

The Arthurian legends tell of the sword in the stone, the lady in the lake, as well as of Arthur's court of Camelot, the magician Merlin, and the love affair between Lancelot and Guinevere.

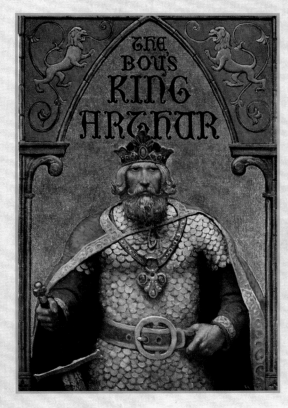

KING ARTHUR
The title page of *The Boy's King Arthur*, based on a fifteenth-century collection of traditional stories about King Arthur.

they settled in Kent. More Germanic tribes began to join them and, eventually, they rebelled against the British.

Toward the end of the fifth century, the rebellion had developed into a full-blown war. It is at this point that one of the warlords is said to have united the British to fight against the Saxons, most notably at the Battle of Badon in the late fifth or early sixth century, which became a famous victory for the British and halted further expansion by the Saxons for many years.

LEGENDS OF KING ARTHUR

The victorious British warlord was not identified as King Arthur until many centuries after the Battle of Badon, about which almost nothing is known other than its name and that it was a British victory. Modern archaeologists have not been able to establish if such a battle was fought, let alone its location and who fought in it. Some now even question the whole Anglo-Saxon invasion of Britain, seeing it as the arrival of Germanic tribes in small-scale movements rather than by major battles and warfare.

The monk and highly regarded historian Bede (ca. 673–735) does not mention a king by the name of Arthur in his major work *The Ecclesiastical History of the English People*, although his main purpose in writing the book was to detail the conversion of the Anglo-Saxons into Christian Englishmen, rather than explore the earlier history of the Britons.

Arthur does get a number of mentions in Celtic poetry, such as in the Welsh poem *Y Gododdin*, parts of which have been dated to the sixth century, which would be the earliest known reference to Arthur in a text. Unfortunately, the earliest text we have of *Y Gododdin* is from the thirteenth century and the poem that mentions Arthur is thought to have been an even later addition.

Much the same can be said of stories about Arthur in other collections of Celtic myths. The problem is the surviving texts we have were copied out at a much later date, and the monks who made these copies may well have replaced a non-Christian god of the Celts with the well-known character of Arthur.

LADY IN THE LAKE
According to the legends of Arthur, he is given his sword by the mysterious lady in the lake.

HISTORY OF THE BRITONS

The earliest known mention of Arthur is in the *Historia Brittonum* (*History of the Britons*), which dates to the early ninth century, three hundred years after the Battle of Badon. Some say the Welsh monk Nennius was responsible for the work although other historians see the *Historia* more as a collection of historical and mythological stories. It includes a discussion of twelve battles in which Arthur fought, concluding with the Battle of Badon. It tells two stories about Arthur: one about his dog Cabal, who left a footprint in a rock while hunting a boar; and the other concerning his son Anir, in which Anir betrays Arthur and is killed and buried by him. The mixing of the historical and the mythological, sometimes within the same story, makes it impossible to know for certain whether Arthur was a real person or not. All that can really be said is that it became an important source for later authors and, in particular, to Geoffrey of Monmouth, which only serves to cast further doubt on the accuracy of what Geoffrey wrote.

In the *Historia Regum Britannia* (*The History of the Kings of Britain*), Geoffrey takes what few historical facts are known about the early kings of Britain and elaborates on them, inventing large parts of what he claims to be history. According to one school of thought, what he was actually trying to do, rather than write a factual document, was to present the Norman kings of his own period in a a good light and as the rightful rulers of the kingdom. If that meant some facts had to be massaged, or invented completely, he was happy to oblige. In such circumstances, attempting to sort out which, if any, parts of his work can be relied on is pointless. He is probably best regarded as the father of the legendary Arthur, rather than the source of information on the possibility of a historical figure.

MAGIC AND MYSTICISM

Over the years, lots of places have claimed an Arthurian connection, with some archaeologists even backing these claims. Perhaps they were trying to raise the profile of their work or they too had

Not one piece of concrete archaeological evidence has ever been found relating to a British king by the name of Arthur.

GLASTONBURY TOR
A ruined church stands on the Tor, thought by some to be the site of Avalon.

been caught up in the mysticism and magic of the legends. Glastonbury Tor in Somerset is said to be Avalon, the island where Arthur was taken after being fatally wounded by his traitorous nephew Mordred and where he is said to be waiting to return should Britain ever need him again. Arthur's court of Camelot has been found any number of times, most famously at Tintagel Castle in Cornwall and South Cadbury in Somerset.

Unfortunately for those of a romantic nature, and for those employed in the tourist industry in various parts of Britain, not one piece of concrete archaeological evidence has ever been found, in Tintagel, Glastonbury, or

anywhere else, relating to a British king of the fifth and sixth century by the name of Arthur. Put this together with the complete absence of any mention of Arthur in texts before the ninth century and what we are left with is virtually nothing at all. Perhaps we should be content with what we do have rather than trying to find what will, like the Holy Grail, always remain just out of reach. Who knows, one day Arthur might come back from Avalon when we are in need of him most. But I, for one, won't be holding my breath.

WHAT CAUSED THE SUDDEN COLLAPSE OF THE MAYA?

ca. ninth century onward

Clue: Maya territory is made up of porous limestone

Main players: The inhabitants of the Yucatán Peninsula

Verdict: A population crash could have been brought on by drought

The European colonization of the Americas after their discovery by Christopher Columbus in 1492 had a devastating impact on the people who were already living there. Within a few decades, Spanish conquerors, known as conquistadors, had begun the process of colonization in Central and South America, all but wiping out the Aztec civilization in Mexico and the Incas of Peru. But the Spanish cannot be blamed for the collapse of the Mayan civilization, which, in its day, was as advanced as any in the Americas. By the time of their arrival, the Mayan culture was already long past its peak. That is not to say it disappeared completely; the Maya still live in the same region today, on the Yucatán Peninsula of southern Mexico and Belize and stretching into the highlands of Guatemala, Honduras, and El Salvador. But their numbers have never recovered to anything like the population levels reached in the period of the Classic Maya Civilization, when step pyramids and temples were being built in Mayan cities, the decorative arts flourished, books were produced using

"The city was desolate. No remnant of this race hangs around the ruins, with traditions handed down from father to son and from generation to generation. It lay before us like a shattered bark in the midst of the ocean... Architecture, sculpture, and painting, all the arts which embellish life had flourished in this overgrown forest; orators, warriors, and statesmen, beauty, ambition, and glory had lived and passed away, and none knew that such things had been, or could tell of their past existence."

—**John Stephens,** *Incidents of Travel in Central America, Chiapas and Yucatan* **(The first description of Maya ruins), 1841**

MAYAN RUINS
Temple 1 and the Great Plaza of Tikal in Guatemala, the Mayan city abandoned in the tenth century.

hieroglyphic writing, and the sciences, particularly mathematics and astronomy, achieved heights not seen anywhere else in the Americas.

Then, in little more than a hundred years, beginning in the ninth century CE, it all fell apart. Cities were abandoned and reclaimed by the surrounding tropical forests and the population crashed, declining by more than 90 percent in some areas. So, what happened?

What caused such a dramatic collapse in such a short space of time?

THE MAYA

The Mayan civilization was by no means a flash in the pan. A recognizably Mayan culture has been identified by archaeologists going back over two thousand years, even if what we now think of as being Mayan, the cities and temples, only began in about 200 CE. Unlike both the Aztecs and the Incas, the Mayan culture never came together into an empire governed by a single ruler. Instead, it developed into numerous city-states, each centered on its own ruler

CALENDAR
A typical colored clay calendar. The Maya developed extremely complex calendars.

extend territory. The fate of those captured was not pleasant. They were often sacrificed in ceremonies conducted by the rulers of the cities, who were regarded as being god-like and were closely associated with maintaining the prosperity and good fortune of the society as a whole.

Agricultural advances at the beginning of the classic period were quickly followed by a rapid growth in population, allowing the elites to become very powerful within their society. It also fueled the building of the cities and the huge monuments that remain today. The extent of this population growth is hotly disputed among academics, but certainly resulted in millions of people living in densely populated areas. One estimate puts the population at eleven million at the height of the classic period in the eighth century, immediately before the start of the collapse.

LANDSCAPE AND CLIMATE
Much of the territory occupied by the Maya, on the Yucatán Peninsula and in the central lowlands, is known as a karst landscape, where the predominant type of rock, in this case limestone, is porous. Rather than remaining on the surface, water seeps through the rock and flows underground, so, for people living in one of these regions, there are few sources of readily available water.

and with its own ceremonial sites. The most highly developed of these, which include Tikal, Chichen Itza, and Copán, are well-known tourist attractions today.

The society as a whole was primarily agricultural, living on a basic diet of corn and beans, with only small domestic animals and wild game to provide meat. No large animals were available for food, transport, or to work on farms and crops, limiting both the agricultural output of Mayan farming and the distances the Mayan could travel.

A great deal of attention has been focused on the violence evident in Mayan society, for the good reason that it was both widespread and brutal. Wars between neighboring city-states were a common occurrence and appear to have been conducted as much for the prestige of the elite classes and to capture prisoners of war as for any ambition to

The consequences of this for the Maya were that they were highly dependent on rainfall for their drinking water and to irrigate their crops. Where the water table is near the surface, usually near the coast, natural sinkholes called cenotes can form, where the limestone has been eroded away from underneath by water until it collapses. But further inland, the Maya were forced to come up with elaborate ways to ensure they had a water supply. At Tikal, for example, a huge reservoir was excavated in the limestone and lined with clay to prevent the water from draining away.

The climate in this region is tropical, and there are distinct wet and dry seasons. For the Maya, preserving enough water during the wet season to last out the dry period was of vital importance, particularly as the population began to increase. In order to feed this growing population, extensive areas of forest would have been cleared to provide more land for cultivation. A consequence of this would undoubtedly have been increased erosion of the already thin tropical soils.

Cutting down large areas of forest can also reduce the amount of rainfall as trees act as a living reservoir and cycle water through the natural processes of evaporation and transpiration (giving off water vapor). So, by cutting down the forest, the Maya were storing up trouble for themselves. But, even though this may have played some part in the oncoming crash, it is not thought to have been the main cause.

DROUGHT AND SOCIAL STRIFE

There are many theories to explain the collapse of the Mayan civilization, chief among them being long-term drought conditions. As well as reducing agricultural production, a drought would have had a domino effect on social stability. If the ruling elite repeatedly promised good harvests that then failed to materialize, it could well have led to revolts in the lower classes. What use is a ruler, after all, if they can't deliver prosperity to their people?

The study of sediments in the bed of one of the few lakes in Yucatán has enabled researchers to develop a detailed picture of the climate going back for thousands of years. It shows that the beginning of the collapse coincided with the onset of the worst drought to hit the region in over seven thousand years. One dry year was followed by another, so city reservoirs could not be adequately refilled nor crops properly irrigated. As a result, Mayan society would have started to come apart at the seams.

The theory of collapse brought on by drought is a long way from being universally accepted. Some don't even accept that the collapse occurred at all, as the Maya still inhabit much of the same territory, if in substantially reduced numbers. That aside, such a dramatic drop in population must surely serve as a warning to us all. Civilizations that have lasted for thousands of years can be brought crashing down by what, at the time, may have been thought of as an insignificant event. We may think it could never happen to us. No doubt the Maya would have thought the same thing.

The collapse of the Maya coincided with one of the worst droughts in over seven thousand years.

WHAT HAPPENED TO THE EASTER ISLAND STATUES?

ca. 1100–1600

Clue: They are a strange presence on the open, treeless landscape

Main players: Rapanuians (inhabitants of the island)

Verdict: A more complicated and involved story than is often told

Easter Island is remote. The people who live there today say it is the most remote inhabited island in the world and, as it is more than 2,000 miles (3,200 km) off the coast of Chile and over 1,000 miles (1,600 km) from the nearest inhabited Pacific island, they may have a point.

Easter Island is justly famous for the stone statues, the moai, which stand on platforms, known as ahu, in numerous locations around the coast of the island. They almost all face inland and are said to represent the ancestors of the islanders who watch over their descendants. With their elongated heads and serious, some might say mournful, expressions, they are an eerie presence in the open, treeless landscape of the island.

Since it was first visited by European ships, beginning with the Dutch explorer Jacob Roggeveen on Easter Sunday 1722, the statues have inspired countless people to attempt to explain their presence in a place where few people lived and where there were hardly any natural resources. Our old friend Erich von Däniken (whom we met on page 72) thinks they were made by extra-terrestrials, but then again, he thinks just about everything was made by aliens. The Norwegian explorer Thor Heyerdahl, who spent several months studying the statues in the 1950s, cited

> *"No nation will ever contend for the honour of the discovery of Easter Island as there is hardly an island in this sea which affords less refreshments and conveniences for shipping than it does; nature has hardly provided it with any thing fit for man to eat and drink, and as the natives are but few and may be supposed to plant no more than sufficient for themselves, they cannot have much to spare to new comers."*
>
> —**Captain James Cook,** *Journals*, **March 17, 1774**

THREE MOAI
The heads of three of the moai sticking out of the ground near Rano Raraku.

of the islanders. They were all quarried in the same place, Rano Raraku, a crater of volcanic rock known as tuff on the slopes of Terevaka, the largest of the three volcanoes on the island. The tuff is a relatively soft rock formed when volcanic ash becomes compacted, and it is ideal for carving into statues. Nearly four hundred of the moai are still in the quarry, some because the carving went wrong before they were finished, some that appear to have been abandoned, and some that have been erected on the slopes around the quarry.

These moai have been buried up to the neck by debris from the quarry, so now often only the heads are visible. Roads lead from the quarry to various parts of the island, and a further hundred moai can be found at different locations along these roads, as if abandoned before they arrived at their final destination. The rest were at one time standing on the ahu—platforms of rubble kept in place by stone retaining walls. By the nineteenth century, all of these had collapsed, some as the result of earth

them as evidence in support of his theory that the Pacific islands were colonized by people from the South American continent. The islanders, many of whom are of Polynesian descent, say their own ancestors erected the statues, which, let's be honest, is by far the most likely story. The mystery, then, is not really who was responsible for putting up the statues, but how, given the impoverished condition of the island, they managed to do it at all.

THE MOAI

Almost nine hundred moai have been identified on Easter Island, or *Rapa Nui*, as it is known in the Polynesian language tremors and others, it would seem, intentionally pushed over.

Over the years, about sixty have been re-erected on the platforms to give an idea of what they would have originally looked like. Only a few still have what appear to be hats, made from a red volcanic stone that had broken into pieces when the moai fell, and none now have eyes. The eyes, made from white coral, with pupils of obsidian rock, were found smashed on the ahu.

It is not possible to carbon date stone, but the coral has shown that most of the moai were put up between the thirteenth and sixteenth centuries, increasing in size as time passed. The largest is 30 feet (9 m) tall and weighs over 80 tons (73 tonnes), with the average being 12 feet (3.6 m) and 10 tons (9 tonnes).

A real monster remains in the quarry, which, if it had ever been erected, would have stood 70 feet (21 m) tall and weighed in at 70 tons (245 tonnes). It is hard enough to envisage how the average-sized statues were moved around the island, but it defies belief that anybody was really intending to transport and erect this one, bearing in mind it could only have been done by manpower alone.

RAPA NUI

When European sailors first began stopping at the island in the eighteenth

ISOLATED ISLAND
The remote position of Easter Island makes it one of the most isolated inhabited places on earth.

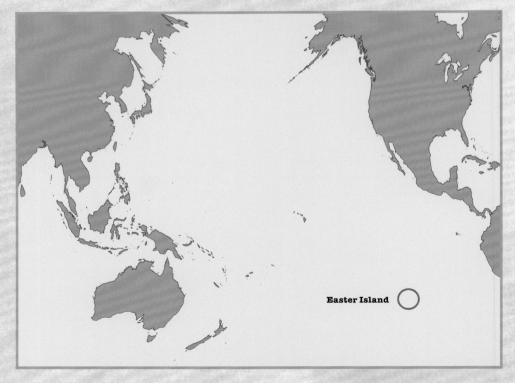

Easter Island

VOLCANIC ROCK
Moai with hat made of red volcanic stone and eyes made from white coral and obsidian rock for the pupils.

century, they found it to be in an impoverished and desperate state; no trees grew on the island, the soils were poor, and there were not very many wild animals. Estimates of the population vary, but there were probably in the region of two to three hundred people living on the island. The modern debate about who these islanders were could have been a lot shorter if those involved had paid attention to Captain Cook. When he stopped at the island in 1774, he had a Tahitian man with him who could talk to the islanders when speaking in his own Polynesian language. In more recent years, DNA testing has confirmed a Polynesian origin for the islanders, and it is now generally accepted that they first arrived in around the tenth century ce, presumably having made a very long oceanic voyage in canoes.

The island as found by these original Polynesian settlers was very different from how it appeared to Europeans in the eighteenth century. The analysis of the types of pollen found in lake sediments have shown that lush forests covered the entire island before people arrived, and it must also have been a haven for seabirds due to the absence of large predators.

POPULATION GROWS
As a result of such abundance, the population of the settlers rose quickly, estimated to have reached perhaps fifteen thousand people (although others vigorously contend that the population was much lower), who had split into twelve clans, dispersed across the island. By this time, the carving of moai had become well established. The artistic style of the statues is similar to that of

The statues are said to represent the ancestors of the islanders who watch over their descendants. They are an eerie presence in the open, treeless landscape of the island.

artifacts made on other Polynesian islands, but the increasing size of the moai was not done anywhere else. The reason they gradually became so big is not known, but may be a consequence of competition between the elites of the clans, each trying to outdo the other by erecting larger and larger statues.

As the population grew, more land was required for cultivation, so the forests were gradually cleared. This process could well also have been stimulated by the competition over the moai, as large amounts of wood would have been required to move and erect them, as well as ever-increasing lengths of rope, which was made from bark.

By about the sixteenth century, all the trees had been cut down, exposing the soils to wind erosion and making

MOAI ABANDONED

By the time Europeans arrived on Easter Island, the islanders appear to have rejected the worship of their ancestors, who had failed to protect them (from themselves mostly) and provide for them. They apparently toppled over and intentionally broke some of the moai. As a replacement, a strange cult had developed whereby each clan selected an individual to take part in an annual competition to collect a tern egg from a small island just off the coast. The winner became "Birdman of the Year," a title that may have given the holder the right to allocate the dwindling resources over the following year.

> **By about the sixteenth century, all the trees had been cut down, exposing the soil to wind erosion and making farming harder and harder.**

farming progressively harder and harder. There would also have been no wood left to build canoes, severely limiting the amount of fishing the islanders could do, which, in turn, probably led them to over-exploit the seabird colonies for food, leading to a population crash in their numbers as well.

At about this time, there was an explosion in the construction of stone chicken coops; the remains of more than a thousand now cover the island. Chickens were the only domestic animal the islanders had, so it would appear they were attempting to compensate for the reduced yields from the land, along with less fish and fewer seabirds, by rearing more chickens.

POPULATION PLUMMETS

Wherever there is a shortage of food, social unrest is bound to follow and it is easy to envisage the islanders rebelling against their leaders. But, with no means of getting off the island, the population began to drop, presumably as a result of fighting between clans for resources and through starvation. By the mid-nineteenth century, Christian missionaries put a stop to what they considered a pagan ritual. At about the same time, slave traders began to kidnap islanders to work in mines in Peru, substantially reducing a population that had already been severely ravaged by the diseases brought to the island by Europeans.

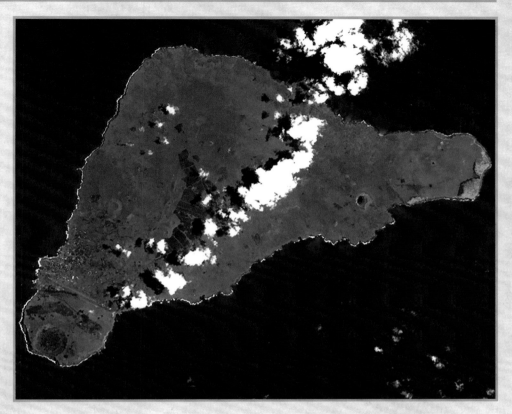

By the time the island was annexed by Chile in 1888, there were only a few hundred people left. For some researchers, the catastrophic effect of disease and slave trading was at least as important in the drop in the population as the decline in the available resources.

LESSONS LEARNED

Given their exploitation of the island's resources, in particular the cutting down of all their trees, it is easy to blame the islanders for their own demise. In doing so, one could use Easter Island as the example of how disastrous humanity's impact on the environment can be.

Yet, while there are lessons to be learned about the extreme fragility of the

ENVIRONMENTAL PROBLEMS

Easter Island offers a case study for people seeking to understand the dangers of environmental degradation.

environment and the sensible management of resources, the devastation that was brought to peoples on Easter Island and in numerous other places around the world, by contact with the Western world should not be forgotten either. The island's elite must also have had a part to play; they appear to have been more concerned with building moai than with ensuring their people had enough food to eat. In combination, these elements form the central planks of what is in reality a much more complicated and tragic story.

WHAT IS THE STRANGE VOYNICH MANUSCRIPT?

ca. fifteenth century

Clue: Voynich said he acquired it from a Jesuit college in Italy

Main players: Roger Bacon, John Dee, book dealers, code-breakers and librarians

Verdict: Still the most mysterious manuscript in the world

The rare book business has always attracted its fair share of colorful characters and Wilfred Voynich (1865–1930) most certainly was one of them. Before going into the book trade, first in London and then in New York, he had been involved in a revolutionary organization in Poland, then part of the Russian Empire. After being caught and sent to Siberia, he escaped and traveled to Britain. The exact circumstances of how he managed to get out of Siberia are, like many other details of his life, not easy to establish, but, after arriving in London, he began to work in the book trade and, in 1895, opened his own store. He began to make regular buying trips to the European continent, looking in particular for old manuscripts and, during one of these trips in 1912, came across the one that still bears his name, and which has been described as the most mysterious manuscript in the world.

A MYSTERY

Everything about the Voynich manuscript is mysterious, including how it actually came to be in the possession of Voynich himself. All he would say was that he had bought it in a castle in southern Europe. Further details only began to emerge in the 1960s, more than thirty years after his death, when it became known that he had acquired it along with a number of other manuscripts from the Villa Mondragone in Italy, then

WILFRED VOYNICH
The Polish book dealer tried without success to sell the manuscript, which many accused him of faking.

UNKNOWN PLANTS
Pages from the herbal part of the manuscript, in which plants are described in strange, indecipherable writing.

identifying it as once belonging to Petrus Beckx, the general secretary of the Jesuits in the 1870s, when the library was first installed in the villa. By not saying exactly where he bought the manuscript and then potentially removing any incriminating labels, Voynich was certainly acting as if he had something to hide.

THE MANUSCRIPT

Anybody viewing the manuscript for the first time could be forgiven for wondering what all the fuss is about. It is a dusty and battered old volume that looks like a notebook in which somebody appears to have compiled drawings of herbal plants with text relating to their medical uses. The remaining pages are then filled with a random selection of additional details of interest to them. There are sections that appear to include astronomical and astrological charts, while others have diagrams that may be biological in nature, and there would appear to be a few recipes of some sort toward the end. Then there are longer pieces of text accompanied by small drawings of figures, mostly naked women cavorting around, giving the impression of an author who grew tired of any serious

a Jesuit college. The exact circumstances of the acquisition remain a little murky because it was not removed from the library catalog. This could have been a genuine oversight or could indicate that Voynich, who had a rather shady reputation, removed it from the college library without the knowledge of the Jesuit librarians.

Suspicions were aroused further because the manuscript was one of the only volumes acquired by Voynich from the villa that did not have a label with it

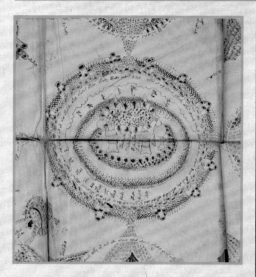

UNFOLDING MYSTERY
Some pages of the manuscript unfolded revealing larger—if equally obscure—diagrams and pictures.

purpose their work might have had and has added some sketches alongside the text for his or her own entertainment.

STRANGE LANGUAGE

The strangeness of the manuscript is clear when you look closely at the text. It is written in a language that so far no one has been able to translate or decipher, despite close attention from professional code-breakers and, in recent years, an army of internet enthusiasts. The characters used by the author to form what appear to be words are not recognizable as letters from any known alphabet. They are made of single or double strokes of a quill pen and ordered into paragraphs without any apparent punctuation. Further analysis has shown that the words are structured in a way that could form a language, but, beyond that, nothing else is known.

The mystery deepens further if the drawings of plants are examined. Very few of them can be identified as being depictions of existing plants, so, if the manuscript was really intended as an herbal (a book of herbal plants) it would have been of little use.

BACON, DEE, AND KELLEY

Voynich claimed that the manuscript was accompanied by a letter when he bought it. It is by a seventeenth-century scientist from Prague and suggests that the manuscript could be by the English medieval philosopher Roger Bacon (ca. 1214–1294), who is known to have been interested in the subjects covered in it. If this were shown to be correct, the manuscript would represent a lost work by Bacon, greatly increasing its value. This possibility was not lost on Voynich, who, in common with most other book dealers, was usually a little strapped for cash, so he spent a considerable amount of time and effort trying to establish its origin. Voynich envisaged the manuscript being taken to Prague by the Elizabethan scientist and alchemist John Dee or his assistant Edward Kelley, both of whom are known to have traveled to the city. Once there, they apparently met Emperor Rudolf II, who, according to the attached letter, had owned it at about that time.

Needless to say, associating the manuscript with such well-known characters as Dee and Kelley, as well as with Bacon, would have further enhanced its value, so it was very much in Voynich's interests to do so. Unfortunately for Voynich, he never managed to prove any of this because the only way of doing so would be to decipher the text.

If the manuscript were a hoax, then the finger would most likely point at Voynich as he stood to gain most from it.

SOME THEORIES

Among the many theories about the origin of the manuscript, there is one that labels it a hoax—a theory that cannot be disproved by the results of carbon dating because old materials may have been used. If it were a hoax, then the finger would most likely point at Voynich as the creator because he was the one who stood to gain the most from it.

However, if he did fabricate it, the quality of his work ultimately worked against him. In his efforts to fool everybody, he managed to mask the manuscript's origins in such a way that its authenticity could not be proved, which prevented him from selling it. It would certainly have made more sense to create a manuscript that bore a closer resemblance to other works by Roger Bacon, rather than one that could not be attributed to anybody at all, let alone Bacon. So, either Voynich wasted an enormous amount of time forging an unsellable manuscript or it is not a hoax, with the latter perhaps being more likely.

Another idea, proposed by Gerry Kennedy and Rob Churchill in their book on the manuscript, is that it is an early example of what has become known as outsider art, work produced by people who have experienced some form of mental breakdown. One of the best known examples is Adolf Wölfli (1864–1930), a Swiss artist who spent most of his life in a mental institution suffering from severe mental disorder and hallucinations. Drawing appeared to have a calming influence on him and over many years he produced an enormous body of work, much of it intricate and intense in nature, and often incorporating musical notation.

The manuscript looks nothing like the art of Wölfli, or any other known examples of outsider art, but that is hardly a surprise given the highly personal nature of the art form. If the manuscript turns out to have been the creation of somebody with one of these illnesses, then trying to ascertain meaning from it may be pointless. As with all the other theories, an understanding of the true purpose of the manuscript is dependent on the strange text being deciphered. With no sign of that happening any time soon, the mysterious nature of the document remains intact.

CARBON DATING

In recent years, carbon dating of the parchment used in the pages of the manuscript suggests they were made in the first half of the fifteenth century. This dating is supported by the style of the handwriting, which has been compared to styles in use at roughly that time in southern France and northern Italy, so ruling out the hand of Roger Bacon. The lack of proof about its origin and a ludicrously high asking price, meant that Voynich failed to sell the manuscript. In the 1960s it came into the possession of another book dealer, who, after also failing to sell it, gave it to the Beinecke Rare Book and Manuscript Library in Yale University, where it remains today.

WHO WAS THE LADY WITH THE ENIGMATIC SMILE?

ca. 1503

Clue: Near-contemporary Vasari says he met the real Mona Lisa

Main players: Leonardo, Lisa, Isabella, Constanza, his mother, his lover

Verdict: Probably Lisa, but who can say for sure?

Leonardo da Vinci (1452–1519) has not made life easy for art historians. Not only did he not sign or date any of his paintings, making the task of attributing work to him difficult, but, in the case of the *Mona Lisa*, there is no reference to it in his notebooks, no trace of a commission, and no records of him ever having received any payment for it. No known written reference to the painting appears to have been made by anybody else while Leonardo was still alive either, except for one possible example, found in the last few years scribbled in the back of a sixteenth-century book. While no one has doubted that the *Mona Lisa* is the work of Leonardo da Vinci, almost everything else about it has been the subject of endless debate.

THE *MONA LISA*

The *Mona Lisa* has proved to be particularly fertile ground because scholars can indulge in debates about when it was painted, who, if anybody,

> "Leonardo undertook to paint the portrait of the wife of Francesco del Giocondo, Mona Lisa. He worked on this for four years, but did not finish it… He used an ingenious expedient: while he was painting Mona Lisa, who was a very beautiful woman, he had her constantly entertained by singers, musicians and jesters so that she should be merry and not look melancholic as portraits often do. As a result, in this painting of Leonardo's there was a smile so enchanting that it was more divine than human; and those who saw it marveled to find it so similar to that of the living original."
>
> —Giorgio Vasari, *The Lives of the Artists*, 1550

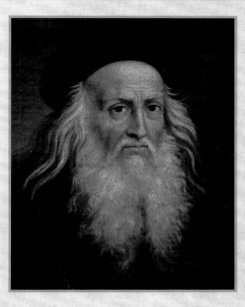

LEONARDO
A portrait of the Florentine master by the Italian painter Lattanzio Querena (1768–1863).

commissioned it, and why Leonardo kept the painting rather than handing it over to the person who commissioned it. And there is also the mystery we will be examining ourselves: who was the woman with the enigmatic smile?

The *Mona Lisa* is on display at the Louvre Museum in Paris, where it has been hung behind bullet-proof glass and, at least according to the Louvre's press office, is seen by six million people a year. Anybody joining the throng in front of it in an attempt to catch a glimpse of that famous smile would most likely agree that it is one of the most viewed works of art in the world, although how many of them leave wondering what all the fuss was about has not been recorded. It has become such a familiar image, reproduced countless times, that

seeing the real thing, which is actually quite small, can come as something of a disappointment.

The fame that the painting now enjoys can be traced back to the nineteenth century, when a succession of romantic writers began to gush about it in terms that can only be described as embarrassing. The English writer and critic Walter Pater famously wrote, "She is older than the rocks among which she sits," whatever that is supposed to mean, while the French historian Jules Michelet, perhaps not wanting to be outdone by the English, said the painting, "attracts me, revolts me, consumes me; I go to her in spite of myself, as the bird to the snake." But the event that really did the trick, getting the painting on to the front pages of newspapers around the world, occurred in 1911, when it was stolen from the Louvre.

CELEBRITY STATUS

In the turmoil following the painting's theft, Guillaume Apollinaire, the French poet who had called for the Louvre to be burned down, was arrested and the artist Pablo Picasso, known to detest the painting, was brought in for questioning. But as there was not a shred of evidence against either, they were both released without charge. Several years later a former employee of the Louvre, Vincenzo Peruggia, was arrested when he tried to sell the painting to the Uffizi Gallery in Florence. His excuse, of being an Italian patriot who was only trying to return the painting to its true home, was rather undermined by a scam he had been involved in to sell copies of it by claiming they were the original. Whatever the truth of the matter, Peruggia got off with a few months in prison, and the painting was returned to the Louvre and to the global celebrity status it still holds today.

GIORGIO VASARI

The reason why the identity of the woman behind the enigmatic smile of the *Mona Lisa* has become so widely discussed is, of course, because the painting has become so famous. Nobody much worries about who the model was for, say, *The Birth of Venus* by Botticelli, other than a few art historians who really don't have anything else to do. The only reason for the speculation surrounding the model for Vermeer's *The Girl with the Pearl Earring* is because of the book and movie of the same name (and, no, it wasn't Scarlett Johansson). But, in spite of how well-known it is, the amount of speculation is still surprising given that

SELF-PORTRAIT?

One of the most common arguments raised against Lisa del Giocondo being the subject of the painting is that her family was of relatively modest means and social standing, while portraits were almost always commissioned by members of the Florentine aristocracy. Over the years, numerous alternatives have been proposed, ranging from the possible to the unlikely and on to the plain ridiculous. The sitter, people have seriously suggested, could have been Leonardo's mother, his male lover, or it could have been a self-portrait of himself in drag.

Giorgio Vasari tells us who she was in his book *The Lives of the Artists*.

Vasari (1511–1574) has been described as the first art historian and his work is the source of a great deal of our knowledge of Italian Renaissance artists. He is not always completely reliable, but he was a near contemporary of Leonardo and, even if he only arrived in Florence after the artist had died, he is thought to have actually met the woman he identified as the subject of the painting. She was, he tells us, the wife of the Florentine cloth and silk merchant Francesco del Giocondo and he names her as "Mona Lisa," which is usually translated as "My Lady Lisa," or more simply "Mrs. Lisa." Her father was Antonmaria Gherardini, a reasonably well off, but by no means wealthy, man who owned land near Florence. In Italy the painting is known as *La Gioconda*, which can be translated as the happy woman or the woman with a sunny disposition. It doesn't take a genius of Leonardo's proportions to figure out that it could also be a play on the name of Lisa del Giocondo, whom the artist painted with a smile on her face.

OTHER CANDIDATES

That would, you might think, be enough to settle the matter, but such a thought could hardly be further from the truth. Countless other people have been put forward as the identity of the *Mona Lisa*. One of the more serious stems from the

Painting the portrait of an old family friend's daughter could well have kept Leonardo going until other opportunities presented themselves.

THE LOUVRE
The *Mona Lisa* has hung in the Louvre since being seized during the French Revolution.

writing of Antonio de Beatis, who visited Leonardo in France during the later years of his life, while he was staying at the palace of Fontainebleau as a guest of King Francis I. De Beatis writes of seeing a painting that he describes as being a portrait of a Florentine lady, without giving any further details other than to say Leonardo told him it was commissioned by Giuliano de' Medici (1479–1516). If this was the case, then it would be difficult to understand why a member of such a noble family would commission Leonardo to paint a lowly merchant's wife.

A whole host of alternatives, mostly wealthy and well-connected women linked to de' Medici in some way, have been proposed, including Constanza d'Avalos, who became the Duchess of Francavilla, and Isabella d'Este, the Marchesa of Manchua. As far as being aristocratic goes, these two fit the bill perfectly, the only problem being that neither of them was from Florence.

The cases made for all the other candidates are similarly not impossible but not very likely either. An alternative solution sees Leonardo attempting to paint the portrait of an idealized woman rather than a specific subject, even if it started out as a commission that he did not complete.

LISA DEL GIOCONDO

In more recent years the tide of opinion has swung back in favor of Lisa del Giocondo, particularly after the discovery in 2005 of a note written in the back of a book by Agostino Vespucci, a contemporary Florentine official, naming her as the subject of a portrait being undertaken by Leonardo. It also gives a date of 1503, which fits with what we know about Leonardo's movements at that time. He had just come back to Florence after a period in Cesena and there is no record of what he was working on immediately after his return. Lisa's father, Antonmaria Gherardini, is thought to have been a friend of Leonardo's father, so painting the portrait of an old family friend's daughter could well have kept Leonardo going until other opportunities presented themselves.

There is, of course, no way of proving this scenario, just as there is no way of proving the claims made on behalf of any other potential candidate. But, on the balance of evidence, Lisa del Giocondo, the merchant's wife from Florence, carries the day ahead of all those other ladies, however aristocratic they may have been.

WAS CHRISTOPHER MARLOWE MURDERED?

May 30, 1593

Clue: Marlowe had links with the Elizabethan underworld

Main players: Christopher Marlowe and a large cast of Elizabethan spies, plotters, atheists and Catholics

Verdict: The plot thickens

The circumstances of Christopher Marlowe's death at the age of twenty-nine were set out shortly after the event in the official report of the coroner. On the evening of May 30, 1593, he was killed by a single stab wound just above the right eye, from which he died instantly. He had spent the day with three men in the house of the widow Eleanor Bull in Deptford, which was, at the time, a small town on the River Thames a few miles to the east of London and less than a mile from Queen Elizabeth's palace at Greenwich. Two of the three men, Robert Poley and Nicholas Skeres, were witnesses, while the third, Ingram Frizer, was the man who inflicted the fatal wound.

The account given, backed up by all three, says that an argument started over the payment of a bill for food and drink. It resulted in Marlowe grabbing Frizer's dagger and attacking him with it.

Frizer stabbed Marlowe above the eye in what was described as an act of self-defense.

In the ensuing fight, Frizer stabbed Marlowe above the eye with the same dagger in what was described as an act of self-defense. This version of events, told by the only three people who were there, was accepted by the jury of the coroner's court. Almost immediately after the inquest, Marlowe's body was buried in an unmarked grave at the church in Deptford. Frizer was held in custody for a further four weeks and then released after being granted a royal pardon.

THE QUESTIONS

These are the bare facts of the case and it would not be until the report was rediscovered in the 1920s, that any serious questions were raised about the death of the man who, in his day, was regarded as the greatest playwright of his generation. What was Marlowe doing in that house in Deptford? Who were the other three men with him? What was their relationship with him and with each other?

The author Charles Nicholl in his book *The Reckoning* has tried to answer these questions, at least as much as he can four hundred years after the event.

> *"Quod me nutrit me destruit."*
> *("What nourishes me also destroys me.")*
>
> —Latin motto on a portrait thought to be of Christopher Marlowe

He discovers connections between all four of the men present on that day, connections linking them with the Elizabethan underworld of criminal gangs and espionage, of plots against the queen, and the measures taken by what would now be known as her secret service. In doing so, Nicholl casts the event of that day in 1593 in an entirely different light. Rather than the traditional story of Marlowe being killed in a tavern brawl, the picture that emerges is far murkier.

MARLOWE?

A portrait thought to be of Marlowe was found in Corpus Christi College, Cambridge, in 1952.

THE LEAD PROTAGONISTS

Christopher Marlowe is well known to us today as the author of such plays as *Dr. Faustus* and *Tamberlaine*. He was the same age as Shakespeare and came from a similar background; he was born in the provincial town of Canterbury and his father was a shoemaker. After attending the King's School in Canterbury, he won a scholarship to attend Cambridge University, where it is thought he began to work in some capacity for the government, possibly for Sir Francis Walsingham (1532–1590), who ran an extensive secret spy network for the queen. After graduating from Cambridge, Marlowe almost immediately began to have his plays produced on the London stage and, from what little we can gather about his life away from the theater, continued to work for Walsingham until Elizabeth's spymaster, as he is sometimes called, died.

Clear evidence of Marlowe's connection with Walsingham does not exist. He was certainly connected to Walsingham's nephew Thomas, who became Marlowe's patron and is known to have worked for his uncle. One of the most probable explanations for Marlowe's frequent absences from Cambridge, which nearly cost him his degree before the government intervened on his behalf, and also for the trips to France he made in the late 1580s, is that he was engaged as some form of secret agent or courier. He also turned up in the Low Countries, involved in a conspiracy to forge money, but even though he was caught, the charges against him were never pursued. The guess is he was involved in government service, perhaps in an effort to infiltrate one of the groups of Catholic plotters known to have been in the Low Countries at the time.

This tactic of placing spies at the heart of plots against the queen had been used by Walsingham on a number of occasions in the past and in one of them, known as the Babbington Plot, Robert Poley had played a leading role by posing as a Catholic sympathizer in order to get inside and inform on a plan to kill the queen. The other two, Skeres and Ingram, can also be placed on the fringes of the world of spies, although at a lower level than Poley. Both had worked for one or the other of the Walsinghams and other high-ranking government officials.

ELIZABETHAN SPYMASTER
Sir Francis Walsingham, Elizabeth I's private secretary, who may have recruited Marlowe as a spy.

They had also been arrested and questioned in the cases of a number of scams, in which gullible young men had been parted from their money. The overall picture, then, of the meeting in Mrs Bull's house is not one of four old friends getting together to share a meal and a few drinks; it is of a nest of spies and underworld fraudsters meeting in a place where they could talk in private.

THE BACKGROUND

Ten days before he was killed, Marlowe had been ordered to attend a meeting of the Privy Council to answer questions arising from information obtained from his friend and fellow playwright Thomas Kyd. Under torture, Kyd had said that documents promoting atheism found in his possession had belonged to Marlowe, putting him in potentially serious trouble as the offense of blasphemy was, at the time, punishable by death. No doubt the Privy Council also wanted to talk to him about the Dutch Church libel, which had led to them questioning Kyd in the first place. Large numbers of Protestant refugees had been fleeing to London from Europe as a result of Catholic persecution and the sudden influx had caused serious social unrest. Papers had been posted around London threatening these foreigners, including one pinned to the wall of the Dutch Church in London. It was written in verse that clearly alluded to several of Marlowe's plays and was signed, "Tamberlaine," again in reference to Marlowe.

Marlowe presented himself to the Privy Council and was bailed until a further round of questioning. A few days after this, a note by another figure from the espionage world named Richard Baines was handed in to the council.

It contained all manner of accusations against Marlowe, saying he was an atheist, a blasphemer, and a homosexual. The note ends, "I think all men in Christianity ought to endeavor that the mouth of so dangerous a member may be stopped." Two conclusions can be drawn from this and the Dutch Church libel, which, surely, Marlowe was not stupid enough to have written himself. The first is that Marlowe really was a radical atheist intent on spreading subversive and blasphemous material; the second is that there were shadowy figures in the spy game who were out to get him.

THE RECKONING

Returning to the scene of the crime, there were many aspects of Marlowe's death that were not covered by the coroner's inquest. All of the men present had been involved in espionage to some extent and all were connected to one other through their work for some of the most powerful people in England at the time—in particular, the Walsinghams. Only those present could know what they spent the day talking about, but surely they must have discussed the trouble Marlowe had found himself in with the Privy Council, so perhaps they were meeting to formulate a plan about what he should say. It is also possible that the other three were there to find out how much he knew about subjects they, and the people who paid them, didn't want the Privy Council to know.

The overall picture is of a nest of spies and underworld fraudsters meeting in a place where they could talk in private.

VIOLENT TEMPER

There is an alternative reading of events, one in which Poley, Skeres, and Frizer were not lying to the coroner and Marlowe had really been killed by Frizer in self-defense. Marlowe certainly gives the impression of having had a violent temper. He had been involved in a number of fights in the past, including one in which a man had been killed, and it is by no means impossible that he really did attack Frizer after an argument over paying the bill.

It would appear unlikely that Poley, Skeres, and Frizer met Marlowe with the intention of killing him. If this had been the case, then surely they would have done it in a more discreet way. A more likely scenario is that the three of them failed to get the assurances they were looking for from Marlowe and decided to kill him in order to silence him once and for all. The final decision to kill Marlowe would most likely have rested with Poley, the most experienced espionage agent.

The truth of the matter lies buried beneath so many layers of secrecy and deceit that it has become impossible to untangle the truth from all the other intriguing possibilities All we can say for sure is that Marlowe suffered, in Shakespeare's words, "a great reckoning in a little room." He left us with a body of work still regarded as being some of the finest in the English language and what he might have gone on to achieve had he lived beyond the age of twenty-nine can only be guessed at now.

WHO PENNED SHAKESPEARE'S PLAYS?

ca. late sixteenth–early seventeenth century

Clue: Nothing exists to link Shakespeare with his work

Main players: Shakespeare, Sir Francis Bacon, Christopher Marlowe, the Earl of Oxford

Verdict: Looks like it was the Bard of Avon after all

There is an obvious answer to the question posed in the title of this entry: Shakespeare wrote Shakespeare's plays. No doubt, no mystery, and nothing to suggest he should be included in a book like this one. This is the man, William Shakespeare, born in Stratford-upon-Avon in 1564 where he would also die in 1616 at the age of fifty-three, who was responsible for many of the greatest works in the entire canon of English literature, and whose plays continue to be performed around the world four hundred years after his death.

What, you might reasonably think, is the problem then? Well, for almost two hundred years after the plays were first performed, there was no problem. It took until the late eighteenth century for any doubts about Shakespeare to surface and another fifty years before these doubts were expressed in any published form. The central question revolves around how a man from a modest background in a provincial town could become the genius of the dramatic arts that we consider him to be today.

AUTHOR OR FRONT MAN?

As well as being beautifully written, the plays exhibit great learning and a familiarity with the workings of the royal courts of Elizabethan and Jacobean England, together with a knowledge of numerous foreign countries. So did Shakespeare write the plays attributed to him or was he really just the front man for somebody else who wished to remain anonymous? Could a highly educated and well-traveled gentleman, perhaps one who preferred not to have his good name stained by association with the low-life of the theater, be the real author and genius?

In essence, the argument against Shakespeare is that he couldn't have written the plays and poetry attributed to him because he wasn't from a wealthy family and he wasn't educated at

The central question revolves around how a man from a modest background in a provincial town could become a genius of the dramatic arts.

Cambridge University. No serious Shakespearean scholar today, of which there are many, accepts this argument in any part and most prefer not to engage with the question at all, seeing it as a distraction and a waste of their time. So, is this simply a case of social and intellectual snobbery or is there any substance to these claims?

WILLIAM SHAKESPEARE

The first thing to strike anybody researching this question is just how little we actually know about Shakespeare the man. Beyond the works themselves, what we know for certain comes from official and legal sources—births, marriages, and deaths in the family, business and property deals, and a handful of legal documents. This includes his will, in which he famously only left his "second-best bed" to his wife of more than thirty years. No manuscripts, no work in progress, no letters, no notebooks. In fact, nothing to associate him with a life in writing.

The only certain examples of his handwriting in existence are six scratchy signatures on various documents and there is no evidence at all that he actually owned any books himself. And he appears to have had little interest in seeing his own plays published; his collected plays, known as the First Folio, did not appear until seven years after his death. Shakespeare's birthday is celebrated on April 23, but we don't know for sure if this is the right day. He was baptized on April 26, 1564, and it is reasonable to assume he was born a few days before that date. His father, John Shakespeare, was a glover and became an alderman, or town councillor, in Stratford; his mother, whose maiden name was Mary Arden, came from a landowning family in the Forest of Arden, a few miles north of Stratford.

Nothing is know for certain about his education. The records of attendance at the grammar school in Stratford, the King's New School, have been lost, but, considering it was close to where he lived and would have been the sort of school attended by a boy from his background, it is reasonable to assume he went there. In 1582, at the age of eighteen, Shakespeare married Anne Hathaway, a woman eight years his senior. Six months later, their first daughter, Susanna, was

FIRST FOLIO

Title page of the first collected edition of Shakespeare's plays, published seven years after he died.

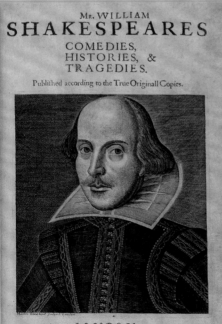

Mr. WILLIAM
SHAKESPEARES
COMEDIES,
HISTORIES, &
TRAGEDIES.
Published according to the True Originall Copies.

LONDON
Printed by Isaac Iaggard, and Ed. Blount. 1623.

SIR FRANCIS BACON

The first to be proposed as a potential author of the plays, in the mid-nineteenth century, was the eminent philosopher and statesman Sir Francis Bacon. During his lifetime, however, he never seemed to have the slightest interest in the theater. A further stumbling block is that, during a long writing career, he tried his hand at writing poems with, at best, mixed results. Even his closest friends would have struggled to describe his poetry as Shakespearean, and Bacon himself declared he was not a poet.

born and two years later, their twins, Hamnet and Judith, after which there is a deafening silence.

The next time we hear anything of Shakespeare, seven years later, he is an actor with a theater company, the Lord Chamberlain's Men, in London and he has already had a number of his own plays performed. Nothing is known about how this occurred, or even where he was during this critical period in his life. Stories of how he was forced to leave Stratford after being caught poaching deer and of how he first became involved in the theater by being employed to hold patron's horses during performances are nothing more than the inventions of biographers desperate to fill in the gaps.

In the absence of some miraculous discoveries, it appears unlikely we will ever get a clear picture of how Shakespeare began his career in the theater. It is the vacuum created by these so-called "lost years," more than anything else, that has fueled the speculation. There is an ever-growing cast list of potential authors, some more fanciful than others.

CHRISTOPHER MARLOWE

Christopher Marlowe is one of the more likely candidates. He was undoubtedly a talented playwright and, being a contemporary of Shakespeare, was in the right place at the right time. But, as we learned in the previous entry, he was stabbed to death in suspicious circumstances in 1593, while Shakespeare's plays continued to appear for a further twenty years. Marlovians, as his supporters are known, contend that the killing was staged so he could avoid a charge of blasphemy and that, in reality, he escaped to the continent to continue writing under Shakespeare's name. While this is not completely impossible, this would have required an elaborate conspiracy. In addition, the plays of Marlowe and Shakespeare are as different as day and night.

EARL OF OXFORD

The current front runner is Edward de Vere, the Earl of Oxford. Now here we have a candidate who really fits the bill. He was as aristocratic and educated as an Elizabethan gentleman could be, as well as being intimately connected with the Elizabethan court, and he had traveled extensively in Europe, particularly in Italy, where he visited

The Earl of Oxford had a long association with the theater as the patron of several acting companies and wrote both poetry and plays.

almost every Italian location used in Shakespeare's plays. He had a long association with the theater and wrote both poetry and plays himself, as well as owning an estate near the Forest of Arden. He would be the perfect candidate if it were not for one small problem: he died in 1604, before *King Lear*, *Othello*, *Macbeth*, *The Tempest*, and a host of the other plays were written. People have tied themselves in knots attempting to explain it away, but in the end there is no getting past it.

MAIN CONTENDER

Contenders further down the list have little going for them. What tends to happen with all of them is that a likely candidate is selected, one who fits in with the conception of what a literary genius should be. Then, if the facts don't quite match up, explanations are cobbled together, no matter how convoluted they

may be, and gaps are filled in with pure speculation, while attempts are made to stain Shakespeare's character by insisting he was nothing more than an illiterate grain merchant and money lender.

Conclusive proof that Shakespeare wrote the plays does not exist, but equally nor does overwhelming evidence proving the opposite. The circumstantial evidence weighs heavily in favor of Shakespeare and it will take the discovery of something irrefutable for a change in the attribution of the plays to be made. The opinion that a glover's son from Stratford could not have been intelligent enough to be the true author is clearly not enough.

WAS KASPAR HAUSER A FOUNDLING OR A FRAUD?

1812–1833

Clue: It was said that Hauser grew up as a wild boy in the woods

Main players: Hauser, the people who believed the stories about him and those who didn't, and the House of Baden

Verdict: An enigma at the time and an enigma now

The story of Kaspar Hauser remains a very familiar one in Germany, even if it is not often told anywhere else these days. Over the years, its mysteries and ambiguities have allowed many different interpretations to be placed on it. To some, Hauser was an innocent soul who was manipulated by those around him, while to others he was a cunning fraudster exploiting his situation for all it was worth. The story has been cast as an almost mythological tale of a wild boy of the woods (which he never was nor claimed to be) and as a royal conspiracy involving babies being swapped at birth. If all this sounds like it comes out of a fairy tale, then perhaps that explains the enduring appeal of the story of Hauser's strange and ultimately tragic life. By one estimate, more than three thousand books have been written about him since March 26, 1826, when he stepped into the Bavarian city of Nuremberg, beginning the mystery that, despite intense scrutiny and several DNA tests endures to this day.

ARRIVAL IN NUREMBERG

On his arrival in Nuremberg, Hauser asked to be taken to the house of the captain of a cavalry regiment stationed in the city. He had almost no possessions with him, except letters, one from a man who said he had been given custody of Hauser in 1812 when he was an infant, making him about sixteen at the time. Another letter from his mother said his father was dead and she wanted Hauser

"To be delivered.
Hauser will tell you exactly what I look like and where I come from.
To spare Hauser the trouble I will tell you where I come from myself.
I come from ____ on the Bavarian frontier ____ on the river ____
I will even tell you the name M.L.O."

—**Translation of the letter found in a purse at the scene of Hauser's fatal stabbing**

KASPAR HAUSER
A portrait of Hauser, painted in about 1830 when Hauser was around twenty.

family, the House of Baden. Whichever story people chose to believe, the sudden appearance of this mysterious boy became a media sensation in Germany and across Europe.

At first Hauser was looked after by a teacher, who, as well as giving him lessons, began to conduct experiments into homeopathic remedies on him. When these treatments yielded few results, and after an incident in which Hauser sustained an injury to his forehead, caused, he said, by the man who had brought him to Nuremberg, he was adopted by the English aristocrat, Lord Stanthorpe. Stanthorpe appears to have lost interest when Hauser's connection to the nobility could not be established, saying Hauser was really an attention-seeking fraud.

to join the same calvary regiment as his father had been in. After being taken into the care of the city council, he told how he had been confined to a small, windowless room and fed only bread and water. By this time, stories had already begun to circulate about how he had grown up as a wild boy in the woods and people were asking questions about his real identity. According to different versions of the gossip, he was either a fraud or the son of nobility, perhaps even a member of the old German noble

FATALLY STABBED

Hauser was then placed in the care of another teacher, who quickly formed the same low opinion of him that Lord Stanthorpe had held. Nevertheless, he had progressed well in his schooling, and he found a job as a clerk. Interest in him was beginning to fade until, in December 1833, he returned to his lodgings with a stab wound in his chest, saying he had been attacked by the same man again, his former guardian and jailer. At first he was not believed, the teacher thinking he was attention seeking again, but as the severity of the injury became clear, a doctor was finally called. Hauser said he had dropped a purse containing a letter at the scene of the stabbing in a park. When this was recovered, it appeared to be a confession by Hauser's assailant, except there were blank spaces where details of the identity of this person should have been.

Suspicions were immediately aroused that the letter had been written by Hauser himself and that the wound was self-inflicted in an attempt to regain the attention he had formerly enjoyed. A few days later, Hauser died and, during the subsequent investigation, witnesses were found who had seen him in the park with another man, seeming to confirm that he had not been alone at the time of the stabbing. The exact circumstances of his death, like so much else in Hauser's short life, have never been fully explained, adding another layer of mystery to this enigmatic story.

SON OF A GRAND DUKE?

The rumors that Hauser was really a lost prince of the House of Baden began almost as soon as he first arrived in Nuremberg and, after his mysterious death, were enhanced by claims he had been murdered to prevent him claiming his birthright. Charles, the Grand Duke of Baden, had two sons with his wife, Stéphanie de Beauharnais, the adopted daughter of Napoleon, both of whom died in infancy. One of these boys was born in September 1812, making him almost exactly the same age as Hauser, and he had died a few weeks later. With no surviving male heir, Charles was succeeded by his uncle Louis on his death in 1818, who was in turn succeeded by his half-brother Leopold. Hauser, so the story goes, was the real son of the Grand Duke and had been swapped by Leopold's mother, the Countess of Hochberg, for the dead body of a baby boy shortly after his birth, so

THE LETTER
The mysterious letter, which was written in mirror writing, found at the scene of Hauser's stabbing.

of DNA testing in the 1990s, when tests were carried out on blood stains found on underpants said to have belonged to Hauser. A comparison with DNA from a descendant of Stéphanie de Beauharnais appeared to show that she was not Hauser's mother—a development, you might think, that would have brought the matter to an end. But doubts about the authenticity of the clothing quickly emerged, prompting a second test on a lock of Hauser's hair and, on this occasion, matches were found in the DNA, even if not enough to be conclusive one way or the other.

So, despite the intervention of modern forensic science, the mystery remains. The story is summed up in the inscription on Hauser's gravestone, "Here lies Kaspar Hauser, an enigma in his own time, his origins unknown, his death mysterious."

that Leopold could become Grand Duke. The countess then gave the boy to the man who had brought Hauser to Nuremberg and he kept him confined and isolated until after his sixteenth birthday, when, presumably because he didn't know who he was, he was released in the city.

DNA TESTING

This story, such as it is, stayed much the same, impossible to either fully prove or reject completely, until the development

Hauser, so the story goes, was the real son of the Grand Duke and had been swapped by Leopold's mother, the Countess of Hochberg, for the dead body of a baby boy shortly after his birth.

ABOMINABLE SNOWMAN OR BROWN BEAR?

1840s onward

Clue: Some Himalayan Sherpas are convinced yetis exist

Main players: Mountaineers, Sherpas, explorers, and, of course, the yetis themselves

Verdict: The yeti lives on

Eric Shipton's famous photographs of yeti (nicknamed the Abominable Snowman) footprints, taken during his Himalayan expedition of 1951, caused a media storm around the world. The fact that the prints are so obviously fake appears to have escaped everybody's notice at the time and, given the fuss they had stirred up, Shipton, who was noted for his keen sense of humor, wasn't about to own up. He was either enjoying the joke too much or thought, after all the attention the photos had received, he would be better off keeping quiet until it had all calmed down.

Shipton never did come clean and the photos still appear whenever yetis are discussed. Rather than dismissing them, perhaps they should be taken in the spirit in which they were meant, as a bit of fun not to be taken too seriously.

But when a mountaineer of the stature of Reinhold Messner (b. 1944), widely regarded as the finest climber of them all, writes about his own encounter with a yeti and obviously takes what he has seen seriously, then perhaps it is time to do the same. His account, quoted in this entry, is both detailed and convincing; nothing at all like most yeti sightings, which usually give the impression of the author having had a few too many sherries around the camp fire after a hard day's climbing.

TAKING IT SERIOUSLY

In his wonderful book *The Snow Leopard*, Peter Matthiessen writes about his journey, both physical and spiritual, through the Nepalese Himalayas in the company of the eminent biologist George Schaller. Matthiessen, an accomplished naturalist himself, is prepared to at least

Depictions of yetis have been found in Buddhist monasteries in Nepal and Tibet. They are rare, but have been found alongside paintings of existing animals, suggesting that they were regarded by some as real animals.

entertain the idea of there being an undiscovered species of primate inhabiting the remote regions of the Himalayas. He is surprised also to find that Schaller, a man not known for frivolous speculation, does not dismiss the idea out of hand either. He goes on to discuss depictions of yetis in Buddhist monasteries in Nepal and Tibet. They are rare, but have been found alongside paintings of existing animals, suggesting that, while the yeti may have mythological significance in stories told by the different peoples of the Himalayas, it has also been regarded by some as a real animal as well.

SHERPA STORIES

In conversation with Tukten, a Sherpa (Himalayans who are known for their skill in mountaineering), whom Matthiessen holds in very high regard, he finds that he is in no doubt about the existence of yetis. Tukten says that, while he has never seen one himself, if he ever does, he will turn away from it and pretend he has not because they are considered to bring bad luck. This could explain why, in almost all the stories about yetis told by Sherpas, they describe how other people have seen the creatures rather than themselves. Of course, it could also be the case that nobody describes having seen a yeti because they don't exist and the stories are simply tall tales made up to fool gullible foreigners. Tukten goes on to tell Matthiessen that yetis were much more common in his grandfather's day, but is reluctant to discuss the subject in any further detail, even though, Matthiessen suspects, he knows a great deal more than he is prepared to reveal.

COLD FOOT
Eric Shipton's photographs of yeti footprints fooled lots of people at the time.

"Out of the corner of my eye I saw the outline of an upright figure dart between the trees to the edge of the clearing, where low-growing thickets covered the steep slope. The figure hurried on, silent and hunched forward, disappearing behind a tree only to reappear again against the moonlight. It stopped for a moment and turned to look at me... I guessed it to be over seven feet tall. Its body looked much heavier than that of a man of that size, but it moved with such agility and power toward the edge of the escarpment that I was both startled and relieved... No human would have been able to run like that in the middle of the night. It stopped again beyond the trees...and stood motionless in the moonlit night without looking back."

—Reinhold Messner, *My Quest for the Yeti*

THE BEAST FROM THE EAST

At a yeti conference held in 2011 in the Russian province of Kemorevo, people describing themselves as scientists announced they were 95 percent certain they had found evidence of the yeti. The giant Russian boxer Nikolai Valuev, known as the Beast from the East, was said to be joining the hunt for the elusive creature. Seeing as Valuev is over 7 feet (2 m) tall and weighs over 280 pounds (127 kg), it's hardly surprising the yetis are hiding from the huge huntsman.

EARLY HOMINID

Matthiessen goes on to discuss the theory of yetis being a surviving population of an early hominid species (a primate species that includes humans and their ancestors). At the time he was writing, in the 1970s, this was highly speculative, but, as we have already seen in the chapter on the hobbit of Flores, such an idea has been shown to be possible. As well as Neanderthals in Europe and Central Asia, evidence of a number of other early hominids has been found in unexpected places, including the Densovians in Siberia and the Red Deer Cave people in China, who have yet to be formally described as belonging to a different species than modern humans, but certainly appear to be.

The evidence places different species of hominid, some of which are thought to have existed up to ten thousand years ago, in a number of locations around the Himalayan region, so it would not be a great leap to speculate that either one of these species, or another as yet undiscovered one, inhabited that region as well. It is even possible to suggest that such a species could have existed into much more recent times in the remote and inaccessible mountains and valleys of the Himalayas; and it could have been remembered in the stories of the Sherpas and other tribes in the region as the yeti, much as the hobbits may have been in the stories of the people of Flores.

Not one shred of credible evidence has been found in support of the yeti being an early hominid species. Messner concluded he had probably been watching a brown bear.

BROWN BEAR

Having almost managed to convince myself of the existence of yetis, I should point out that not one shred of credible evidence has been found in support of the argument I have presented above. In the end, Reinhold Messner concluded he had probably been watching a Himalayan brown bear, an animal well capable of walking on its hind legs and that fits many of the less fanciful descriptions of yetis given by mountaineers and travelers. And, let's be honest, the chances of there being a snowman, abominable or otherwise, roaming the mountains of the Himalayas are slim, even if it makes for a good story.

REINHOLD MESSNER

The great climber and yeti enthusiast, Reinhold Messner (right) pictured during one of his numerous expeditions.

DID ANYONE SURVIVE THE FRANKLIN EXPEDITION?

May 1845–June 1847

Clue: The Northwest Passage is a maze of islands and inlets, and shifting pack ice

Main players: Sir John Franklin, the Royal Navy, and the frozen north

Verdict: Chances of survival are slim

In August 1845, a whaling ship sighted the HMS *Terror* and HMS *Erebus* in Baffin Bay, an extension of the Atlantic Ocean between Baffin Island and Greenland. The two Royal Navy ships of the Franklin expedition were seen heading west toward the entrance to Lancaster Sound. From here they would attempt what the British Admiralty described as the "final push" to prove the existence of the Northwest Passage, a sea route linking the Atlantic with the Pacific Ocean through the ice and islands north of the Canadian mainland. The report from the whaler would prove to be the last record of the expedition; none of the 129 officers and men on board the two ships were ever seen alive again.

UNCHARTED WATERS

Before the Panama Canal was opened in 1914, the only way of sailing between the Atlantic and Pacific Oceans was the long voyage around the tip of South America, through the treacherous waters of Cape Horn. The attractions of a northern route were obvious to all and numerous attempts had been made to establish the Northwest Passage over the course of the previous three centuries. The maze of islands and inlets in the uncharted waters, together with shifting pack ice and the short Arctic summer when the sea was ice-free, had thwarted all previous expeditions. In the Victorian era of empire and expansion, the Royal Navy led the way in mapping uncharted waters and with characteristic confidence, bordering on arrogance, was determined to be the first to discover a viable route. The stated aim was to open up a trade route, but, at a time of empire and expansion, there can be little doubt that the British had wider concerns.

After victory at the Battle of Trafalgar in 1805, the Royal Navy really did rule the waves. The final defeat of Napoleon at Waterloo ten years later was the

> **None of the 129 officers and men on board the two ships of the Franklin expedition were ever seen alive again.**

FRANKLIN
A portrait of Sir John Franklin from the period of his tenure as governor of Tasmania.

the territory that would eventually form the country of Canada. In charting the waters off the northern coast of the American landmass, the British were consolidating their claims in the region and preventing the Russian Empire expanding farther east from the territory it already held in Alaska

THE MAN WHO ATE HIS BOOTS

Sir John Franklin was a navy man through and through. He joined the senior service at the age of fourteen, served at the Battles of Copenhagen and Trafalgar, and had been to the Canadian Arctic on three previous occasions, including an overland trip in which eleven of the twenty people involved had died and the rest had resorted to eating the leather of their boots in order to survive, earning Franklin the nickname of "the man who ate his boots" in the process.

The published accounts of these expeditions had made him a well-known public figure and, if he had not been fifty-nine years old in 1845, he might have been the perfect man to lead the Admiralty's proposed expedition to map

prelude to a long period of prosperity and peace in Europe, in which Britain began to look further afield for opportunities to expand its empire and to establish trade links. The role of the navy, with no more battles to fight, was to protect British interests around the world and, as part of this and to make use of its manpower and resources, the Admiralty began a huge program of surveying and map-making. In any disputes over territorial claims, those with the best maps would hold a significant advantage. In the 1840s, Britain was facing competition from both America and Russia over the extent of

TWO SHIPS

This print shows two ships, probably the *Enterprise* and the *Investigator*, ice bound in Baffin Bay off Devil's Point in the Arctic. The crews work to break up the ice and tow the ships to open water.

the remaining 300 miles (500 km) of coastline left uncharted after previous expeditions to the region.

FRANKLIN EXPEDITION

Initially, the preferred choice for the Arctic expedition was Captain James Clark Ross, who had recently returned from the Antarctic with the *Terror* and *Erebus*, but he had turned down the offer of commanding the expedition. Franklin had recently been recalled from his position as Governor of Tasmania, having fallen out with the locals there, so he was in need of an opportunity to restore his reputation and jumped at the chance when it was offered by the Admiralty. The expedition was to be the largest and best prepared ever sent to the region and, if it succeeded in finding the Northwest Passage, would make its commander a national hero.

The two ships had been designed as bomb vessels, used by the navy to carry huge mortars to shell targets inland. Both had been strongly built, making them ideal for Arctic exploration, and they had been further reinforced and fit with steam engines to power propellers so they could make headway whatever the weather conditions. The ships were

---

The Franklin Expedition was to be the largest and best prepared ever sent to the region. If it succeeded in finding the Northwest Passage, it would make its commander a national hero.

provisioned for three years, including a huge supply of canned meat, and a steam-powered heating system had been installed for the comfort of the officers and crew.

The ships left London on May 19, 1845, with much fanfare and celebration, heading first for Greenland and then on through Baffin Bay and into Lancaster Sound.

LOST

No communication could be expected from Franklin while he was in uncharted territory and even though some optimists thought he might achieve the aims of the expedition in a single season, most thought it would take at least two. After a second year went by with no word,

concerns began to mount and, in the summer of 1848, a search party was sent out. No trace could be found and, after further extensive searches and the posting of a huge reward for information, the situation remained much the same until, finally in 1851, evidence of Franklin's first winter camp was discovered on Beechey Island, to the north of Lancaster Sound, including the graves of three sailors and a food dump. No message was found concerning Franklin's future intentions and nothing else was found for four years, when a surveying party on the Boothia Peninsula recovered a few pieces of the expedition's kit from a party of Inuit people. They told the surveyors about the bodies of

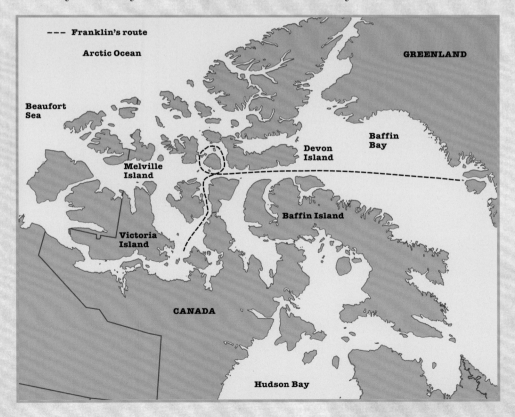

forty sailors they had come across on King William Island to the west. All had apparently starved to death.

Over the next few years more reports from Inuit people were gathered and some remains recovered, which included evidence of cannibalism among the last survivors. In 1859, a document was found under a mound of stones, known as a cairn, on King William Island. It included messages from James Fitzjames and Francis Crozier, the commanders of the *Terror* and *Erebus*. The last of these messages, dated April 25, 1848, read in part, "H.M.'s ships *Terror* and *Erebus* were deserted on April 22, having been beset since 12 Sept. 1846… Sir John Franklin died on June 11, 1847." Rumors persisted for some years of survivors living with the Inuit, but these were more in hope than expectation and would come to nothing in the end.

NORTHWEST PASSAGE

The search for Franklin may have failed, but one of the consequences of the number of ships involved was the completion of the maps of the coastlines of northern Canada and its islands. In 1850, Captain Robert McClure led a search effort to enter the region from the west, by way of the Pacific Ocean and through the Bering Straits. He sailed far enough to observe a point from which a route to the Atlantic was already known, so, in effect, he had discovered the Northwest Passage, even if he could not complete the passage after becoming

LAST WORDS
The document found on King William Island in 1859, fourteen years after Franklin had gone missing.

trapped in pack ice himself. Unlike Franklin, however, he was rescued.

It would be more than fifty years before the Norwegian explorer Roald Amundsen finally made the passage, setting out in 1903 on a much smaller boat with a crew of seven and staying as close as possible to the Canadian mainland. It took him three years and

After the ships became icebound in the second year of the expedition and then remained stuck throughout that winter and the following year, supplies began to dwindle.

involved a voyage through waters too shallow to allow the passage of commercial shipping. In 1969, a US oil tanker, the SS *Manhattan*, with the help of several icebreakers, smashed its way through, and, in recent years, climate change has caused the passage to be largely ice-free during the summer months. But, since the opening of the Panama Canal, there has been little need for a commercial sea lane by this northern route.

These days, the use of the open channel has more to do with disputed territorial claims between Canada, America, and Russia, together with the ownership of resources associated with these claims, than it does with any perceived commercial trade benefits.

WHAT WE KNOW TODAY

Since the Franklin Expedition first went missing, our knowledge of the circumstances of their demise has gradually increased to the point where we can be reasonably sure about what happened to them. Modern science has certainly helped to shed some light on one of the great Victorian mysteries, which, in part, had been brought about by a combination of over-confidence and a lack of experience in polar travel among the crew.

Franklin himself was experienced in the Arctic and, perhaps, should have known better, but, in the end, bad luck also played a part. He could not have known that King William Island was actually an island rather than being part of the Boothia Peninsula, as it was thought to be at the time. Had he continued to sail south into the James Ross Strait, rather than turn west, in the second year of the expedition, he most likely would not have become trapped in pack ice. The decision to turn west may have been the right one given what Franklin knew of this uncharted region, but it also sealed the fate of both himself and his crew.

LEAD POISONING

In more recent times, forensic tests have been carried out on the expedition remains that were found, including on the bodies of the three sailors whose graves were found on Beechey Island. The results have indicated that lead poisoning from the solder used to seal cans of meat, or possibly from the water pipes on the ships, may well have been a contributing factor to the deaths of so many men. After the ships became icebound in the second year of the expedition, and then remained stuck throughout that winter and the whole of the following year, supplies began to dwindle. As well as dying from the effects of the extreme cold and from starvation, men had also been suffering from a number of diseases, including pneumonia, tuberculosis, and scurvy. The symptoms of lead poisoning, of exhaustion, depression, and various disorders of the central nervous system, could only have exacerbated the problem. Those who were still alive after eighteen months set out to walk to safety in a last desperate effort to save themselves but died in the attempt.

DID OUR LADY OF LOURDES APPEAR TO BERNADETTE?

1858

Clue: After being dazzled by light, the apparition appeared

Main players: Saint Bernadette, the people of Lourdes, and Catholic pilgrims from around the world

Verdict: It is all a matter of belief

The small town of Lourdes, tucked away among the foothills of the Pyrenees in the southwest of France, is today the destination of Catholic pilgrims from all over the world. They have come to worship in the Sanctuary of Our Lady of Lourdes and to take the waters from the spring in the Grotto of Massabielle. Since the apparition of Our Lady first began appearing to Bernadette Soubirous in 1848, on one occasion directing her to find the source of the spring, Lourdes has become the most famous Marian shrine in the world.

To the faithful, the vision of Our Lady and the healing properties of the waters are more miraculous than mysterious, and the Catholic Church has recognized sixty-seven miracles related to the shrine. However it is viewed, there can be little doubt that strange and inexplicable events have occurred at the grotto, ones that have touched the lives of many millions of people.

FIRST APPARITION

The first of the apparitions occurred on February 11, 1848, when the fourteen-year-old Bernadette was collecting firewood on common land near the town with her sister and another young girl. At the Grotto of Massabielle, Bernadette paused to take her stockings off so she could cross a stream without getting them wet while the other two went on ahead. While she was doing this, an apparition appeared to her after she had been dazzled by a light coming out of the grotto. She would later describe the apparition as being of a small young lady dressed in white robes and used the word *aquero* to refer to it, which, in the Gascon dialect she spoke, simply means "that."

Despite the initial disapproval of her family and of the church, Bernadette was drawn back to the grotto many times, accompanied by a growing number of people as word of the apparitions spread, and she apparently fell into a trance

Bernardette would later describe the apparition as being of a small young lady dressed in white robes.

when she was having a vision. On a number of occasions, the small lady spoke to her, most notably to tell her how to find the spring and also asking her to have a chapel built on the spot so that processions could come to it.

OUR LADY OF LOURDES

In total, Bernadette had eighteen visions, most of which were simple calls for prayer and penitence. During the sixteenth and longest one, lasting over an hour, Bernadette asked the apparition who she was and received the reply that she was the "Immaculate Conception," providing a direct link to the Virgin Mary, who, according to Catholic teachings, was free from the stain of Original Sin. Although Bernadette never specifically said that the apparition was of the Virgin Mary, the association was made almost as soon as the phenomenon had become more widely known, and the words "Immaculate Conception" was taken as confirmation by many people.

The veneration of Mary has a long history in the region, together with the tradition of making pilgrimages to shrines associated with her. There were already numerous other shrines at locations where apparitions had occurred, so perhaps it was the story of Bernadette herself that led to Lourdes becoming the destination of so many pilgrims.

Bernadette was from a very humble

BERNADETTE SOUBIROUS
A portrait taken in 1863, five years after Bernadette saw the Marian apparitions.

HEALING WATERS

Pilgrims who visit the Sanctuary of Our Lady of Lourdes drink its waters as the sick are reputed to be miraculously healed by it and the water itself is a strong symbol of devotion. Many also bathe in the water or buy small statues and rosary beads containing small vials of it. Tests carried out on samples of Lourdes water to ascertain if they really do have any healing properties have come up negative, adding to the impression that claims of miraculous events have, at best, been a little exaggerated. But, then again, if people are cured of their ailments as a consequence of what doctors would call the placebo effect, by simply willing themselves and believing they will get better, the end result is much the same as being cured by the application of medical science.

background and, at the time of the apparitions, her large family were living in a one-room basement and hardly had enough for them all to eat. As a young child, she had suffered from severe illnesses, limiting her education to the extent that she was considered by some to be simple-minded, and she was also very small in stature. Before coming back to her family in Lourdes, she had worked as a shepherdess. Bernadette's story provided a sharp contrast to the formal institutions of the Church, which could appear distant from everyday experience. She appealed to ordinary people because she was one of them, a simple shepherdess

who had experienced the miraculous and who had been blessed by the mother of Christ.

Bernadette does not appear to have been comfortable with the attention she received as the story of her apparitions became more widely known. At the age of twenty-two she left Lourdes to live with the Sisters of Charity of Nevers, a religious institution hundreds of miles from the town. She spent the rest of her short life there, dying at the age of thirty-five from tuberculosis. More than fifty years after her death, in 1933, she was officially made a saint by Pope Pius XI, becoming popularly known as Saint Bernadette of Lourdes.

RATIONAL EXPLANATION

Over the years attempts have been made to explain the visions in rational and scientific terms, including by those who consider the apparitions to have been no more than hallucinations brought on by hysteria. Those of a more skeptical nature do not accept any explanation, no matter how straightforward it may be, instead dismissing the entire episode as being a hoax.

Bernadette, according to this line of thought, would have been well aware of the stories of apparitions of the Virgin Mary, which were quite common at the time in both France and Spain, and simply made the whole thing up. Once she had started, she kept up the

Some consider the apparitions to have been no more than hallucinations brought on by hysteria. Others dismiss the entire episode as a hoax.

OUR LADY
A statue of Our Lady of Lourdes was placed in the Grotto of Massabielle in 1864.

vision. According to the official website, there are twenty-two places of worship encompassed within the Domain, the largest of which is capable of holding twenty-five thousand people, and spreads out over more than a hundred acres of ground.

Some find the commercialization of the town distasteful, believing it has turned into a tourist trap rather than a site of pilgrimage. Either way, it's hardly surprising—the people of Lourdes have to make a living one way or another, just the same as everybody else.

pretense either so that she wouldn't have had to own up to the truth, or because she was enjoying the attention she was receiving too much to stop.

PILGRIMAGE SITE

The Sanctuary of Our Lady of Lourdes, usually known as the Domain, has grown to accommodate an ever-expanding number of pilgrims since the first chapel was built in response to Bernadette's

If pilgrims want to buy their own little statue of Our Lady to take home with them as a souvenir of their visit, it is hard to know what is wrong with somebody selling one to them.

After all, the pilgrimage to Lourdes developed in the first place as the response of ordinary people to the miracles experienced by Bernadette. If you don't believe in it, then there is an easy option for you to take: don't go.

WHERE DID THE PEOPLE ON THE *MARY CELESTE* GO?

December 4, 1872

Clue: All on board the *Mary Celeste* seemed to have vanished

Main players: The captain, his family, and the crew of seven

Verdict: Still lost at sea

On December 4, 1872, the *Mary Celeste* was found in the Atlantic Ocean, about 400 miles (650 km) east of the Azores, with some of the sails still set, but no sign of anybody on board. The ship, a 100-foot (30-m) American-registered brigantine, had left New York three weeks earlier, bound for Genoa in Italy with a cargo of seventeen hundred barrels of commercial alcohol, to be used to fortify wine. It was commanded by the experienced sailor Captain Benjamin Briggs, who was accompanied on the voyage by his wife and two-year-old daughter, and a crew of seven, all of whom were old hands at sea. No trace of any of them has ever been found and the story, described as the greatest maritime mystery of them all, has been told countless times, both as fact and fiction, and, more often than not, as a mixture of the two.

ARTISTIC LICENSE

In the story *J. Habakuk Jephson's Statement*, published in 1884, the young Sherlock Holmes author Sir Arthur Conan Doyle renamed the ship as the *Marie Celeste* and embellished the tale with details of his own, many of which have gone on to be treated as established fact. Conan Doyle wrote of the lifeboats still being on the ship and half-eaten meals found in the cabins, where hot coffee remained on the stove and cigar smoke hung in the air, as if the people who had been on board had simply vanished off the face of the earth. It was fiction, but caught the imagination of the reading public, prompting any number of theories about what happened, spanning the entire spectrum of probability.

At one end of the scale, there are theories straight from the Erich von Däniken school of thought—if you can't explain it, blame it on aliens. At the other

No trace of the ship's captain, his family, or the crew of seven has ever been found, and the story is described as the greatest maritime mystery of them all.

end, people have attempted to reconstruct what might have happened based on an interpretation of the available evidence, such as the testimony of the people who found the ship, given at the official inquiry held in Gibraltar. In between, there are sea monsters, pirates, mutinies, seaquakes, and even the Bermuda Triangle, even though, if it exists at all, it is all the way across the other side of the Atlantic from where the *Mary Celeste* was found. As life is short and none of us is getting any younger, what follows concentrates on some of the less fanciful theories, even if there can be no way of knowing for certain what really happened.

THE *AMAZON*

The ship was built in 1860 in Nova Scotia, Canada, and initially called the *Amazon*. After a series of unfortunate incidents, including the death of one of its captains on board from pneumonia, and a number of accidents, it was renamed as the *Mary Celeste*, perhaps in an attempt to change its run of bad luck. It was sold to a group of businessmen, including Captain Briggs, in New York. Before leaving New York in November 1888,

THE *MARY CELESTE*

A painting of the *Mary Celeste*, as it was found by the crew of the *Dei Gratia*.

the ship was refitted with an extra deck to accommodate extra barrels of alcohol, a change that, although possibly affecting the seaworthiness of the vessel, does not appear to have played a part in subsequent events. Alcohol is, of course, highly flammable and Briggs was apparently concerned about carrying it, although it did not prevent him from taking his family along on the voyage.

ABANDONED

The weather in the Atlantic was rough that November, resulting in the loss of a number of vessels. The ship's log of the *Mary Celeste* shows the captain steering a course to avoid the worst of the weather;

HARD TIMES

The 1880s were difficult times for merchant shipping, not least because wooden-hulled ships like the *Mary Celeste* were rapidly becoming obsolete and being replaced by those with a steel hull. This may account for the measures taken by the ship's owners to save money. There was only one small boat, known as a yawl, on the ship that could act as a lifeboat and the captain only appears to have taken one chronometer with him. Keeping accurate time was an important element in navigation, necessary for establishing the latitudinal position of a ship, and it would have been normal practice for a ship to carry a number of chronometers on any voyage in case one developed a fault or was running fast or slow.

> **The overall appearance was of an orderly but rapid abandonment, an event made inexplicable because the ship was found to be perfectly seaworthy.**

it has been suggested that he may not have been sure of his position, possibly due to a faulty chronometer. Whatever the reason, he changed course on November 24 to pass to the north of Santa Maria, the most southeasterly island of the Azores. The last entry in the log was written the following morning, which indicates that the captain ordered the ship to be abandoned at that time. The reason for this is unclear.

When the ship was found ten days later, the yawl was gone and a piece of the ship's railing had been removed, presumably in order to launch the yawl. Some sails were still up, some blowing loose, and the rigging was in a poor state of repair, with one long rope trailing behind the ship.

The sailors who first boarded the abandoned ship found that one of the two bilge pumps had been dismantled. Bilge pumps are vital pieces of equipment in any wooden-hulled ship because water constantly seeps in and collects in the bilges at the bottom of the vessel. It has to be pumped out on a regular basis to maintain seaworthiness, so any problems with the pumps can have serious consequences if not fixed immediately. There was also 3.5 feet (over 1 m) of water in the bilge, a significant but by no means dangerous amount. The chronometer, sextant (used for measuring distances), and some

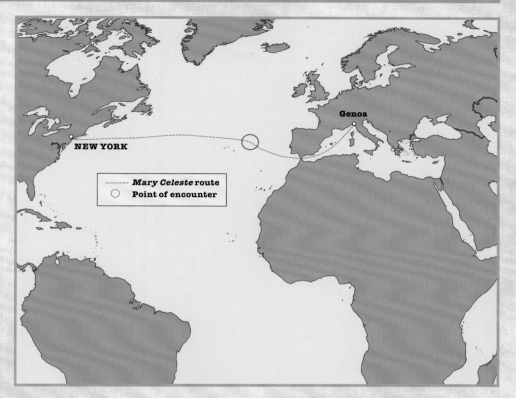

Genoa

NEW YORK

- - - - - - - - *Mary Celeste* route
○ Point of encounter

charts were gone, but, otherwise, everything else, including the possessions of those who had been on board, had been left behind. The overall appearance was of an orderly, rapid abandonment, an event made inexplicable because the ship was found to be perfectly seaworthy; the sailors who found it had no difficulty in sailing it into Gibraltar.

FOUL PLAY

The inquiry in Gibraltar initially focused on foul play. The captain of the *Dei Gratia*, the ship that found the *Mary Celeste*, was a close friend of Captain Briggs and there were suspicions that they had conspired together in an insurance fraud, a common occurrence with old wooden-hulled vessels at the

FOUND ADRIFT

The *Mary Celeste* was adrift in the Atlantic east of the Azores when it was spotted by the *Dei Gratia*.

time. In 1885, the *Mary Celeste* was intentionally wrecked on a reef off Haiti for exactly this reason. No evidence could be found and, as the captains and crews of both vessels had unblemished records, it could not be pursued. It would also appear unlikely that Captain Briggs would have taken his family on the voyage if he had been planning any sort of fraud, let alone if it involved abandoning the ship in the middle of the ocean.

No signs of any violence were found on the *Mary Celeste*, ruling out the possibility of a mutiny by the crew or the likelihood of piracy. This also suggested that accusations against the crew of the *Dei Gratia*, of killing everybody on board the *Mary Celeste* and dumping their bodies over the side in order to claim what remained (salvage rights), were simply attempts by the insurers to find a reason not to pay out rather than a credible explanation for what had happened. Reports of a sword being found in the captain's cabin with blood stains on the blade turned out to be false. An old sword was found, but when it was checked, the stains turned out to be rust. Eventually, the inquiry awarded salvage rights to the crew of the *Dei Gratia*, paid at only one-sixth of the value, indicating that doubts remained about their innocence in the matter.

The ship sailed on to Genoa and, when the barrels of alcohol were unloaded, nine were found to be empty. These nine barrels were made of American red oak, while all the others were white oak. Red oak is more porous, so it is likely that the alcohol leaked out of them during the voyage.

In an alternative theory, the captain abandoned the ship because he thought it had taken on much more water than it actually had.

HUGE EXPLOSION

One theory as to why the captain abandoned the *Mary Celeste*, a course of action that would have only been undertaken if the ship was in imminent danger of sinking, proposes that, when the hatches to the hold were opened, alcohol vapor from the leakage was released. With so much alcohol on board, there could have been a huge explosion if the vapor ignited. So, according to the theory, the captain ordered everybody into the yawl, which was then tied to the ship so they could return to it once the alcohol had fully evaporated away. If the wind rose while they were all in the yawl, a sudden acceleration of the ship could have broken the rope, casting everybody adrift.

Name	Status	Nationality	Age
Benj. S. Brigg	Captain	American	37
Albert G. Richardson	Mate	American	28
Andrew Gilling	2nd Mate	Danish	25
Edward Wm. Head	Steward and Cook	American	23
Volkert Lorenson	Seaman	German	29
Arian Martens	Seaman	German	35
Boy Lorenson	Seaman	German	23
Gottlieb Gondeschell	Seaman	German	23
Sarah Elizabeth Briggs	Captain's Wife	American	30
Sophia Matilda Briggs	Daughter	American	2

—Crew and Passenger List for the *Mary Celeste*

ABANDONED SHIP
The *Mary Celeste* found abandoned in the Atlantic Ocean in 1872 by *Dei Gratia*.

levels, then, with no way of pumping it out, the captain may have decided that he, with his wife and daughter should take to the yawl and make for Santa Maria. According to the ship's position given in the log, Santa Maria would not have been all that far away. If the sea then became rough, and with the yawl being overloaded with ten people, it could easily have been swamped or overturned.

LOST AT SEA

The two theories presented above are as close as we are likely to get, given the evidence, to what happened on board the *Mary Celeste*, but both rely heavily on speculation to interpret facts that otherwise don't entirely add up. It is probably safe to say that the ship was abandoned, rather than everybody on board was abducted by aliens or eaten by sea monsters, but the reasons why a sailor as experienced as Captain Briggs would take such drastic action, risking the lives of his family and crew by taking to a yawl in the middle of the Atlantic Ocean, are difficult, if not impossible, to understand. The real story of the *Mary Celeste*, like those who sailed her, remains lost at sea.

An objection to this theory is that, when the ship was found, two small hatches were open, but neither of these led directly to the hold, while the main hatch over the hold was still secure. If the intention was to release the alcohol fumes then come back to the ship when it was safe, then surely the main hold would have been opened as well.

ABOUT TO SINK

In an alternative theory, the captain abandoned the ship because he thought it had taken on much more water than it actually had and, with one pump out of action, thought it was about to sink. Immediately before setting out to cross the Atlantic, the ship had carried a cargo of coal, so it is possible that the debris and dust from the coal had collected in the bilge and clogged up at least one, if not both, of the pumps. If, for some unknown reason, the water in the bilge seemed to be building up to dangerous

WHO WAS JACK THE RIPPER?

1888

Clue: The Whitechapel murderer wrote letters to the police

Main players: An unknown serial killer and the thousands of people who have tried to identify him

Verdict: Still the most famous unsolved murders of all time

In the Victorian age, the East End of London had an infamous reputation for violent crime, drunkenness, and prostitution. It was a desperately deprived area, where appalling slums were situated alongside gin palaces, brothels, and opium dens. Tensions were at breaking point, heightened by the arrival of huge numbers of destitute people from outside the city, from rural areas of Britain and Ireland, together with the mass immigration of Jewish refugees escaping from persecution in Europe. Concerns had been raised of the likelihood of serious social unrest, most particularly because of its potential to spread out into other parts of the city. But all of this was overshadowed by a series of murders committed between August and November 1888 in Whitechapel, then a warren of narrow streets and back alleys notorious even by the standards of other parts of the East End.

It soon became apparent that a maniac was on the loose, one who was murdering women, all of them prostitutes, in a progressively more violent and depraved manner. The motive appeared to be sexual and, as a pattern to these dreadful

> *"I keep on hearing the police have caught me but they won't fix me just yet... I am down on whores and I shant quit ripping them till I do get buckled. Grand work the last job was. I gave the lady no time to squeal. How can they catch me now. I love my work and want to start again. You will soon hear of me with my funny little games... My knife's so nice and sharp I want to get to work right away if I get a chance. Good Luck.*
> *Yours truly, Jack the Ripper"*

> **—Text from the "Dear Boss" letter, the first of several allegedly written by Jack the Ripper**

FROM HELL
The letter sent on October 15, 1888, by somebody claiming to be Jack the Ripper.

crimes emerged, it was obvious that what would later become known as a serial killer was responsible for the killings.

UNSOLVED MYSTERY

Lurid press reports fanned the flames of hysteria already surrounding the case and provided a name for the unknown murderer, Jack the Ripper. In the process the media frenzy established a precedent for the way journalists treat such terrible crimes that persists to this day. Numerous letters purporting to be by the man himself were sent to newspapers and the police investigating the murders. Most of them were obvious hoaxes, some probably written by

journalists trying to sensationalize the case even further, but three of them seemed more credible, including the one quoted at the beginning of this chapter.

The murders stopped as suddenly as they began and, despite investigating numerous suspects, the police failed to uncover the identity of the killer. Since then, an ever-increasing number of candidates have been proposed as being Jack the Ripper. In common with other mysteries in which the evidence is open to all sorts of interpretation, well-known personalities have come under scrutiny and elaborate conspiracy theories have been constructed. The speculation continues more than 120 years after the murders were committed, making the Whitechapel murders among the most famous and widely discussed unsolved crimes in history. Ripperologists can browse through hundreds of books and websites on the subject, go on guided tours of the locations of the crimes, and, as libel laws don't apply to the dead, are free to point the finger at whomever they choose, however unlikely their guilt may be. Yet, despite an unprecedented level of attention, what has been described as the greatest Victorian mystery remains to be solved.

THE WHITECHAPEL MURDERS

The murder of prostitutes was an all too common occurrence in 1888 in the East End of London. The police investigated the deaths of 11 women as being potentially by the same man, of which six do not fit with the known methods of Jack the Ripper. The rest, known as the "canonical five," have all the hallmarks of being the work of a single serial killer. The first victim was Mary Ann Nichols, who was found in the early hours of

DUKE OF CLARENCE
The most famous suspect, Prince Albert Victor, Duke of Clarence, elder son of the future king Edward VII.

Friday, August 31, lying in a stable doorway on Bucks Row. Her throat had been slashed and her body mutilated. A week later, on Saturday, September 8, Annie Chapman's body was left in the backyard of a barber's shop in Hanbury Street, not far from where Mary Ann Nichols had been found. She had been killed in the same way and her body even more badly mutilated than in the previous attack. A doctor who examined the body thought the killer must have had some knowledge of anatomy and was skilled in the use of a knife, leading some to conclude that he was either a doctor, butcher, or slaughterman.

The police received the "Dear Boss" letter toward the end of September, in which the Ripper, if it was really him, said he would cut off the ear of the next victim and that he would soon strike again. At about one o'clock on the night of Sunday, September 30, Elizabeth Stride was murdered in a yard off Berner Street. The killer appears to have been disturbed by a horse and cart pulling into the yard and only had time to partially sever the victim's ear after slashing her throat. Apparently not satisfied with his night's work, he struck again half an hour later, murdering Catherine Eddowes between 1:30 and 1:45 am in Mitre Square. Minutes before the body was found, a policeman had seen a man coming out of an alley leading off the square but had not stopped him. The killer had used a piece of the victim's apron to clean his hands and, above the spot where he had discarded the cloth, a message was scrawled on the wall that said, "The Juwes are the men That Will not be Blamed for Nothing." The police washed the message off, hoping to avoid an escalation in the rising tide of anti-Semitism (hostility to Jews) already sweeping through the area.

A few days later, the "Saucy Jack" postcard arrived, written in the same handwriting as the previous letter and describing the latest murders as the "double event." Another letter was received by the man who was organizing a vigilante group in Whitehall.

Over the years, more than a hundred people have been identified as Jack the Ripper. The killer's identity is still not known — it was as if he had disappeared off the face of the earth.

The "From Hell" letter, as it is known, contained half a human kidney, the writer saying it was from Catherine Eddowes and that he had eaten the other half. Nothing further occurred until the night of Friday, November 9, when the mutilated body of Mary Jane Kelly was discovered in her room by her landlord. It was to be the Ripper's last known victim. A man had been seen accompanying Kelly toward the house where she lived earlier in the evening and, in a place where he was confident he would not be disturbed, the killer had apparently taken his time with the body. After this killing, there was a deafening silence—no more murders, no more letters, and, for the police and successive generations of amateur detectives, no conclusive evidence pointing to the identity of the killer. It was as if he had disappeared off the face of the earth.

CHIEF SUSPECTS

The police investigation into the killings at the time concentrated on suspects who had a good knowledge of Whitechapel. Documents drawn up in 1894 by Sir Melville Macnaghten, then the Chief Constable of the Metropolitan Police, came to light in 1959 and named three men whom the police considered to be the chief suspects. The first on the list, according to Macnaghten, was Montague Druitt, a barrister and teacher whose body was recovered from the River Thames in December 1888 after he had apparently committed suicide. No direct evidence linked Druitt to the crimes, other than he died at about the same time as the murders had stopped and he had lived in Blackheath, not all that far from the East End. The second suspect was Aaron Kosminski, a Polish Jew living in

FAMOUS SUSPECTS

The most famous suspect was Prince Albert Victor, the Duke of Clarence. He was Queen Victoria's grandson and second in line to the throne, until his death in 1892 in the influenza epidemic then sweeping across Britain. Rumors about the prince were already in circulation, although these did not link him to Jack the Ripper. That accusation only arose in the 1960s, despite the prince having a cast-iron alibi. In late September 1888, when the double murder occurred, he was a member of a royal shooting party at Balmoral in Scotland, more than 400 miles (650 km) from the scene of the crime. Attempts to implicate the royal doctor Sir William Gull and the artist Walter Sickert, either as the killer or being involved in a conspiracy to cover up the identity of the real killer, have met with little success either.

Whitechapel at the time of the killings, who was committed to an insane asylum in 1891, where he appears to have been regarded as not being dangerous. Even less evidence links the third suspect, Michael Ostrog, to the crimes, and subsequent research has placed him in France at the time anyway.

If, after six years of inquiries, these three were considered the chief suspects, then the police really had no better idea who was responsible than anybody else has had since. Like the man himself did at the time, the true identity of the Ripper continues to lurk in the shadows.

DID THE PRIORY OF SION REALLY EXIST?

1890s onward

Clue: The unlikely wealth of a lowly French priest

Main players: Bérenger Saunière, Pierre Plantard, the authors of *The Holy Blood and the Holy Grail*, and Dan Brown

Verdict: As real as a fake Rolex watch

The tiny hill-top village of Rennes-le-Château, in the Languedoc region of southern France, is an unlikely location for numerous mysteries and conspiracy theories. If it were not for the throngs of tourists attracted to the place as a result of accounts of the mysteries, and recent elaborations of them, the village would probably have remained in the rural obscurity it had enjoyed for much of its history.

The original source of all the fuss dates back to the late nineteenth century, when people began to ask questions about the local Catholic priest, Bérenger Saunière. In particular, they queried how he had been able to pay for the extensive renovations of his church and for other building work he had undertaken in the village considering the modest salary his position commanded. It might not appear to be the basis for much, other than some local gossip; in fact, it was of no significance until the 1950s and '60s, when the fun really started.

THE PRIORY

Pierre Plantard, a draftsman from Paris, came across the old story of Bérenger Saunière's supposed wealth, as told by Noël Corbu, a hotelier from Rennes-le-Château who had inherited the priest's estate. Unsatisfied with the story as it was, he decided to elaborate on it. According to this new version of events, Saunière had found some ancient parchments in a hollow pillar in his church that led him to a secret treasure, accounting for his supposed great wealth and setting in motion a story that remains with us today.

The parchments, according to Plantard, also referred to a secret society, the Priory of Sion, which was dedicated

The Holy Blood and the Holy Grail **explains how the members of the Priory of Sion are the keepers of the secret of the ancestral bloodline of Jesus Christ and how he married Mary Magdalene and had children.**

to maintaining the bloodline of the Frankish Merovingian kings of the fifth to seventh centuries. The three authors of *The Holy Blood and the Holy Grail*, Michael Baigent, Richard Leigh, and Henry Lincoln, picked up the thread of this story and knitted it together with other mysteries to come up with one almighty theory that, according to the authors at least, would shake the foundations of the Christian faith.

In a nutshell, the book explains how the members of the Priory of Sion are the keepers of the secret of the ancestral bloodline of Jesus Christ and how, contrary to what it says in the Bible, he married Mary Magdalene and had children. After the Crucifixion, Mary brought her family to France, where, some four hundred years later, their ancestors would marry into the Merovingian dynasty.

BLOODLINE OF JESUS

After the Merovingian king Dagobert II was murdered in 679, his son (according to the theory at least) was brought up in secret in Rennes-le-Château, so the bloodline of Jesus continued through him, becoming the dynasty of the House of Lorraine. During the First Crusade (1096–1099), Godfrey of Bouillon, of the House of Lorraine, became the king of Jerusalem and founded a priory on Mount Zion. The secret of the bloodline passed from generation to generation of priory members under the direction of a Grand Master, until it reached none other than Pierre Plantard.

The original documents found by Saunière, now known as Les Dossiers Secrets, turned up in the Bibliothèque Nationale in Paris and included a list of previous Grand Masters. It was something of a Who's Who of the great and the good through the ages and including such luminaries as Leonardo da Vinci, Isaac Newton and Victor Hugo.

The end result of all this was that Plantard was shown to be the direct descendant of Dagobert II, making him the inheritor of the bloodline of Jesus.

ENORMOUS HOAX

The fact that Plantard, the person who publicized the story in the first place, was the one who stood to gain the most out of it might have made some people rather skeptical about the whole episode right from the start and, in France at least, this is exactly what happened. Several French writers and journalists did a little digging and quickly showed it to be one

> "And it is not hard to be amazed by Lincoln's [one of the authors of The Holy Blood and the Holy Grail] own recollections…of how the sacred Merovingian bloodline occurred to him and his colleagues. During a discussion one of them remarked that there was something 'fishy' about the Merovingians. And then, said Lincoln, 'the penny dropped with an almighty clang!' Merovingians, fishy. Fish, early Christian symbol. Early Christian symbol, Jesus. Jesus, Jesus's kids. Therefore Merovingians, Jesus's kids."
>
> —**David Aaronovitch**, *Voodoo Histories*

enormous hoax, cooked up by Plantard and a couple of his buddies. The hollow pillar in Saunière's church turned out to be solid, the documents were modern forgeries, and the priest was shown to have made his fortune, such as it was, by selling masses through the mail—a practice that would get him booted out of his post in Rennes-le-Château.

The Priory of Sion, which is central to the whole theory, only came into existence in 1956 when it was founded by Plantard himself, and everything else, from the bloodline of Christ to the involvement of Leonardo da Vinci, was just nonsense. To be fair to Plantard, he never actually made the claim that he was related to Jesus, and denied it when *The Holy Blood and the Holy Grail* was published. But he had inserted plenty of clues that pointed toward that conclusion, so he cannot be absolved of all the blame either.

By the time *The Holy Blood and the Holy Grail* was published in 1982, full details of the hoax had been exposed in France. Nevertheless, the authors stood by their conclusions and the book went on to become a bestseller. The whole episode may well have faded into obscurity after that, had not Dan Brown's 2003 novel *The Da Vinci Code*, about an American academic who stumbles on the secret of the Priory of Sion, sold more than forty million copies around the world and been made into a movie starring Tom Hanks.

SEE YOU IN COURT

A few months before the release of the movie, Michael Baigent and Richard Leigh issued a writ for infringement of copyright against Dan Brown, alleging he had plagiarized their book. Henry Lincoln had long since acknowledged

RENNES-LE-CHATEAU CHURCH
A devil figure in the entrance of the Church of Saint Mary Magdalene.

that he had been duped by Plantard's hoax and took no part in the subsequent trial and, in maintaining their insistence of the validity of their theory, Baigent and Leigh were sowing the seeds of their own downfall. If the information presented in *The Holy Blood and the Holy*

Grail was true, in that it was a matter of historical fact, then there was nothing to stop anybody from writing a novel based on the same material as long as the author didn't directly quote large parts of the original book.

It was no surprise, then, when Dan Brown won the case. In the process, both the book and the movie of *The Da Vinci Code* received a huge amount of publicity as the trial was reported around the world. TV pictures showed Brown and his wife, who, it emerged, had done most of the research for the book, smiling broadly as they left the court after the judge had found in their favor. Not only had they won the case, but sales of *The Da Vinci Code* had gone through the roof. Who could blame them if they laughed all the way to the bank?

GRAND MASTER?

The great English scientist, Sir Isaac Newton, was said to be one of the Grand Masters of the Priory of Sion.

DID BUTCH AND SUNDANCE DIE IN A SHOOT-OUT?

ca. 1908

Clue: The bodies of the two outlaws were never identified before they were buried

Main players: Butch, Sundance, and the mythology of the Old West

Verdict: They either died in Bolivia or they didn't

In the final scenes of the movie *Butch Cassidy and the Sundance Kid*, the two heroes have been wounded and are holed up in a building in a small town in Bolivia. They decide to make a run for their horses, not knowing that a unit of the Bolivian army has the building completely surrounded. The two of them burst out of their hiding place, six shooters in hand, and the image freezes at the exact moment when a volley of fire from the army begins. The picture then gradually changes from color to a sepia-tinted black and white, as if consigning these two outlaws back into history as mythological figures of the Old West, a period that, if it really existed at all, was long gone by the time they made their last stand.

The movie is very much a Hollywood version of events and its success had much to do with the wit and charm of both William Goldman's Oscar-winning script and the engaging performances of Paul Newman and Robert Redford, who portrayed Butch and Sundance as likeable rogues rather than desperate outlaws. The final scenes were based on an incident that happened in the Bolivian town of San Vicente on November 6, 1908. Two Americans were recognized in the town as being the bandits who had robbed the payroll of a silver mine and they were cornered by a handful of soldiers and people from the town. In the ensuing gunfight, one of the soldiers was killed and, after a stand-off lasting into the following morning, the siege ended when one of the gunmen shot the other before turning his gun on himself. The two could not be identified and were buried in unmarked graves in the cemetery at San Vicente. It was assumed at the time that the two outlaws were

Butch
[getting his guns ready]
"The next time I say let's go somewhere like Bolivia,
let's go somewhere like Bolivia."

—William Goldman, *Butch Cassidy and the Sundance Kid*

Butch Cassidy and the Sundance Kid, or Robert LeRoy Parker and Harry Longabaugh, to give them their real names, but the bodies were not positively identified before they were buried and, as they were by no means the only American outlaws in Bolivia at the time, it is impossible to be certain if it was really them. Several attempts have been made to locate the graves in the cemetery, beginning in the 1990s, so that DNA tests can be carried out and compared to their living descendants. As yet, the remains have not been found, and neither has a definitive solution to the mystery of whether Butch and Sundance were really the two Americans killed that day. Some reports would have us believe that it was not them and, far from dying in Bolivia, they returned to the United States to live out their lives in anonymity.

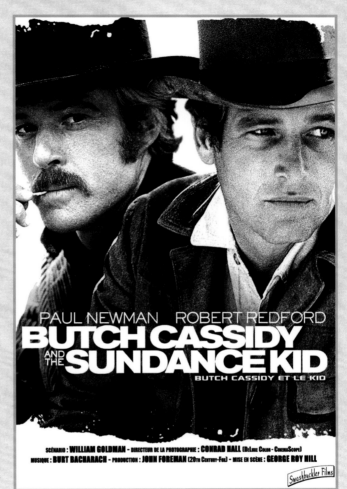

HOLE-IN-THE-WALL GANG

Butch and Sundance fell in together in the mid-1890s as members of an outlaw gang known as the Wild Bunch or, sometimes, as the Hole-in-the-Wall Gang. Butch and Sundance both prided themselves on not using violence in their robberies, and there is no evidence that either of them ever killed anybody, but

HOLLYWOOD TREATMENT
Paul Newman and Robert Redford starred in the movie *Butch Cassidy and the Sundance Kid*.

the same cannot be said of other members of the gang. Kid Curry, known as the wildest of the bunch, killed at least eleven people, nine of them lawmen. Butch did most of the thinking for the gang because, as Sundance remarks on several occasions in the movie, that is

WILD BUNCH
Back row, left to right: Will Carver and
Kid Curry. Front row: Sundance, Ben
Kilpatrick, Butch.

what he was good at. He meticulously
planned bank jobs and train robberies,
surveying the locations at great length
and paying particular attention to the

getaway. Fast horses would be left at
specific places along the route of their
proposed escape, enabling the gang to
outrun the pursuing posse.

In the winter months, the gang
returned to the Hole-in-the-Wall, often
accompanied by female friends. Ethel
Place, or Etta as she was commonly
called, had been with Sundance for a

WANTED MAN

A wanted poster from 1900 offering a $4,000 reward for the capture of Butch Cassidy either "dead or alive."

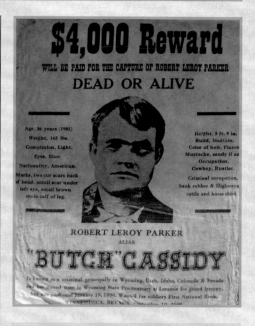

number of years and, together with Butch, the three of them formed a tight-knit little group within the gang. By the end of the century, the number of robberies carried out by the gang had made them notorious, particularly with one of their principle targets, the Union Pacific Railroad. They were being tracked by lawmen and the Pinkerton Detective Agency, and several members of the gang were either caught and sent to prison or killed. Butch wanted to negotiate an amnesty for himself and Sundance, in which both would promise not to commit any more robberies if past crimes were forgotten.

SOUTH AMERICA

By 1901, and after attempts at setting up a deal to get themselves an amnesty had failed, Butch and Sundance appear to have grown tired of life on the run. They left the West with Etta, traveled first to New York, where they appear to have spent a leisurely few weeks sightseeing, and then on to Argentina by ship, traveling under the names of Mr. and Mrs. Harry Place and James Ryan. For the next four years they made a determined effort to go straight, buying a ranch near the town of Cholila in the Patagonian Andes and raising cattle, sheep, and horses. By 1905, Pinkerton agents had tracked them down and they were forced to leave their ranch in something of a hurry. As far as we know, Etta went back to America, while Butch and Sundance returned to their criminal careers in Argentina and Bolivia.

THE EARLY YEARS

Butch and Sundance both drifted into crime in the early 1880s, when still in their teens, and took jobs, mostly on ranches in Wyoming and Montana, when they were not breaking the law. Cassidy grew up on the family ranch near Circleville, Utah. He took his assumed surname from Mike Cassidy, the man who had first introduced him to cattle rustling, and acquired the nickname of Butch during a short spell working as a butcher. Longabaugh, who was originally from Pennsylvania, was initially known simply as the Kid because of his youth, with the addition of Sundance coming later, after he had spent time in prison in the Wyoming town of that name.

her as a schoolteacher who has left her husband to be with Sundance. Others suggest she was a prostitute from San Antonio, Texas, while still others describe her as being a schoolteacher who also worked in a brothel. The only credible report we have of her after she returned to the United States from South America comes from 1909, when a woman matching her description inquired about the possibility of obtaining a death certificate for Sundance so she could settle his estate. After that, nothing further was ever heard from her and none of the countless stories about her, of her running a brothel in Texas or marrying a wealthy man in Paraguay, can be backed up with any solid evidence at all.

ETTA

Despite extensive investigations by Pinkerton agents at the time and by numerous other people since, we still know next to nothing about Etta. Nobody has been able to establish her identity, so we don't even know her real name or where she was born, or, in truth, anything about her at all other than her involvement with Butch and Sundance. In the movie, William Goldman makes use of one of the most common stories about her, portraying

BUTCH AND SUNDANCE

Much the same can be said for Butch and Sundance after their alleged deaths in San Vicente, which, according to some people at least, they used as a cover story to enable them to return to the US. Numerous sightings of both of them in America after 1908 have been reported, but, somehow, the evidence is never quite enough to be able to say for sure. Sundance, it has been claimed, lived until 1936 under the name of William Henry

Long, a rancher in Utah who told his grandchildren stories of how he rode with Butch Cassidy back in the old days. Long never claimed to be Sundance, but, then again, if he was living under an assumed name, he would hardly want to reveal himself, and there are undeniable similarities between photographs of the two of them. Unfortunately for those who have promoted Long's claims, DNA analysis carried out in 2008 on his exhumed body does not provide a match with the DNA of Sundance's known descendants.

Reports about Butch are much more numerous than they are of Sundance, even if most of them have more to do with wishful thinking on the part of the people making the reports than they do with accuracy. The most credible story was told by Lula Parker Betenson, Butch's younger sister, who continued to live in Circleville, Utah, until 1980, when she died at the age of ninety-six. In her later years, she told how Butch returned to the family home in Circleville for a visit in 1925 and, while it may be possible to question the memory of an old lady, in truth there can be few other reasons to doubt her word. One of the people she talked to was the author Bruce Chatwin, who was collecting stories about Butch and Sundance for his book *In Patagonia*, which included a number of references to the two outlaws. Chatwin was not always the most reliable of witnesses, but he clearly believed what he was told by Lula, who described eating blueberry pie with

---

In her later years, Lula Parker Betenson told how Butch returned to the family home in Circleville for a visit in 1925.

Butch when he visited in 1925 and that she thought he had died of pneumonia in the late 1930s, by which time he was living in the state of Washington.

Reports from the city of Spokane, Washington, lend some support to this theory. It has been claimed that Butch took the name William Philips and lived with his wife and two daughters in the city, where he ran a manufacturing business and became a member of the local Masonic lodge. But no actual evidence can back up these claims, which could, in truth, simply be wishful thinking or just outright lies.

MYTHS OF THE OLD WEST

There is one line of evidence supporting the theory that Butch and Sundance did not make it back to the US and were really killed in a Bolivian shoot-out. Both had been in regular contact with their respective families by mail while they were in South America and no more letters were received from either of them after the date of the deaths of the two American bandits in San Vicente.

Of course, if Butch and Sundance were trying to use the incident as cover for their return to the United States, they would have had to stop writing letters, otherwise the game would have been given away. If that was the case, and they went on to live quiet lives so as not to bring attention to themselves, then they did so with great success. To this day and despite all the research, we still don't know for certain what happened to them. If their bodies really do lie in unmarked graves in Bolivia, perhaps it would be best to leave them to rest in peace and allow the mythological versions of their lives in the Old West, like the one told in the film, to act as their memorial.

WHAT CAUSED THE HUGE EXPLOSION AT TUNGUSKA?

June 30, 1908

Clue: Many eyewitnesses saw a column of fire shooting up into the sky

Main players: Alien spacecraft, asteroids, and comets

Verdict: The answer is still out there, somewhere

The basic facts of what happened at just after seven o'clock on the morning of June 30, 1908, in the remote and sparsely populated Tunguska region of what is now Krasnoyarsk Krai, the Siberian federal subject of Russia, are straightforward enough. A massive explosion occurred, estimated as being hundreds of times more powerful than the blast of the atomic bomb dropped on Hiroshima at the end of World War II. The shock waves from the explosion flattened something like eighty million trees over an area of about 800 square miles (2,000 km²) of the taiga forests which stretch for thousands of miles across Russia. The blast knocked people off their feet and broke windows hundreds of miles away, and the aftereffects, atmospheric disturbances like the northern lights, were recorded as far away as London.

SCENES OF DEVASTATION

As a consequence of Russia's turbulent history of wars and revolutions in the early twentieth century, no scientists investigated the explosion until the late 1920s, when a Soviet Academy of Science expedition was sent to the area. Even twenty years after the event, they found scenes of devastation; near to where the blast must have occurred, they found the stumps of incinerated trees still standing, while, farther away, vast swathes of trees had been knocked over in a pattern radiating out from the center. What they didn't find at the scene was anything that could explain what had caused the explosion. There was no sign of an impact crater or of any of the sort of debris that might have been expected had something crashed into earth. In fact, there was nothing at all in the vicinity of the explosion that could

A massive explosion occurred, estimated as being hundreds of times more powerful than the blast of the atomic bomb dropped on Hiroshima. It knocked people off their feet and broke windows hundreds of miles away.

account for what had happened. And now, more than a hundred years later, we are not a great deal wiser about the event than we were then. There have been plenty of theories, ranging from the bizarre to the plain ludicrous, but as yet, no solid evidence has been found to confirm any of them.

ALIENS AND BLACK HOLES

There are people, as there always are for unexplained events, who don't just have a theory to account for what happened at Tunguska, but know the answer to the mystery with an unshakable certainty that borders on religious fanaticism. And if you were thinking that Erich von Däniken might be one of these people, then you would be correct. Apparently, an alien spacecraft got into a bit of difficulty during a flight over Siberia and blew up. In an effort to keep extra-terrestrial visitations of this nature secret, the Russian government collected up all the wreckage and deposited it in a warehouse of unknown location, presumably storing it next to all the other flying saucers that have banged into the planet over the years.

In another version of events, rather than their spaceship blowing up and crashing, the aliens did us all a massive favor by destroying a meteor that had been on course to smash into the earth, preventing untold death and destruction.

SHOCK WAVE
The blast from the Tunguska event flattened trees over a huge area of Siberia.

REINDEER HERDERS
People of the Tunguska region, Siberia, in Russia in the early twentieth century.

IMPACT THEORY

Eyewitness reports gathered in the 1920s from the Evenki people, the nomadic reindeer herders of the region, tell of the tents, their animals, and themselves being thrown into the air by the shock wave of the explosion. Accounts of the blast itself are by no means consistent, but mostly involve a column of fire shooting up into the sky, followed by a blast of intense heat and a shock wave that knocked the observers off their feet. Some reported seeing a fireball in the sky immediately before the blast, which has led to the theory that it was caused by a celestial body—an asteroid or a comet—that, as no impact crater has been found, must have exploded in the atmosphere rather than hitting the ground.

The main problem with this theory is that, even if the asteroid or comet had

So, rather than being afraid of aliens invading the planet or demolishing it to make way for a hyperspace bypass, what we should be doing is offering them a great big thank-you for saving our necks.

A marginally less fantastic theory describes how the planet collided with a microscopic black hole and, had the author of this book been Stephen Hawking, he most probably would have been able to explain what that is supposed to mean. Unfortunately, he was otherwise engaged and your current author hasn't got the slightest idea.

Some reported seeing a fireball in the sky immediately before the blast, which has led to the theory that it was caused by a celestial body—an asteroid or comet.

> *"There were three of us in the tent; my husband Ivan, me, and old man Vasilii… Suddenly someone gave our tent a powerful shove. I got frightened, cried out, woke up Ivan, and we started to crawl out of the sleeping bag… Ivan and I had not even managed to get all the way out and stand on our feet when once again someone gave our tent a powerful shove and we fell to the ground. Old man Vasilii fell on top of us, as if someone had thrown him. All around we heard a noise, like someone banging on the roof of the tent. Suddenly it got very bright, like the sun was shining on us, and a strong wind blew. Then someone fired a powerful shot, as if the ice was cracking on the river in winter, and right away a dancing whirlwind swooped down, grabbed hold of the roof, whirled it around and dragged it off somewhere."*
>
> **—Eyewitness account by Akulina Lyuchetkana, an Evenki woman interviewed in 1926**

vaporized in the atmosphere, scientists would have expected to find debris or dust on the ground and, as yet, nothing has been detected. In the summer, the terrain of the taiga forest becomes very wet, forming swamps as the top levels of frozen soil melts, so it is possible that any debris simply sank out of sight. However, the inability of researchers to detect anything at all remains a mystery.

In recent years, Italian scientists from the University of Bologna have suggested that Lake Cheko, about 5 miles (8 km) from the epicenter of the blast, could have been formed by the impact of a large piece of debris. Unlike other lakes in the region, Cheko is relatively deep and conical in shape, consistent with what would be expected from a large impact. Others have raised doubts about this, citing anecdotal accounts from the Evenki saying that the lake existed before the event took place in 1908, together with the lack of any rings of soil displacement around the lake that are typically found after a large impact. The Italians have not been deterred and are currently engaged in further research in the lake to recover evidence of material from the celestial body.

"EARTH BELCH"

An entirely different theory speculates that, as no indications of any extra-terrestrial material has ever been found at the site, then perhaps the blast was not caused by an impact in the first place. The "earth belch" theory, as it is called, was developed in the University of Bonn in Germany and suggests that the blast was caused by the sudden release of high-pressure natural gas through weak points in the earth's crust. If this was the case, then these vents through which the gas escaped should be detectable by the presence of shocked quartz, which is formed by the extreme pressure created by shock waves. So far, neither the vents nor shocked quartz have been found, which leaves the theory as unproven as the impact theory.

The race is on, then, between the Italians and Germans to come up with the evidence that proves their respective theories, unless, of course, somebody finds a piece of a flying saucer first.

IS THERE REALLY A MONSTER IN LOCH NESS?

1934 onward

Clue: Sightings of Nessie are usually fleeting glimpses in twilight

Main players: Many, many monsters of all different shapes and sizes

Verdict: Oh for goodness sake!

The modern phenomenon of Loch Ness monster sightings more or less began in 1933, when a road was constructed along the banks of the loch. Sightings had been a bit thin on the ground before easy access to the loch was afforded by the road but, immediately after it opened, a rush of reports of strange occurrences in the water began to appear.

That is not to say there were not any sightings before the road was constructed. The presence of a monster in Loch Ness has a long recorded history going back to the seventh century, when writings about the life of St. Columba, the Irish monk who spread Christianity among the Pictish tribes of Scotland, told how he encountered the burial of a man said to have been killed by the monster. As well as being the oldest, it is also the only account of the monster behaving in such a manner.

These days reports are almost always of fleeting glimpses in twilight conditions, occasionally bolstered by grainy photographs of some strange shape poking out of the water. Rather than the fearsome beast of St. Columba's day, the modern monster is a shy and retiring creature, who apparently prefers to stay out of the media spotlight.

MURKY WATERS

The loch is the largest of a series of lakes in the Great Glen, a geological fault running all the way through the Scottish Highlands from Inverness on the North Sea to Fort William at the head of Loch Linnhe, a sea loch that runs out into the Atlantic Ocean. Loch Ness is the second largest freshwater lake in Great Britain, after Loch Lomond, and the deepest, reaching down to a depth of about 800 feet (250 m). Rainwater drains down to the loch from the Highlands and through the surrounding peat bogs, which stains it to a deep brown color and makes it looks as if a giant tea bag has

> The murkiness of the water explains why sightings have almost all been of a monster on the surface of the loch. Some of these sightings have provoked intense media interest.

LOCH NESS
A view of the loch with no monsters in sight—those bumps in the foreground are just stones.

been dipped into it. As a consequence, visibility in the water is very low, leading to a scarcity of life because sunlight cannot penetrate very far down into it.

The murkiness of the water explains why sightings have almost all been of a monster on the surface of the loch. Some of these sightings have provoked intense media interest in the monster, beginning with one of the first, and still the most famous, photographs, taken in 1934 by Dr. Robert Wilson. Known as the surgeon's photograph—its author interestingly refused to be publicly

associated with it—it shows what appears to be the head and neck of some kind of animal projecting out of the water (see page 150). Although various theories have been put forward to explain what it could be, it was eventually exposed as a hoax. Forty years after its publication, a then 93-year-old model maker Christian Spurling owned up to perpetrating a hoax, explaining that he had made the head and neck himself and glued it on to a toy submarine. An examination of the pattern of ripples on the water around the object would tend to support this description, as they indicate that it was only a few feet long and was probably being towed along by a line.

LARGE PREDATORS

Interest peaked again in the 1970s after photographs taken from a submersible vehicle appeared to shown the fins of a large animal. It was claimed that it was a *Plesiosaurus*, a prehistoric marine reptile that is otherwise thought to have died out sixty-five million years ago during the Cretaceous-Tertiary extinction event.

Attempts to explain how a dinosaur could have survived through the ice ages have not been very convincing. Loch Ness in its current form only emerged after the retreat of the glaciers at the end of the last ice age, about ten thousand years ago; before that, it would have been frozen solid and covered in a very thick layer of ice—not an ideal habitat for a cold-blooded animal like a *Plesiosaurus*.

In general, the outlook for monsters in Loch Ness from an ecological point of view, even if ice ages are ignored, is not

THE HOAX
The ripples in the water are either very big or the monster is very small.

particularly great. The relatively low levels of aquatic life in the loch would not be able to support a population of large predators, or at least the numbers needed for a realistic breeding population. So, if a monster had ever really existed in the first place, its prospects would have been rather bleak.

OTHER THEORIES

A vast range of other possibilities have been put forward to explain the sightings over the years and, in truth, most of them have not been any more convincing than the one about the *Plesiosaurus*. They include suggestions that it is really the upturned keel of a submerged Viking longboat, a primitive whale, and an unknown species of long-necked seal. The fact that most sightings have been made at dusk could mean that Nessie is a nocturnal creature, or else people have seen a monster in the loch while driving home after having one too many rounds at the bar.

In recent years, sightings have become less frequent, perhaps reflecting the fact that the drinking and driving laws are now more strictly enforced in the Highlands than they used to be. Or maybe it is because you no longer actually have to go to the loch to catch a sight of Nessie. These days, she (Nessie, it turns out, is a lady monster) has her own website, where you can catch up with what she's been up to by reading her blog. Should you feel the need, you can even send her an email.

A MODERN FOLKTALE

In a rare outbreak of serious scholarship on the subject, the Swedish naturalist Bengt Sjögren has proposed a link between modern stories of the Loch Ness monster and the ancient Celtic mythology of the kelpie. According to the folktales, kelpies were supernatural shape-shifting water horses who would lure unwary people into riding on their backs and then dive into deep lochs, vanishing completely so that their unsuspecting riders were never seen again. According to Sjögren, these old stories have undergone a transformation themselves, being updated for modern audiences by substituting kelpies for creatures such as dinosaurs, which we are now familiar with through watching films and documentaries on TV.

TOURIST ATTRACTION

These days, the more cynical of us might say that the stories about the Loch Ness monster have been promoted in an attempt to stimulate the tourist industry. But that being said, it's probably not needed as anyone who has been to the region hardly needs to be encouraged to return to what remains one of the most beautiful parts of the British Isles.

These days, she (Nessie, it turns out, is a lady monster) has her own website, where you can catch up with what she's been up to by reading her blog. Should you feel the need, you can even send her an email.

WHY DID AMELIA EARHART'S PLANE VANISH?

July 2, 1937

Clue: Amelia's plan to fly around the world was always risky

Main players: Amelia Earhart and Fred Noonan

Verdict: The plane is still lost somewhere in the Pacific

Howland Island is a tiny speck of land in the Pacific Ocean, a little over 1 mile (1.5 km) long and less than half a mile (0.8 km) wide. The coral island emerged from complete obscurity on July 2, 1937, as the destination of the Pacific stopover in Amelia Earhart's attempt to fly around the world. Before their scheduled stop on the island, Earhart and Fred Noonan, her navigator, had already flown over 20,000 miles (32,000 km), traveling across the US, down to South America, across the Atlantic Ocean to Africa, and all the way through Asia. They took off from Papua New Guinea to begin the last part of their trip by crossing the Pacific. To reach Howland Island, they had to fly 2,500 miles (4,000 km) over water and, once they had established radio contact with the island's US Coast Guard, the plan was to use radio direction to navigate to the airstrip.

For some reason only intermittent contact was established, and Earhart and Noonan could not get a bearing on the ship. They never arrived at the island. Despite a massive search effort, no trace of the aircraft or its pilot and navigator have ever been found.

"THE QUEEN OF THE AIR"

In the ten years before her disappearance, Amelia had become an international celebrity. In 1928 she became the first woman to cross the Atlantic by air. Even though she had not actually flown the plane, describing her own role in the flight as being "like a sack of potatoes," she was given a hero's welcome when she returned to the US. Afterward, she embarked on a series of aviation challenges in which she did the flying herself, becoming in 1932 the first woman to fly solo across the Atlantic. By that time she had married George P. Putnam, the man who had promoted her first record-breaking flight. He was a highly skilled publicist, who arranged speaking tours and book publishing deals for her. With her boyish good looks and easy-going manner, she was rarely out of the news. Even though there were plenty of other female fliers around at the time, some of whom were

Amelia's aviation exploits made front-page news around the world, the press labeling her "the Queen of the Air."

THE ELECTRA
Amelia pictured in 1937, in front of the
Lockheed Electra she was flying when
she disappeared.

arguably better aviators, the press labeled Earhart "the Queen of the Air."

Amelia's family had initially been able to finance her flying ambitions. Like many other people at the time, they lost much of their money in the stock market crash of 1929 and the subsequent Great Depression of the early 1930s. From then on, she had to find the money to pay for her exploits herself, which she did with the help of Putnam. As well as writing books and going on speaking tours, she began her own flying school and endorsed a number of commercial products, including her own range of clothing and luggage. She also continued to set aviation records; in 1935, she was the first person, man or woman, to fly solo from Honolulu in Hawaii to Oakland, California. In the same year she then flew nonstop from Los Angeles to Mexico City and then on from there to New York.

ROUND THE WORLD

With aviation records being set regularly by other people, Amelia was always looking to stay ahead of the game with further exploits. In 1935, the Department of Aeronautics at Purdue University in Indiana agreed to finance her next expedition, including buying her a new plane, a twin-engined Lockheed Electra. It cost $50,000 and required $30,000 more to be spent on it to fit it out for Amelia's plan, to fly around the world by a route along the equator that had never been attempted before.

Amelia's first attempt at a round-the-world flight, beginning on March 17 in Oakland, almost ended in tragedy. She was flying with Noonan and another navigator, Harry Manning, from east to

JAPANESE CAPTIVES

One theory proposes that Amelia and Noonan were picked up by the Japanese and held in captivity as spies. Anecdotal evidence, which emerged in the 1960s, recounts how witnesses on the island saw two Americans, a man and a woman, in the custody of Japanese soldiers, who, according to some of the reports, took their captives into the forest and shot them. This led to a theory that Amelia and Noonan had been engaged in spying on Japanese positions in the Pacific for the American government—an idea that has now been widely discredited.

west, crossing the Pacific first. The first leg to Honolulu was mostly uneventful, with her business partner Paul Mantz doing some of the flying. But, on take-off from Honolulu, the Electra went into a spin while still on the ground, causing the landing gear to collapse. Fuel spilled everywhere, but, miraculously, did not ignite and, except for a few bumps and bruises, nobody was hurt. The cause of the crash could not be established, although the plane had been extensively damaged and the attempt to fly around the world had to be abandoned.

After the plane had been repaired and additional funds raised, Amelia set off on her second attempt on June 1, this time flying from west to east, and with just Noonan to accompany her. Over the next month, they made their way around the world. It was an arduous trip, with little opportunity for rest, but they arrived in New Guinea on June 29 without having encountered any major problems, other than some difficulty using the radio navigation equipment. Given how far they had traveled, they must have been looking forward to the final leg of their journey over the Pacific, even though it would be the most difficult and dangerous part of it. They took off three days later, the Electra lumbering into the sky on account of its heavy fuel load, and headed toward Howland Island.

PLANE VANISHES

The reason why they didn't make it has been debated ever since. The most obvious answer is that they simply could not find the island and ran out of fuel, forcing Amelia to ditch the Electra in the ocean. Such a maneuver would have been difficult, even in perfect conditions, and after twenty hours in the air, Amelia must have been extremely tired. In such circumstances, it is not hard to imagine the plane crashing into the water. Even if she had managed to put it down safely, it wouldn't have stayed afloat for long, and the chance of being rescued in the vast expanse of the Pacific Ocean, would also have been remote.

The exact reason why they became lost is impossible to say for certain. The failure to establish proper radio contact most probably played a part and

Amelia was an aviation pioneer who pushed the boundaries of what was possible. In the end, all we can say is that her plane was lost at sea.

HOWLAND ISLAND
The tiny speck in the Pacific Ocean that Amelia and Frank Noonan failed to find.

THE SEARCH

In the absence of a definite answer, all sorts of theories have been put forward to explain the disappearance. At the time, some people thought Amelia and Noonan could have turned back when they couldn't find Howland, leading to an intensive search effort around the islands the plane would have passed over, but nothing was found. Renewed searches have occurred over the years, notably on the island of Nikumaroo. There are signs that people had been on the island at about the right time, but nothing could be explicitly connected to Amelia or Fred Noonan.

that could have been the result of a problem with the transmitter on the plane or because both pilot and navigator were not accustomed to using the equipment. Some people have speculated that the radio antenna could have been damaged during take-off, but it would only be possible to know for sure if the aircraft were ever found—an unlikely prospect given how deep the water is in that part of the Pacific.

The radio messages received from the plane were of sufficient strength to indicate that it was not far away. According to the last message, Noonan seemed to indicate that they had flown far enough east to have reached Howland and were now flying from north to south in an effort to find the island. It has since emerged that the position of Howland was wrongly marked on US naval charts—a discrepancy of 5 nautical miles (9 km; 5.75 miles). When the Electra failed to turn up at the scheduled time, the Coast Guard began to put out black smoke that would have been visible for miles around. Had the plane been anywhere near the island, they should have seen it.

In the end, all we can really say is that the plane was lost at sea. Even today, despite all the technology available to track planes, occasionally one will go missing for no apparent reason. When Amelia was flying, radio technology was in its infancy. She was an aviation pioneer who pushed the boundaries of what was possible. In doing so, she demonstrated that, given the opportunity, women were just as capable of flying an airplane as men. Flying at the time was a dangerous occupation and numerous people lost their lives in pursuit of their ambitions. We can't be sure what happened to Earhart, and we may never know for certain, other than to say that, on that fateful flight, her luck ran out.

DID HITLER SEND RUDOLF HESS TO SCOTLAND?

May 10, 1941

Clue: Hess flew to Scotland on his own and parachuted into a field

Main players: Hess, Hitler, Albrecht Haushofers, the Duke of Hamilton, and a widow from Cambridge

Verdict: The lone loony theory looks to be the most likely

Shortly after 11 o'clock on the night of May 10, 1941, Rudolf Hess, the Deputy Führer of Nazi Germany and close personal friend of Adolf Hitler, parachuted into Scotland from a plane that he himself had been flying. He landed in a field about 10 miles (15 km) south of Glasgow and was found by David McLean, a local farmer, who took him into his house and offered him a cup of tea. Hess told McLean that his name was Captain Alfred Horn and that he was bearing an important message for the Duke of Hamilton, one of the most prominent members of the aristocracy in Scotland. McLean phoned the Home Guard, who took Hess into custody and handed him over to the British army. Hess, still claiming to be Alfred Horn, said he would only talk to the duke, who, when told of this strange occurrence, visited the prisoner. In the subsequent meeting, Hess revealed his true identity to the duke, who immediately afterward sent a report of the conversation directly to Winston Churchill.

> "*I was in the house and everyone else was in bed late at night when I heard the plane roaring overhead. As I ran on to the back of the farm I heard a crash and saw the plane burst into flames in a field about 200 yards away... I hurried round by myself again to the back of the house and in the field there I saw [a] man lying on the ground with his parachute near by. He smiled, and as I assisted him to his feet he thanked me, but I could see that he had injured his foot in some way.*"
>
> —Account of the capture of Rudolf Hess by David McLeand published in the *Daily Record*, May 12, 1941
>
> "*Hess or no Hess, I'm going to watch the Marx Brothers.*"
>
> —Winston Churchill's response on being told the news

LURED TO BRITAIN

It was one of the most bizarre occurrences of World War II and has led to endless speculation about the reason for Hess's actions, including doubts about his mental state at the time. The British government's obsession with secrecy over the affair, which has led to some of the files relating to it still being classified more than seventy years later, has left huge gaps in our understanding of what happened. Predictably, these gaps have been filled with a wide selection of half-baked theories concerning, among other things, the role played by the government and its intelligence services in luring Hess to Britain under false pretenses. The objective of such an action seemed either to be the capture of Hess or the initiation of a process of mind-boggling complexity that would eventually ensure Germany attacked the Soviet Union, thereby relieving some of the pressure on Britain, which had been fighting alone against Nazi Germany after the fall of France.

COUP AGAINST CHURCHILL

An alternative theory suggested that the affair was part of a much wider plot aimed at removing Churchill from power in Britain so a government more favorable to Germany could be installed in its place. In this scenario, Hess had come to Britain to make contact with a supposed "peace party," made up of former appeasers, such as Lord Halifax, together with members of the aristocracy who had shown sympathy toward Nazi Germany before the war had started. One of these was the Duke of Hamilton, the man Hess had flown over to meet, according to the theory at least, in order to offer the support and cooperation of Germany in the formulation of what would be, in effect, a coup against Churchill.

A BRITISH PLOT

Needless to say, most of these conspiracy theories owe more to the imaginations of their authors than they do to the facts as we know them, even if it is currently impossible to say for certain what really happened. One line of reasoning, supposedly linking the British secret services to the affair, says that the RAF allowed Hess to fly into Britain unchallenged because they had been told not to stop his plane. Studies into the response of Fighter Command on that night don't support this theory.

RUDOLF HESS
The reasons why the Deputy Führer of Nazi Germany took it upon himself to fly to Scotland remain mysterious.

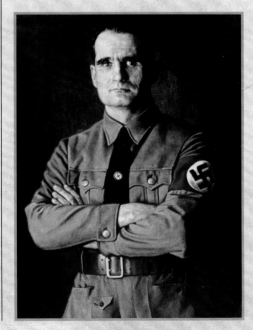

The RAF may have been surprised at the arrival of a single German plane over the country, but, once it was detected, several squadrons of Spitfires were rushed to intercept it. Only Hess's ability as a pilot prevented him from being shot down—he was observed from the ground flying over the coast at no more than 50 feet (15 m) and then continued across Scotland at a low altitude to avoid being seen by the RAF.

If it had been a British plot, you might think that some sort of plan would have been put in place to deal with him once he had been caught. As it was, his arrival was greeted with astonishment and the response was, at best, confused, suggesting that the British had no prior knowledge. There is a possibility that British Intelligence was involved in encouraging the belief among Germans

AN IMPOSTER

One theory states that the man who landed in Scotland was not Hess at all, but an imposter. He then continued the pretence, playing the role of Hess even after he was given a life sentence in 1946 at the Nuremberg Trials and took the secret to the grave after his death in 1987 in Berlin's Spandau Prison. However, the idea that the man captured in Scotland was an imposter is easily shown to be a fantasy—a British Foreign Office official, who had met the real Hess on numerous occasions in Berlin before the war, confirmed his identity shortly after his arrival.

that a British "peace party" was actively working to end their country's participation in the war. It was certainly what Hitler wanted to believe, as a settlement with Britain would have left Nazi Germany free to pursue its aims of expansion in Eastern Europe and Russia. But, beyond a small number of Nazi sympathizers and British fascists, there is no evidence of any such a movement in Britain. So, with the conspiracy theories easily dismissed, we are left with a rather more difficult question: what on earth was really going on?

HESS AND THE HAUSHOFERS

The conspiracy theories all concentrate on the role of the British in the affair. If the focus is switched to what Hess was doing in Germany immediately before he set out for Britain, a rather different picture emerges. Both Hess and Hitler were familiar with the geopolitical work of Professor Karl Haushofers and, in *Mein Kampf*, Hitler had adapted the professor's ideas into the concept of *Lebensraum*, literally "living space," which emphasized the necessity of an eastward expansion in order for Germany to grow and prosper. In his book, Hitler had also expressed the view that Germany's great mistake in World War I had been to fight on two fronts. In an attempt not to make the same mistake himself, he was actively investigating the possibility of a settlement with Britain.

If the Battle of Britain had been won by the Germans, then Britain would either have had to come to the negotiating table or face invasion and the loss of the war. Thankfully, the RAF successfully repelled the German attack, forcing Hitler to rethink his strategy. He was well aware that, as long as

CRASH SITE
Members of the Home Guard and police officers pose for a photograph with the remains of Hess's plane.

Churchill remained prime minister, there would be no chance of doing any sort of deal, so he appears to have asked Hess to find a way of overcoming this impasse. Hess turned to Professor Haushofers's son Albrecht, who had followed his father into the same field of study. Despite Albrecht's assessment that nobody in Britain, of any political persuasion, would consider a pact with Hitler, between them they came up with a plan.

Albrecht Haushofers had met the Duke of Hamilton in 1936, when the duke had been in Berlin for the Olympic Games, and there are indications that the duke may have been introduced to Hess as well at the same time. The plan devised by Hess and Haushofers involved contacting the duke to set up a meeting in a neutral country, most probably Portugal, to discuss a plan for peace. This was to be done through an intermediary in Britain who, coincidentally, had just written to Professor Haushofers. She was Mrs. Violet Roberts, the widow of a Cambridge academic, who had known

The RAF may have been surprised at the arrival of a single German plane over the country, but, once it was detected, several squadrons of Spitfires were scrambled to intercept it.

the professor before the war and had apparently written to him to express her regret that the war had come between them and to suggest that they communicate via a post office box she had opened in Lisbon. What a widow from Cambridge was doing behaving in this way in the middle of a war is anybody's guess; although no proof exists, it could point to the possible involvement of British Intelligence.

Whatever the truth of the matter, Albrecht Haushofers wrote back to Mrs. Roberts in November 1940, signing his letter only with the letter "A" and asking her to forward a message to the Duke of Hamilton. If British Intelligence had not been involved before, they certainly were now, because MI5 intercepted this letter. We don't know exactly what they did about it, although it is fair to assume that they launched an investigation into Mrs. Roberts and the duke. Nothing more is known about Mrs. Roberts and we can

only assume that the duke, a serving officer in the RAF, was found to be entirely innocent. Ultimately, it seems that MI5 decided to do nothing.

HITLER FURIOUS

The message was not delivered to the duke and the letter remained unanswered, leaving Hess with a dead end in his plan to make contact with somebody involved with a British peace party. As the chance of setting up a meeting in Portugal was now gone, Hess appears to have begun considering other ways of getting in touch with the duke, including taking the matter into his own hands by going to Scotland himself. It is not certain if Hitler was aware of any of this, but he personally banned Hess from

said to have flown into a violent rage, ordering anybody who had helped Hess to be arrested, including Albrecht Haushofers, and for Hess to be shot as a traitor should he return to Germany.

FANCIFUL SCHEME

The picture that emerges from Germany is of Hess becoming increasingly desperate to succeed in the mission he had been given by Hitler. Over the course of 1940 and into 1941, Hess had gradually been sidelined in the Nazi party by more able politicians—in particular, by Martin Bormann. What Hess needed was a spectacular success that would restore his reputation in the eyes of Hitler. So, rather than being an elaborate conspiracy, the affair can perhaps be better explained as the fanciful scheme of a deluded man who had convinced himself that he could resolve the conflict between Britain and Germany all on his own.

In truth, attempting to find a rational explanation for the behavior of an irrational man is always going to be a fool's errand. That said, should all files relating to the affair ever be declassified, information might come to light that finally solves the riddle. For now, however, it looks as though the mystery of the Hess affair will endure for a long time to come.

flying at about this time, so it is possible that Hess had put the idea to him and he turned it down. If this is the case, then Hess disregarded Hitler and went ahead on his own initiative. On being told that Hess had traveled to Britain, Hitler is

> **Rather than being an elaborate conspiracy, the affair can perhaps be better explained as the fanciful scheme of a deluded man who convinced himself he could resolve the conflict all on his own.**

WAS GLENN MILLER KILLED IN A PLANE CRASH?

December 15, 1944

Clue: There was never any search for the missing aircraft

Main players: Lt-Col. Norman Baessell, Major Glenn Miller, Flight Officer John Morgan, and a United States Army Air Forces UC-64 Norseman

Verdict: Most likely took a nose-dive into the Channel

The disappearance of one man during World War II, which cost the lives of millions of people, may not have received so much attention had the man in question not been one of the most popular musicians of his era. Glenn Miller came to prominence as the leader of his own big band in the mid-1930s, playing smooth arrangements of the band's signature tune "In the Mood," as well as hits like "Moonlight Serenade" and "Chattanooga Choo Choo." He joined the US army in 1942, at the height of his fame, to do his bit for the war effort by taking a band to Europe to entertain the troops. His subsequent disappearance provoked much speculation about the circumstances surrounding it. As he was last seen boarding an airplane to fly from England to France, the most likely explanation is that something went wrong on the flight, such as a mechanical failure or the plane being hit by what we would now call friendly fire. Needless to say, such straightforward scenarios have not satisfied everybody and numerous rumors and alternative explanations have circulated ever since he was first reported missing.

CONCERT IN PARIS

By December 1944, Major Miller had been in Britain for almost six months, leading his band in concerts and making regular radio broadcasts on the BBC. An American general described the effect of Miller's music on the morale of American servicemen in Britain and Europe as being the next best thing to a letter from home. As Allied forces continued to advance through France toward the German border, Miller planned to take the band to Paris to play

"By the time you receive this letter we shall be in Paris, barring of course a nose-dive into the Channel."

—From a letter by Glenn Miller to his wife, dated December 4, 1944

GLENN MILLER
The band leader and trombonist, one of the most popular performers of the swing era.

for soldiers who were on leave from the front line. The first concert was scheduled for Christmas Eve and Miller had already made several trips to the city to make arrangements. On December 13, Don Haynes, the band manager, was supposed to fly over to make sure everything was in place for the arrival of the fifty-piece band three days later, but was prevented from going by bad weather. At the last minute, the plan was changed and Miller decided to go himself instead of Haynes, who would follow with the band. The only thing holding him up was the fog, which was blanketing southern England.

On December 14, Haynes met Lieutenant Colonel Norman Baessell, who was flying to Bordeaux in the morning and offered to give Miller a lift,

dropping him off in Paris before continuing on to his destination. The purpose of Baessell's trip remains unclear, but it appears that he was only going to France to obtain supplies of champagne for a Christmas party. On the morning of the scheduled departure date, the weather was still cold and foggy and Miller and Baessell were forced to wait until after lunch before the plane they would be flying in, a single-engined UC-64 Norseman piloted by Flight Officer John Morgan, was given clearance to fly. Although the fog did begin to lift, conditions were far from ideal for flying. According to Haynes,

who saw them off, Miller expressed some concern over the flight when he was getting into the plane. Baessell is said to have replied by asking Miller if he wanted to live forever. It was the last time any of the three people on board the plane were seen alive.

Three days later, on December 18, Haynes and the rest of the band arrived in Paris expecting Miller to be at the airport to meet them. At first nobody was greatly alarmed by his absence, but over the next few days, as it became apparent that the plane he had been traveling on had not landed in Paris and as no trace of him or his companions could be found anywhere, concerns began to mount. By Christmas Eve, his wife was informed and he was posted as missing. Over the years, questions have been asked about the slow response of the American military in searching for the missing aircraft.

FRIENDLY FIRE?

The official report into the disappearance stated that a crash would likely have been caused either by engine trouble or by the build-up of ice on the wings. The lack of a search for the missing aircraft can be explained by the delay in raising the alarm; three days had elapsed between the plane taking off and it being reported missing, greatly reducing the chances of finding anyone alive. Nobody had any idea where the aircraft might have come down, so a search, even if it had begun, would have had to cover an enormous area. Another factor was the progress of the war at the time; on December 16, the Germans had mounted a huge offensive in the Ardennes region, known now as the Battle of the Bulge, and it is perhaps understandable that resources were not diverted away from the fighting in order to search for three people who, in all probability, were already dead.

Thirty years later, in 1985, it emerged that crew members of a British Lancaster bomber, returning from an aborted mission over Germany, had seen a plane crash into the English Channel on the same day as the Norseman went missing. The Lancaster was jettisoning its bombs over a designated area of the Channel because it was too dangerous to land with the bombs still on board. The navigator, who was watching the bombs fall, spotted a small plane, which he identified as a Norseman, spinning out of control and crashing into the water. Two other crewmen saw the same thing and, years later, the pilot, who had not seen it for himself, confirmed that he had been told over the radio what had happened. It appears incredible now that nobody on board the Lancaster reported the incident at the time; it was, after all, a friendly plane that had crashed. The pilot explained that his main concern was to get his plane home safely and it had not occurred to him to say anything about the incident.

THE RUMORS

Some doubts have been raised over this account, particularly concerning the location of the drop zone and whether the Lancasters were crossing the Channel at the same time as the plane carrying Miller. The ability of the navigator to identify the type of plane that crashed has also been the subject of some speculation, as the UC-64 Norseman was uncommon in Britain at the time. The navigator, it turned out, had trained in Canada, where the aircraft was widely used, making it much more likely that he would have been able to recognize one, even in poor weather conditions. Although it is the only account we have backed up by credible eyewitness reports, it is impossible to confirm the accuracy of the account.

Almost as soon as Miller was posted as missing, rumors began to circulate about what had happened to him. They were all based on the assumption that he

---

The most ludicrous of the rumors is that Miller had been ordered by General Eisenhower to conduct secret talks with German officers concerning a surrender.

KILLED IN A FIGHT?

One of the most persistent rumors about Miller is that, rather than dying in a plane crash, he was killed during a fight in a Parisian brothel and the incident was kept quiet because of fears over the effect it would have on morale. This particular theory, however, does not account for what happened to the other two people on the plane. Both Baessell and Morgan were also missing and neither of them was ever seen again, leading to the only sensible conclusion that all three, who were last seen together as the plane took off from Bedfordshire, disappeared in the same incident.

did not die in a plane crash over the Channel, but had died after arriving in Paris, with the incident covered up by the American military. The most ludicrous of these rumors is that Miller had been ordered by General Eisenhower, the overall commander of Allied forces in Europe, to conduct secret talks with German officers concerning a surrender. Why Eisenhower would pick a big band leader with no military experience of any description to go on such a sensitive mission is, of course, not fully explained in this theory.

The exact circumstances of the disappearance may never be known for certain, but the most likely explanation is that, either as the result of mechanical failure or friendly fire, their plane went down in the Channel and sank without leaving a trace.

WHERE IS THE MISSING NAZI GOLD?

1945 onward

Clue: Gold was hidden underground and in bank vaults abroad

Main players: Nazis, Allies, Swiss banks, and various people with sticky fingers

Verdict: Still missing

E ven before war had been officially declared in 1939, the Nazi regime in Germany had begun the financial preparations for war, initiating processes that would finance a military buildup and pay for the import of essential commodities and war materials. After the occupation of Austria, Czechoslovakia, and the free city Danzig, the gold reserves of all three were transferred to Berlin and held in the vaults of the Reichsbank. The process continued after the invasion of Poland, with much of the wealth of invaded countries, including the Netherlands, Belgium, and France, as well as those of Eastern Europe, being looted and transferred to Germany.

As well as gold from the central banks, other precious metals, jewels, and works of art were taken and the assets of

Alongside the hoard of gold reserves, jewels, and works of art, anything of value was taken from the victims of the concentration camps, such as gold teeth, rings, and eyeglasses.

Jewish businesses and individuals in Germany and throughout Nazi-occupied zones were seized. Anything of value taken from concentration camp victims, such as gold teeth, rings, and eyeglasses, were added to the hoard, held in the Reichsbank and at other locations around Germany as the property of the SS. In the immediate aftermath of the war, much of this loot was recovered by the Allies, but in the chaos that accompanied the surrender and subsequent occupation of Germany, huge amounts went missing.

GOLD HIDDEN

The Nazi regime had also transferred large quantities of gold to financial institutions in neutral countries (nations that were not fighting on any side in the war). Some of this gold would be used to buy foreign currency, in what would now be called money laundering, and some of it would be put in personal accounts. Many of these institutions were Swiss banks, which also held numerous accounts of Jewish people who had been murdered during the war, and it would be many years before serious attempts

NAZI LOOT
Gold, sacks of paper currency, SS loot, paintings, and the contents of museums were stored for safe keeping in a potassium mine near Merkers, Germany.

were made to return these deposits to their rightful owners or, where that was not possible, to find their heirs. Despite a policy of more openness from Switzerland in the past few decades, prompted in part by legal action taken by Jewish organizations, suspicions remain that large quantities of gold are still hidden away in the vaults of the country's banks and in those of a number of other countries around the world.

STEEL PRODUCTION
Two of the most important commodities that Nazi Germany needed to import in large quantities were iron ore and tungsten, both of which were used in the production of steel. Supplies of iron ore

> "The most significant finding…was the overall movement of looted gold from occupied countries and individual victims flowing to and through Switzerland—primarily the Swiss National Bank—from Germany, and used by Germany to pay for its wartime imports. The Swiss National Bank must have known that some portion of the gold it was receiving from the Reichsbank was looted from occupied countries, due to the public knowledge about the low level of the Reichsbank's gold reserves and repeated warnings from the Allies."
>
> —Senator Stuart Eizenstat, quoted from a briefing given in 1998 on the release of a State Department report on Nazi Gold

came from Sweden, while the metal of tungsten was sourced from mines in Spain and Portugal. All three countries had declared themselves to be neutral at the outbreak of war and, while maintaining that status, continued to supply Germany with materials vital to its war effort, right up until it became obvious who was going to win the war. Payment for these supplies was mostly made in the form of gold looted from various European sources, particularly after it became known that Germany had been using counterfeit currency to finance these deals at the start of the war.

MISSING LOOT

On February 3, 1945, the American Air Force mounted a huge raid on Berlin that destroyed the Reichsbank. Although

NEUTRAL TRADING

The Swedish economy benefited enormously from maintaining its neutral status while trading with Germany. Its postwar prosperity was in large part based on the money it made from the sale of iron ore and other war materials. The Portuguese chose to keep hold of their gold supplies after the war, and were allowed to do so by the Allies. According to some estimates, they acquired somewhere in the region of a hundred tons of gold and it is thought that much of it remains in the vaults of Portuguese banks, held in the form of gold bars stamped with the swastika of Nazi Germany.

the vaults underneath the bank, which contained about 93 percent of the financial wealth of Nazi Germany, remained intact, the decision was made to move all the reserves out of the city to protect them from the rapidly advancing Allied forces. They were taken to the Kaiseroda potassium mine near Merkers in the state of Thuringia, 200 miles (320 km) southwest of Berlin, where the contents of many of Germany's museums, together with many looted artworks, were also being stored for safe keeping. In total, at least 100 tons (91 tonnes) of gold and a thousand sacks of paper currency of various denominations were placed in the mine.

The speed with which General George Patton's Third Army advanced across the country after the successful crossing of the Rhine on March 22, 1945, took the Germans by surprise. Those units of the German army and employees of the Reichsbank responsible for moving the reserves were slow to react, and all but about four hundred sacks of currency were captured. This was done with a little help from people living near the mine, who tipped the Americans off about the location of the loot. The entire contents were removed and sent to Frankfurt in a heavily armored convey, consisting of thirty-two trucks and armed escorts. Rumors have persisted ever since that one of the trucks never arrived in Frankfurt and, while there is no evidence to support this, various artworks known to have been in the mine have turned up for sale in America over the years.

After the bulk of German reserves had been lost, Hitler himself ordered that the remaining 7 percent, held in branches of the Reichsbank in parts of the country

currency, and works of art at $2.5 billion. Many of those who had access to the loot appear to have had sticky fingers, including numerous Americans. Sayer and Botting also found evidence of a US government cover-up to keep the illegal activities of their servicemen as quiet as possible.

yet to be overrun, was to be hidden in various locations in the Bavarian and Tyrolean Alps. These caches would then be available for use, at least according to the fantasy Hitler still apparently believed, to finance a Nazi stronghold in the mountains until a resurgence and eventual breakout became possible.

By this stage of the war, with Germany only weeks away from surrender, the transport situation was chaotic. Efforts were made to hide the reserves, but many of those involved may have dipped into the loot themselves. In their book on the subject, published in 1984, Ian Sayer and Douglas Botting estimated the value of the missing gold,

Ian Sayer and Douglas Botting estimated the value of the missing gold, currency, and works of art at $2.5 billion.

GOLD RETURNED

After the war, attempts were made to return gold recovered during the war to the central banks of the countries from which it had been stolen. As records detailing the amount of gold taken from concentration camp victims were lost at the end of the war, attempts to return it to the families of those people murdered by the Nazis have been complicated and drawn out. In 1997, an agreement was reached to give all the remaining gold to a fund set up to help people who survived the Holocaust. After an initial reluctance to act, most financial institutions that were involved with the Nazis have for the most part come clean about their role in the war. The notable exception is the Vatican Bank, which still maintains that it had nothing to hide in the first place, despite abundant evidence to the contrary.

DID AN ALIEN SPACECRAFT CRASH AT ROSWELL?

Summer 1947

Clue: Footage released of an alien autopsy was a hoax

Main players: Ufologists, the residents of Roswell, the US Air Force and government, and some aliens

Verdict: US Air Force maintain debris is from a weather balloon

Over the years, the Roswell Incident has become the most prominent and debated of all the reported encounters with UFOs and aliens. Enthusiasts, or ufologists as they are sometimes called, have access to a huge body of material on the subject, from movies and TV series to hundreds of books and more websites than you can shake a stick at. And, since the good people of Roswell in New Mexico decided to embrace the event that bears the city's name, those who are really keen can go to the UFO festival held there every summer, where, among many other attractions, they can enter their pets in an alien-themed fancy dress contest. In case anybody is unclear about what this might entail, the festival's website includes a photo of a girl, dressed in an alien costume, holding what appears to be a large ferret wearing alien head

boppers (if you don't believe me, have a look at the website).

DEBRIS IN THE DESERT

So, what happened in the New Mexican desert near Roswell to inspire such enthusiasm and why did this particular incident become so famous when most other accounts of extra-terrestrial encounters have quickly faded into obscurity? It is difficult to pin down the exact date, but toward the end of June or the beginning of July 1947, a ranch foreman called William Brazel came across some strange debris in the desert about 30 miles (50 km) to the north of Roswell. He would later describe it as being made up of "rubber strips, tinfoil, a rather tough paper and sticks" and, at first, appears not to have been over-excited by what he had found. He left it where it was for a few days before

Stories told not only of the crash of an extra-terrestrial spacecraft, but the recovery of the bodies of the aliens who had been flying it and a huge government conspiracy to cover up the details.

coming back with his family and collecting up as much of it as he could find, throwing it in the back of his pick-up, taking it home, and putting it in the barn.

That summer, the newspapers were full of articles about sightings of mysterious flying disks and, being a responsible citizen, Brazel thought he had better report what he had found in case it turned out to be one of them. As he didn't have a phone, he popped into the Sheriff's office the next time he was in Roswell. The Sheriff informed the Roswell Army Air Field and the following day Major Jesse Marcel and another man who was not in uniform drove out to the ranch to pick up the debris. On July 8, a press officer at the air base, who would later say he had not seen the debris, put out a release to the local papers (quoted over the page), saying that a flying disk had been found. It was quickly retracted, but by then a number of newspapers had already run the story. The debris was sent to Fort Worth Army Air Base, where it was identified as being the remains of a weather balloon.

THE DEBRIS
Major Jesse Marcel (on the left) examines the debris recovered from a New Mexican ranch.

MEDIA SPOTLIGHT

After about a week, media interest in the story died away and, with the spotlight moving elsewhere, Roswell returned to being the sleepy town it had always been. It would be more than thirty years before the world's attention returned, but, once

"The many reports regarding the flying disk became a reality yesterday when the intelligence office of the 509th Bomb Group of the Eighth Air Force, Roswell Army Air Field, was fortunate to gain possession of a disk through the cooperation of one of the local ranchers and the sheriff's office of Chaves County. The flying object landed on a ranch near Roswell sometime last week. Not having phone facilities, the rancher stored the wreckage until such time as he was able to contact the sheriff's office... Action was immediately taken and the disk was picked up at the rancher's home. It was inspected at the Roswell Army Air Field and subsequently loaned by Major Marcel to higher headquarters."

—Press release from Roswell Army Air Field on July 8, 1947, which was withdrawn the following day

it did, what at first sight appeared to be a minor incident in the desert that had been explained away in such a straightforward manner, took on vast proportions.

ALIEN SPACECRAFT

The story now encompassed not only the crash of an extra-terrestrial spacecraft, but the recovery of the bodies of the aliens who had been flying it and a huge government conspiracy to cover up the details. Since the first book on the subject appeared in 1980, successive authors have added layer upon layer of mystery to the story and, as the years have gone by, found an ever-increasing number of witnesses who have been able to confirm each different version of events. There have been descriptions of the recovery of the flying saucer and its alien crew by secret service agents, no doubt all wearing black suits and sunglasses. There have also been endless discussions about the material used to make the craft, which, it turns out, was not rubber, tinfoil, wood, and paper as

first reported, but various strange and extraordinary substances with properties unlike anything seen on earth before. Witnesses are said to have been bullied into keeping quiet and military documents forged to cover up the real events, while the dead aliens were spirited away to a secret location where autopsies were carried out on the bodies.

What started out as a trickle of information had, by the 1990s, turned into a deluge. To top it all off, in 1995, film of the autopsies emerged, creating a media frenzy around the world. Debate raged over the authenticity of the footage, with expert opinion divided between those who insisted it was real and those who thought the whole thing was a total wind-up. Ten years later, the person who had made the movie finally owned up to the hoax, explaining that it had been knocked up in a flat in London using a couple of dummies, several sheep brains he had bought from the butcher and a generous helping of raspberry jam.

US AIR FORCE

While all this was going on, the US Air Force, perhaps feeling left out of the proceedings, released a report giving more details of the weather balloon, which, they were still claiming, was what had really crashed in the desert. It was, they said, part of a secret program called Operation Mogul, aimed at using high-altitude balloons to detect Soviet nuclear tests. If the report was intended to damp down the fervor surrounding the Roswell Incident, then the air force was going to be disappointed. Even though ufologists had split into various factions supporting alternative versions of events, not too many were buying the weather balloon story. If anything, the descriptions of what had supposedly happened became even more extreme.

By this time, the story had taken on a life of its own, no longer relying on, or even resembling, the facts on the ground. Just how much the wider public, beyond a few diehard fanatics, believed any of this nonsense is hard to tell. As well as spawning a media and publishing industry all of its own, it is not hard to see the Roswell Incident becoming the subject of academic studies

ROSWELL UFO FESTIVAL
Two purple-headed aliens in the Roswell alien costume contest at the UFO festival.

into how modern myths develop and adapt over the years. These days, it no longer matters much if the real event involved a weather balloon, a flying saucer, or just about anything else for that matter. The story has gone beyond the facts and people have the option of either buying into it or ignoring it. Or, if you happen to live in Roswell, you can invite people to come to the city, give them the opportunity to dress up as aliens, and try to persuade them to part with as much cash as possible.

It was claimed spacecraft had been crashing all over New Mexico for years and the government's secret mortuaries were filling up with debris and dead aliens.

DOES THE BERMUDA TRIANGLE EXIST?

1950 onward

Clue: Strange forces have led to unexplained disappearances

Main players: Flight 19 and other lost ships and aircraft

Verdict: It's all a big load of nonsense

The existence of a region of the Atlantic Ocean where both ships and planes have disappeared under mysterious circumstances first became widely publicized during the 1950s and '60s. News reports cited an area off the coast of Florida and to the north of the Bahamas as being particularly prone to strange occurrences. It became known as the Bermuda Triangle and encompassed a section of sea between the tip of Florida and the islands of Puerto Rico and Bermuda. A full range of paranormal and extra-terrestrial explanations have been put forward at one time or another to account for the supposedly unexplained disappearances, and some authors have made a comfortable living writing about their particular theories. The choice available between one type of weirdness or another is really quite amazing; from alien abductions to a force emitted by the lost continent of Atlantis, and from craft disappearing into some strange kind of fog to them slipping into a parallel universe through a time

> *"Draw a line from Florida to Bermuda, another from Bermuda to Puerto Rico, and a third line back to Florida through the Bahamas. Within this area, known as the 'Bermuda Triangle,' most of the total vanishments have occurred.*
>
> *This area is by no means isolated. The coasts of Florida and the Carolinas are well populated, as well as the islands involved. Sea distances are relatively short. Day and night, there is traffic over the sea and air lanes. The waters are well patrolled by the Coast Guard, the Navy and the Air Force. And yet this relatively limited area is the scene of disappearances that total far beyond the laws of chance."*
>
> **—From an article by Vincent Gaddis in *Argosy* magazine, February 1965**

THE AVENGER
Grumman TBM Avenger torpedo bomber,
similar to the ones involved in Flight 19.

vortex never to be seen again. So, is it as
big a load of nonsense as it sounds, or is
there really something strange going on?

THE LOST PATROL

It was one tragic event, which occurred
on December 5, 1945, that sparked the
development of the concept of the
Bermuda Triangle. Five US Navy
planes, Grumman TBM Avenger torpedo
bombers, left Fort Lauderdale naval base
in Florida for a routine training flight
involving a practice bombing run and
navigational exercises. The squad did not
return, resulting in the loss of all fourteen
airmen. Flight 19, as it was designated,
was led by Lieutenant Charles Taylor, an
experienced aviator, and it appears to
have gotten into trouble after the
bombing run had been completed about
60 miles (100 km) off Florida.

Radio contact with Taylor established
that both the compasses on his plane
were malfunctioning, which caused him
to lose his bearings. He appears to have
mistaken islands in the Bahamas for the

Florida Keys and, instead of heading
west, which would have taken him
back to Florida, set out on a northerly
heading, then turned east, taking him
farther out into the ocean. A radio
message from one of the trainee pilots in
another plane was heard saying that if
they headed west, they would reach
land, but all five planes continued in an
easterly direction. In the last radio
message picked up from Taylor, he says
that, unless they reach landfall, they
will have to ditch into the sea, which is
presumably what happened. The
Avenger was a solidly built, heavy
plane and, even if any of the pilots had
managed to make a successful landing on
the water, it is unlikely that they would
have stayed on the surface for long.
To compound the tragedy, one of the
seaplanes sent out to look for the missing
airmen was also lost along with its crew

> **Explanations offered for
> unexplained disappearances in the
> Bermuda Triangle range from alien
> abductions to a force emitted by the
> lost continent of Atlantis.**

AREA KNOWN AS THE
BERMUDA TRIANGLE

Bermuda

Florida

BERMUDA
TRIANGLE

Gulf of
Mexico

Puerto Rico

Caribbean Sea

of fourteen, apparently blowing up not long after it had taken off.

OTHER DISAPPEARANCES

Once the idea of the Bermuda Triangle had become established, other incidents of ships and planes lost in this region of the Atlantic began to be linked together. The USS *Cyclops* was lost at sea with all 306 passengers and crew in March 1918 somewhere between its last stop in Barbados and its destination of Baltimore, so it would have had to sail through the Bermuda Triangle. No wreckage of the ship has ever been found, so it is impossible to say what caused its loss,

BERMUDA TRIANGLE
The region of the Atlantic where ships and planes are said to have mysteriously disappeared without a trace.

or even if it was actually in the region of the Bermuda Triangle when it went down. Various theories have been put forward over the years, but it appears likely that a combination of the ship's poor design, a dangerously large cargo, and bad weather led to its disappearance.

Two other sinkings often cited as being a result of the Bermuda Triangle are those of the SS *Cotopaxi* and the SS *Marine Sulphur Queen*. The *Cotopaxi* disappeared

The loss of the USS *Cyclops* and its 306 passengers and crew remains the largest loss of life in US naval history other than as a consequence of war.

with all thirty-two crew members in December 1925 while transporting a cargo of coal from Charleston, South Carolina to Cuba. A distress call was received from the ship saying it was taking on water and listing, suggesting that it was sinking at the time. Despite this apparently straightforward explanation for the ship's disappearance, it has been linked with strange phenomena ever since, including in Steven Spielberg's *Close Encounters of the Third Kind*. At the start of the movie, a group of scientists, who have already come across the planes of Flight 19, find the *Cotopaxi* in the middle of the Gobi Desert, leading them to the conclusion that something rather odd is going on.

The *Marine Sulphur Queen* was lost with all thirty-nine crew members in February 1963 off the coast of Florida. The US Coast Guard found that the ship had not been in seaworthy condition and should not have been allowed to leave port. All that remained was small pieces of debris on the surface of the water, so the investigation could not determine the exact cause of its sinking. This lack of information invariably led some to link the disappearance with the Bermuda Triangle, despite the fact that the ship was in no condition to go to sea in the first place.

MANUFACTURED MYSTERY

In his book on the subject, first published in 1975, Lawrence Kusche found that in almost every case cited by those who believe in the existence of the triangle, a more likely account of how they were lost could be given, usually involving human error, poor weather conditions, or just plain old bad luck. He described it as being a "manufactured mystery," created by people who had either jumped to wild conclusions from the minimum of facts or had deliberately falsified the details to fit in with their theories. The US Coast Guard and the marine insurers Lloyd's of London tend to agree with Kusche. Both have said that, while ships and aircraft have been lost in the region, the numbers are not particularly high given how much traffic passes through it. Perhaps the real mystery is not what happened to those ships and planes lost in the region, but why people would believe it had anything to do with the Bermuda Triangle in the first place.

DISAPPEARED
USS *Cyclops*, a collier ship launched in 1910 and lost at sea in 1918. Probably shown during the 1911 naval review in New York City.

DID THE ESCAPEES FROM ALCATRAZ MAKE IT?

June 11,1962

Clue: The FBI found what was left of their raft on Angel Island

Main players: Frank Morris, John and Clarence Anglin, the FBI

Verdict: It's not very likely that they made it, but it's not impossible either

If Hollywood movies are anything to go by, then a jail warden telling a convict that his jail is escape-proof is probably not a very good idea. In Clint Eastwood's movie *Escape from Alcatraz*, Patrick McGoohan's warden runs through the full list of inadvisable things to say to a newly arrived prisoner. To be fair, the movie is a surprisingly sober and accurate portrayal of real events, a few jail movie clichés aside. It depicts in detail how three men, Frank Morris and the brothers John and Clarence Anglin, devised and executed one of the most audacious jail escapes ever attempted.

In the movie, the last we see of the three escapees, after they have managed to get out of the jail itself, is of them paddling out into San Francisco Bay, away from Alcatraz Island, on a homemade raft. The final scene of the movie shows the warden and various law enforcement officers finding the remains of the raft on a beach and, while they are trying to convince themselves that all three escapees have drowned in the bay, the warden picks up a chrysanthemum from the sand. It is the same type of flower he had previously taken from Frank Morris in the jail and the suggestion is that, by finding it on the beach, he knows that they didn't really drown, but is not prepared to admit it.

The situation in real life is, needless to say, a little less clear-cut. The raft was found on Angel Island, just over 1.5 miles (2.5 km) across the bay from Alcatraz, but it is impossible to say for sure what happened to the three men. Since June 11, 1962, the day of the escape, no sign of them has ever been found; no bodies were recovered from the water at the time and, over the course of the following fifty years, no sightings of them have ever been reported. If they did make it, then they have successfully avoided detection by one of the largest manhunts ever mounted by the FBI.

Since June 11, 1962, the day of the escape, no sign of them has ever been found; no bodies were recovered from the water and no sightings of them have ever been reported.

THE ROCK

The federal jail on Alcatraz Island, known as the Rock by its inmates, really was intended as a place to send the bad apples of the US jail system. It was a punishment block for those who had caused trouble in other federal jails, and Morris and the Anglin brothers were all sent after a number of escape attempts. Prisoners were held in individual cells and had to earn the right to privileges, such as family visits or access to the jail library, by conforming to the rules. When a prisoner was thought to have been sufficiently reformed, he would be transferred to another federal jail to complete the remainder of his sentence, so most of the prisoners on the Rock had not been there for all that long. It was also comparatively small, holding about 250 convicts at any one time, and although some of the prisoners were well-known gangsters and racketeers, like Al Capone and Machine Gun Kelly, the majority were career criminals who had been in and out of jail for most of their lives.

THE ESCAPE

Frank Morris is generally credited with being the brains behind the escape. He had been through every stage of the jail system, from reform school at the age of thirteen to a ten-year stretch in the Louisiana State Penitentiary for bank robbery. After escaping from there and being recaptured during a burglary, he was sent to Alcatraz, where he would meet up with John and Clarence Anglin, whom he had known in other federal jails. The Anglins had been in numerous jails over the years, mostly for burglaries and armed robbery, and had finally been sent to Alcatraz after repeated attempts to escape. All three were held in cells

THE ROCK

The infamous jail occupied most of Alcatraz Island in the middle of San Francisco Bay.

from papier-mâché and real hair from the barber shop in their beds so that the jail guards would not realize they were gone when passing. They then squeezed out through the holes in the walls at the back of their cells and got the raft. From there, they climbed up onto the roof of the jail building, carefully crawled across it to a drain pipe, and then lowered themselves down to the ground. They then had to climb over two perimeter fences and they were out of the jail. They used a concertina to inflate their raft and pushed off into the bay, using pieces of plywood as paddles.

near to one other and began planning their escape along with a fourth man, Allen West, who, in the end, did not manage to get out of his cell.

The plan involved digging through the concrete around air vents at the back of their cells with spoons, giving them access to a narrow utility corridor that was rarely used. From there, they climbed up on to the top of the cell block, where they began to make a raft from jail issue raincoats. The hole in their cells was disguised by cardboard painted the same color as the wall and they each worked while another kept watch. If they had to do something that would make a noise, they would do it while Morris played the accordion in his cell.

On the night of the escape, all three of the prisoners left dummy heads made

DID THEY MAKE IT?

The following morning, jail guards found the papier-mâché heads and the alarm was raised. A huge manhunt began, led by the FBI, who were provided with details of the plan by Allen West, the man left behind. The escapees were going to row over to Angel Island, then swim the short distance to Marin County on the mainland. Once there, they would attempt to steal some clothes and a car to make their getaway. The FBI found what was left of the raft on Angel Island the following day, together with some paddles and a bag containing the belongings of one of the Anglins. With little else to go on, they came to the conclusion that all three convicts had most likely drowned in the bay and the bodies had been washed out to sea. There were several reported

sightings of bodies in the water over the next few days, but nothing was recovered.

The FBI investigation made little further progress and the file was closed in 1979, when Morris and the Anglin brothers were officially pronounced dead. However, the US Marshalls Service file on the case remains open until positive proof has been found that the three are dead or they are recaptured, even if all of them would now be well into their eighties.

In 2011, a TV documentary stated that the FBI had found footprints in the sand leading away from the raft on Angel

MUGSHOTS

From the left: Clarence Anglin, John Anglin, and Frank Morris, the brains behind the escape.

Island and that a car had been reported stolen in Marin County on the night of the escape. These two new revelations are not enough on their own to conclusively prove that Morris and the Anglins successfully escaped, but, if correct, then it certainly points in that direction. If they did make it and are still alive today, then they are hardly likely to let the cat out of the bag now.

> *"Extensive search being conducted under FBI direction of Bay Area waters, Angel Island, Marin County, San Francisco, and East Bay areas. Inmates' photos and descriptions being widely circulated by all news media.*
>
> *Prevailing tide charts reflect that, from 9 pm to 3 am, strong prevailing tides flowed in westerly direction from Alcatraz out through the Golden Gate toward the ocean. Experts advise that it would be extremely difficult for anyone to proceed from Alcatraz to Angel Island to the north in the manner contemplated by the convicts."*
>
> **—Extract from an FBI report on June 12, 1962, the day after the escape**

WHO WAS BEHIND THE ASSASSINATION OF JFK?

November 22, 1963

Clue: Lee Harvey Oswald could be linked to all sorts of conspirators

Main players: The leader of the free world, Lee Harvey Oswald, the mafia, the Cubans, the CIA—the list goes on...

Verdict: It was either a lone gunman or a wider conspiracy

One of the few things it is now possible to say about the assassination of President John F. Kennedy with any degree of certainty is that he was definitely killed that day, November 22, 1963, in Dallas. Everything else has been the subject of so much speculation, and every shred of evidence interpreted in so many different and often conflicting ways, that it has become next to impossible to separate the credible and fact-based assessments of the event from those of the crackpots and fantasists. Over the years, the waters have become so muddied with disinformation, half-truths, and outright lies that it is hard to imagine a time when a definitive answer to the mystery of who was behind the assassination will ever emerge from the murk.

THE ROAD TO DALLAS

The 1960 presidential election had been one of the closest contests ever fought. Kennedy's narrow victory over the Republican candidate Richard Nixon had in part been due to the support he had received in the key states of Florida and Texas. By the summer of 1963, he was already looking toward the next elections in 1964, when those two states would again be crucial. The prevailing

> "The fact that none of the conspiracy theorists have been able to offer convincing evidence of their suspicions does not seem to trouble many people. The plausibility of a conspiracy is less important to them than the implausibility of someone as inconsequential as Oswald having the wherewithal to kill someone as consequential—as powerful and well guarded—as Kennedy. To accept that an act of random violence by an obscure malcontent could bring down a president of the United States is to acknowledge a chaotic, disorderly world that frightens most Americans."
>
> —**Robert Dallek**, *John F. Kennedy: An Unfinished Life*, 2001

JFK
Kennedy campaigning in 1960. He became president at the age of forty-three.

opinion in the White House was that he had lost some ground in both states. In Florida, this was thought to be a result of his perceived lack of support for the anti-Castro movement among the large and influential Cuban exile community in the US This was heightened when he refused to authorize the American military to fully support the CIA-led attempt to invade Cuba by a force of exiles in 1961, which had ended disastrously.

At the same time, support in the conservative state of Texas had been ebbing away because of Kennedy's backing for the civil rights cause, one of the most pressing and contentious domestic issues faced by America at the time. Trips to both Florida and Texas had been arranged for November and,

despite numerous warnings of the dangers involved, Kennedy was determined to fulfill them. He was well aware of the positive publicity both would generate, particularly because his wife Jackie, who was being treated by the media as if she were a movie star, would be accompanying him. The Florida leg of the trip passed off without major incident and, on Thursday, November 21, Kennedy and his retinue arrived in Houston, Texas. In addition to the stated aims of the visit, he hoped to smooth over a bitter rivalry that had developed between the state governor, John Connally, who was very much at the conservative end of the Democratic party, and a number of his more liberal-minded colleagues.

TOWARD DEALEY PLAZA

Air Force One, the presidential plane, arrived at Love Field airport, about 6 miles (10 km) from the center of Dallas, at 11:25 am on Friday, November 22. After shaking hands with innumerable people, the president and Jackie Kennedy set off for the city center in their specially adapted Lincoln Continental convertible, with Governor Connally and his wife sitting in front of them. They were heading for the Dallas Trade Mart, where the president was due to have lunch with prominent civic leaders and give a short speech, and the motorcade followed the usual route of parades through the city. At Dealey Plaza, it made a right turn onto Houston Street, followed by a left turn onto Elm Street, which dipped down under an overpass and then headed out toward the exit for the Stemmons Freeway, from where it was only a few minutes' drive to the Trade Mart.

GUNFIRE

The Texas School Book Depository is a seven-story brick building on the corner of Houston and Elm. As the motorcade approached Dealey Plaza, a number of people were seen watching from windows on the fifth floor by those in the plaza below, together with a single man at the corner window on the floor above. The limousine turned into Elm Street and, shortly afterward, there was a loud bang, initially thought by almost everybody to have been either a firecracker or a car backfiring. A few seconds later, as the limousine was approaching a low bank with a fence and trees on the top of it, now known as the grassy knoll, two more bangs rang out, this time leaving nobody in any doubt that it was gunfire.

Witnesses would later describe seeing the man at the sixth-floor window of the book depository with a rifle, some seeing him clearly enough to be able to give a

THE MOTORCADE

Crowds lined the streets as the Kennedys traveled into Dallas in a Lincoln Continental convertible.

full description. One of the men watching the motorcade from the fifth floor clearly heard the bolt action of a rifle being worked and the spent cartridges hitting the floor above him after each of the three shots. Abraham Zapruder was standing on a concrete post next to the grassy knoll filming the motorcade on a home movie camera as it went past. The footage he took, now surely the most analyzed home movie ever made, clearly shows Kennedy being shot. The first of the three bullets apparently missed, but the second hit the president in the upper back, exiting through his throat and going on to wound Governor Connally in the back and right wrist. It has become known as the "magic bullet" by conspiracy theorists, who doubt if a single shot could have caused all the various injuries attributed to it.

The Zapruder film shows the devastating effect of the third shot in graphic and distressing detail. It hit Kennedy in the head, causing a massive and obviously fatal wound. This fraction of a second, when Kennedy was hit in the head and his body thrown back and to the left by the impact, is the crucial moment in determining if anybody else, other than the man in the book depository, was involved in the assassination. If there was a fourth shot, it could not have been fired by a single gunman and would most likely have come from a second shooter behind the fence on the grassy knoll, thereby providing direct evidence of a conspiracy, even if it would not necessarily shed any light on who was involved. The Zapruder film certainly gives the impression that Kennedy was shot from the front and to his right, from the direction of the grassy knoll, but it is by no means conclusive. Statements made by different witnesses conflict with one other on this point. Some claimed to have seen people behind the fence shortly after the gunshots and they either heard the bang, saw smoke, or could smell cordite. Others, including a woman who was with Zapruder, making her one of the people closest to the grassy knoll, did not notice anything coming from that direction.

The Zapruder film certainly gives the impression that Kennedy was shot from the front and to his right, from the direction of the grassy knoll.

LEE HARVEY OSWALD

The president was rushed to the nearest hospital, where he was pronounced dead at one o'clock, half an hour after the shooting. About ten minutes later, Dallas police officer J. D. Tippitt stopped a man walking down the street about 3 miles (5 km) from Dealey Plaza, who matched the description he had been given of Lee Harvey Oswald, an employee of the Texas Book Depository who had been reported missing after the shooting.

The man pulled a handgun and shot Tippitt four times, fatally wounding him, and then ran off. He was seen entering a movie theater nearby and was arrested there shortly afterward. It was Oswald, a twenty-four-year-old ex-marine. After initially being charged with the murder of Tippitt, later that day he was also charged with the assassination of the president.

Oswald was held in the Dallas police headquarters where he repeatedly denied both charges of murder. When asked by press reporters if he was guilty, he protested his innocence and claimed that he was a patsy, set up to take the blame. Two days later, on Sunday, November 24, while he was being taken through the basement of the police headquarters, he was shot in the stomach by Jack Ruby, who ran a seedy nightclub in Dallas, and died from the wound later that day. Ruby claimed to have shot Oswald so the city of Dallas could repair its tarnished image and to spare Jackie Kennedy the ordeal of going through a trial. He was found guilty of the murder of Oswald in March 1964 and died of cancer in January 1966, before an appeal against the conviction could be heard. Ever since, persistent allegations have been made that he was involved with the mafia and had been forced to kill Oswald by them.

LONE GUNMAN
OR CONSPIRACY?

The Warren Commission, as it has become known, was set up by the newly appointed President Lyndon Johnson within days of the assassination to investigate the circumstances of the event. It was chaired by Chief Justice Earl Warren and reported in September 1964 that Lee Harvey Oswald had acted alone. The rushed nature of the investigation has led to it being dismissed by many as a cover-up. In 1979, the House Select Committee on Assassinations published a report that

BIZARRE LIFE

Some evidence exists to link Oswald to a number of people involved with mafia figure Carlos Marcello. But there is also evidence to link Oswald to all sorts of other potential conspiracies. He led what can only be described as a bizarre life, defecting to the Soviet Union after being discharged from the marines and living in Russia for over two years before returning to the US, where he became involved with a pro-Castro Cuban group. Some conspiracy theorists have claimed that he was working for the CIA all the time, going to Russia to recruit secret agents and then infiltrating Communist Cuban groups back in America. This, they claim, is the reason why the CIA has not been overly cooperative with any of the investigations into the assassination.

contradicted the Warren Commission, finding that, while Oswald had fired three shots at the president, evidence obtained from a recording of a police radio showed it was possible that a fourth shot had also been fired. This led to the conclusion that a conspiracy had been behind the assassination.

The most persistent conspiracy theory puts the blame on the mafia, often in collusion with rogue elements in the CIA, who, in the early 1960s, had established contacts with organized crime during secret missions to assassinate the Cuban leader Fidel Castro. Kennedy's lack of enthusiasm for regime change in Cuba, together with Robert Kennedy's vigorous attempts to crack down on the mob after being appointed to the position of attorney general by his brother, are given as reasons why prominent mafia figures, including Carlos Marcello in New Orleans and Sam Giancana in Chicago, wanted the president dead. Years later, Marcello is said to have admitted his involvement to a fellow inmate while serving a jail sentence, explaining that in Sicily, if you wanted to kill a dog, you cut off its head not its tail, implying that, if John Kennedy was dead, Robert Kennedy would no longer be in a position to threaten mafia interests.

A different conspiracy theory has Oswald working for the Cuban secret service, who were planning to kill Kennedy in response to CIA attempts to assassinate Castro. Oswald, or, at least, a man claiming to be Oswald, is known to have visited the Cuban Embassy in Mexico City in September 1963, where he applied for a visa to go to Cuba. He made repeated visits to the embassy and was eventually granted a visa, but,

DEALEY PLAZA

The book depository is the first building on the left, while the grassy knoll is in the center foreground.

rather than traveling to Havana, he returned to America instead. Could he have been meeting with Cuban secret agents to plan the assassination attempt and his escape route out of America?

Like everything else to do with Oswald, trying to unravel his intentions in going to Mexico only leads to further unanswerable questions. In the end, it is next to impossible to know what motivated him and who, if anyone, he conspired with. By silencing Oswald, Jack Ruby most probably put an end to any chance of our knowing for sure if there was a conspiracy to kill Kennedy. There were certainly plenty of people in America who were not sorry to hear the news of his death, but that does not necessarily mean they were involved in a plot to kill him. The evidence as it currently stands can only construct theories about the involvement of people other than Oswald. While many people remain convinced a conspiracy was behind one of the defining moments of the twentieth century, in truth, fifty years after the event, we are no closer to knowing what happened for sure than we ever were.

DID THE AUSTRALIAN PRIME MINISTER DROWN?

December 17, 1967

Clue: Harold Holt went for a swim in rough waters

Main players: Harold Holt, an invisible submarine, and the waters of the Bass Strait

Verdict: No submarines, no suicide, just a tragic accident

Over the course of a political career of more than thirty years, Harold Holt enjoyed his fair share of success. He succeeded Sir Robert Menzies as prime minister of Australia in January 1966 and led the Liberal Party of Australia to a decisive victory over their Labor Party rivals in the general election held in November of that same year. But, as is the way of politics, today he is not associated with these considerable achievements. If he is remembered at all, it is for the unwise choice of words he used in a speech made in America in June 1966, and for the way his tenure as prime minister came to a sudden and dramatic end. The speech was made in Washington in the presence of President Lyndon B. Johnson, in which Holt pledged Australia's continuing support for the Vietnam War. He ended it by saying that Australia would remain a staunch friend to America and would be "all the way with LBJ," a direct quotation of Johnson's 1964 presidential election slogan. It came across as a bit grovelling, and was, to use the Australian slang, enough to make a koala spew, and came at a time when public opinion in both America and Australia was beginning to turn against the war.

The following year would be a difficult one for Holt, with deep divisions emerging in the coalition government and an increasing number of Australian soldiers, some of them conscripts, being killed in Vietnam. Then, on Sunday, December 17, 1967, Holt went for a swim off Cheviot Beach, near his weekend home in Portsea, Victoria, and disappeared. He was never seen again and, as his body was not recovered, a month later it was announced that he

Holt went for a swim off Cheviot Beach, and disappeared. He was never seen again and, as his body was not recovered, a month later it was announced that he was presumed to have drowned.

was presumed to have drowned.
Over the years, numerous alternative explanations have been put forward to explain what happened, ranging from the plausible, that he committed suicide because revelations about his private life were about to become public, to the more ambitious, that he had been a Chinese spy for years and, rather than drowning, had been picked up by a submarine and taken to China.

WEEKEND AWAY

Holt was very much an Australian man; he enjoyed a few beers with his pals, liked the occasional bet on the horses,

HAROLD HOLT

Holt had a distinguished political career before becoming prime minister of Australia in January 1966.

and had an eye for the ladies. And when he wasn't working, he spent much of his time outdoors indulging in two of his favorite pastimes, swimming and spear fishing. The week before his disappearance had been a long and hard one. The splits emerging in the coalition government were becoming more serious by the day. The Vietnam War was causing him difficulties along with increasing lack of public support for his government, expressed in the recent loss of two by-elections to the Labor Party. Spending the weekend at Portsea, away from the political strife in Canberra, was a means of finding rest and relaxation, and that fateful weekend in November was no different from many previous occasions.

CHEVIOT BEACH

On the Sunday morning, he went down to Cheviot Beach with a number of friends who had been invited to stay for the weekend and in the company of Marjorie Gillespie, his near neighbor in Portsea and long-term mistress. His friends would later report that the surf was heavy that day and all of them, except Holt, thought better of going into the water. He was a strong swimmer and went in despite the conditions, but, according to Marjorie Gillespie, appeared to get into trouble soon afterward and disappeared after apparently being dragged under by a particularly large wave. It would be the last time anybody saw him. Despite a search involving the police, the army, navy divers, and rescue helicopters, no trace of him could be found. As no body was recovered, a coroner's inquest was not held and it was later decided that, as the circumstances of his death were clear, an inquiry would be a waste of time and money. The lack of an official investigation into the circumstances of Holt's death provided a gap into which all manner of speculation and conspiracy theories have subsequently flowed.

CHINESE SUBMARINE

Other than the usual alien abduction stories you might expect in such circumstances, the most outlandish and surprisingly persistent of the rumors surrounding Holt's disappearance is the one about him being picked up by a Chinese submarine. It has something of the James Bond about it, but, unfortunately for fans of the genre, it appears to be, like Bond himself, a figment of the imagination. No evidence has ever been produced to back it up and, as one witness to the events of that Sunday has pointed out, if a submarine, Chinese or otherwise, was near enough to the beach to be able to meet a swimmer, then how come nobody who was there noticed it? If Holt were a Chinese spy, for which there is not one shred of evidence, it's hard to believe he would choose to swim out into the surf,

> **The theory that Holt was picked up by a Chinese submarine has something of the James Bond about it, but appears to be, like Bond himself, a figment of the imagination.**

in full view of his friends and family, in the hope of meeting up with a submarine, which he would then board without anybody seeing him.

The substory, then, can be easily dismissed as a load of nonsense, most likely concocted in order to sell a book. Another rumor suggesting that Holt disappeared so he could run off with his mistress can be equally easily discounted because Marjorie Gillespie remained in Australia after the disappearance. The only lasting legacy of this story has been the adoption of the Australian expression "doing a Harold," as rhyming slang for running away (Harold Holt—

CHEVIOT BEACH
Holt disappeared while swimming off the beach, known for its strong currents and rip tides.

bolt). What we are left with is the likelihood that he really did drown in the surf and his body was either swept out into Bass Strait, the notoriously rough sea off Cheviot Beach, or it became tangled up in the kelp beds that lie beneath the water along this stretch of coast.

STRONG CURRENTS

A clue to the most likely course of events is contained in the name of the beach Holt visited that day. It was named after the SS *Cheviot*, a passenger steamer sailing out of Melbourne that broke up in rough seas off the beach in October 1887 with the loss of thirty-five lives. Only seven bodies were recovered, the rest being lost at sea. And, in more recent times, the disappearance of people in the water off the Victorian coast has been an all too frequent occurrence. The rough seas of the Bass Strait, combined with strong currents and riptides near the beaches, can cause even the most experienced swimmers trouble. And, as healthy as Holt may have appeared, there are some indications that he had been experiencing problems in the months leading up to his disappearance. He had been prescribed painkillers for a long-standing shoulder injury and had collapsed in the Australian parliament earlier in the year. The official explanation was that he had been suffering from a vitamin deficiency, but the rumors in political circles were that he may have developed a heart condition that was concealed from the press.

On balance, then, the most likely explanation for Holt's disappearance was that he either got into trouble and drowned because he underestimated the severity of the conditions, or he experienced some sort of health-related

SUICIDE?

In recent years, a theory has emerged that Holt committed suicide by swimming out into the surf with no intention of coming back to shore. This is based on an assumption that the pressure of his job was placing an unbearable strain on Holt. Plus it was alleged that he was about to be named by Marjorie Gillespie's husband in divorce proceedings, which would have caused a scandal and cost Holt his job. In the absence of a suicide note, it is impossible to say for certain if he intended to kill himself that day. Those people who knew him well, including his family and colleagues in the government, have dismissed the idea. They acknowledge the pressure he was under at the time, but say there was nothing out of the ordinary in his behavior that weekend to indicate he was contemplating suicide.

issue while he was swimming. When a coroner's report on the disappearance was finally released in 2005, thirty-seven years after the event, it came to the only possible conclusion, given the available evidence, that Harold Holt had taken an unnecessary risk by going into rough water that day and had drowned accidentally. The law in Victoria had been changed by then to allow an inquest to take place despite the absence of a body and, since then, eighty suspected drowning deaths going back to 1957 have been examined. Much the same conclusions were reached in nearly all of them.

WHO WAS THE ZODIAC KILLER?

1968 onward

Clue: The killer sent messages and even phoned the police

Main players: The police departments of the San Francisco Bay Area

Verdict: The file remains open

The series of murders committed in the 1960s and '70s in the San Francisco Bay Area of the United States by a man calling himself "the Zodiac" terrorized local people. Despite a huge police investigation and intense media interest, the identity of the perpetrator remains a mystery to this day. The killer appeared to court publicity, sending letters to a number of newspapers taunting the police over their failure to identify him. On one occasion, a man claiming to be the Zodiac even called a lawyer live on a TV talk show. Even though this particular stunt was generally thought to be a hoax, it fit in with a pattern of behavior in which the killer apparently committed terrible crimes in order to attract attention to himself. If that was his intention, then he was extremely successful.

THE ATTACKS

In one of his letters, the Zodiac claimed to have killed thirty-seven people. Such a figure cannot be confirmed; the police attributed a total of five murders to him, with two other people being attacked but surviving. The first attack that can

definitely be attributed to the Zodiac occurred on December 20, 1968, in a secluded spot near the Lake Herman reservoir, which is not far from the city of Benicia on the northern shore of San Francisco Bay. Two teenagers, David Faraday and Betty Lou Jensen, were in a parked car when they were attacked. Faraday was shot in the head from close range as he sat in the car and died of his wounds later in the hospital. Betty Lou Jensen was shot five times in the back as she tried to run away from the killer and died at the scene. A witness later told police he had seen two cars parked together at the spot, but saw nothing to arouse suspicion.

On July 4, 1969, the Zodiac struck again, shooting Darlene Ferrin, a married woman of twenty-two, and

More than forty years later, numerous movies, books, and TV shows have been produced about the murders, without any further progress being made in solving the crime.

WANTED

SAN FRANCISCO POLICE DEPARTMENT

D. 90-69   WANTED FOR MURDER   OCTOBER 18, 196

ORIGINAL DRAWING   AMENDED DRAWING

Supplementing our Bulletin 87-69 of October 13, 1969. Additional information has developed the above amended drawing of murder suspect known as "ZODIAC".

WMA, 35-45 Years, approximately 5'8", Heavy Build, Short Brown Hair, possibly with Red Tint, Wears Glasses. Armed with 9 MM Automatic.

Available for comparison: Slugs, Casings, Latents, Handwriting.

ANY INFORMATION:
Inspectors Armstrong & Toschi
Homicide Detail
CASE NO. 696314

THOMAS J. CAHILL
CHIEF OF POLICE

THE ZODIAC
Sketches based on witnesses' statements were used on wanted posters, but the Zodiac was never identified.

Michael Mageau, nineteen, while they were sitting in a car at Blue Rock Springs Park in Vallejo, a few miles away from the first shooting and a similarly secluded spot. Despite being shot in the face, neck, and chest, Mageau survived and was able to give a description of his attacker and the circumstances of the shooting. While the couple were in their car, another car pulled up immediately behind them. A man got out and approached their car, shining a light into their faces and shooting at them. Darlene Ferrin was hit nine times and was pronounced dead when her body arrived at a local hospital.

Shortly after the shooting, a man phoned the Vallejo Police Department and claimed responsibility for it and for the previous attack. The call was traced to a pay phone across the street from the sheriff's office and within sight of Darlene Ferrin's house. During the investigation, it emerged that Ferrin may have known the man who had killed her. A white car had been seen outside her house on a number of occasions and the description of the man in the car fit with those given by other witnesses. He was a white man, about forty years old, stockily built and with brown hair.

LETTERS FROM THE KILLER
A few days later, letters were received by three different San Francisco newspapers, signed by the Zodiac and including a symbol of a circle with a cross over it, interpreted by some as being a representation of the wheel of the zodiac. Each letter contained a part of a code and a message from the killer saying that, if his letters were not printed on the front pages of the newspapers, he would go on a rampage, not stopping until he had killed twelve more people.

Another young couple, Bryan Hartnell, age twenty, and Cecelia Shepard, age twenty-two, were attacked on September 27, 1969, while they were picnicking by Lake Berryessa in the Napa Valley, about 20 miles (30 km) from Vallejo. A man with a gun and wearing a mask with the zodiac symbol on it approached them and said he was an escaped convict. He demanded their car and, after tying them up, stabbed both of them multiple times. Hartnell survived, but Cecelia Shepard died of her wounds two days later. The killer phoned the police to report the crime himself and to tell them he had left them a message at the scene to show he was really the Zodiac. He had written the dates of his previous attacks on the door of the couple's car and drawn the zodiac symbol before, apparently, walking casually away.

The last murder attributed to the Zodiac occurred on October 11, 1969, when the same gun that had been used in the previous shootings was used to kill the San Francisco taxi driver Paul Stine. He was shot in the head by the passenger in his cab. Witnesses watched the murderer take Stine's wallet and keys and rip a piece of cloth from his shirt, before wiping the inside of the cab down with it and walking away. The police were on the scene within minutes, but failed to catch the man. One police officer failed to stop a man who was leaving the scene and could possibly have been the killer because he didn't match an inaccurate description given by the radio dispatcher.

ME = 37, SFPD = 0

More letters arrived from the Zodiac, some including pieces of the cloth from

TV SHOW

The most bizarre incident involving the Zodiac was when a man claiming to be him arranged to speak to Melvin Belli, a prominent lawyer, on a TV talk show. Belli had a long conversation with the man and police traced the call to a mental institution, leading them to conclude that it was a hoax. Belli received a Christmas card that year from the Zodiac that contained a piece of a victim's, Paul Stine's, shirt and a message to say that he wanted to be helped but something in his head was stopping him.

In one letter, the Zodiac threatened to blow up a school bus and bragged about how he had been chatting to some policemen shortly after shooting the cab driver.

Paul Stine's shirt to prove they were authentic. In one letter he threatened to blow up a school bus and bragged about how he had been chatting to some policemen shortly after shooting the cab driver.

Messages continued to be received throughout 1970, mostly addressed to the *San Francisco Sun* journalist Paul Avery, who had been covering the case. A number of attacks were investigated as being by the same man, but none could be definitively attributed to him. Then, after March 1971, the messages stopped arriving. After a gap of nearly three years, the *Chronicle* received one final message, which ended with the line, "Me = 37, SFPD = 0," as if the killer had been keeping score and was claiming he had killed a total of thirty-seven people. Numerous hoax messages were received after this, but there were no further murders that could be attributed to him and no further contact that could be authenticated. For reasons that remain unknown, the Zodiac had disappeared.

SUSPECTS

Over the years, the San Francisco Police Department is estimated to have investigated more than two thousand people as suspects in the killings. One of their main suspects was Arthur Leigh Allen, the man also identified as the killer in books by Robert Graysmith, who had worked as a cartoonist at the *San Francisco*

Chronicle at the time of the murders and had maintained an interest in the case right from the beginning. Graysmith initially used a false name for the man he identified as the killer to protect himself from being sued.

By the time of the 2007 movie, *Zodiac*, which was based on the books and starred Jake Gyllenhaal as Graysmith, Allen had died, allowing the filmmakers to name him. The only problem was that the evidence against Allen was entirely circumstantial. He had continued to maintain his innocence up until his death and, in 2002, DNA analysis carried out on the saliva found on the stamps used for the letters sent by the killer did not match Allen's DNA. It ruled him out of the police investigation as a suspect, even if some, including Graysmith, are not fully convinced he was not involved in the murders in some capacity.

Of the numerous other suspects investigated by both the police and amateur detectives who have taken an interest in the case, only a handful can be linked directly to it and then only by circumstantial evidence. More than forty years after the crimes were committed, it appears unlikely that any fresh evidence will come to light. Should that happen, at least the police now have the advantage of being able to use the DNA evidence obtained from the Zodiac's letters. In the meantime, the man behind these terrible murders remains a mystery, together with any motive he may have had for committing them, and the police file on the case remains open.

ZODIAC SPEAKING
Almost all of the Zodiac's letters began with the phrase, "This is the Zodiac speaking."

IS LORD LUCAN STILL ALIVE?

November 7, 1974

Clue: Lucan's younger brother thought he had escaped to Africa

Main players: The playboy earl, the Clermont set, Lady Lucan, and Sandra Rivett

Verdict: Whatever happened, a murderer escaped punishment

More than forty years after Lord Lucan went missing, the case continues to fascinate the British public, at least if stories about him in the newspapers are anything to go by. Whenever a sighting of a man vaguely resembling him comes to light from some far-flung part of the world, or a snippet of new information is revealed after all these years, it is splashed across the front pages under headlines like, "I Helped Lord Lucan Live a Secret Life in Africa" or "UK Expat Denies He Is Lucan." The members of the old aristocracy may have lost much of their power and prestige these days, but they can still enthrall us, particularly if there is some lurid story or juicy gossip associated with them. Lucan managed to provide us with plenty of both and, in

By 1974, Lord Lucan's life began to spiral out of control. As well as being broke, he was separated from his wife and involved in a bitter battle for the custody of their three children.

photographs of him, he certainly looked the part. He usually had an aloof and disinterested expression on his face, as if barely able to conceal his disdain for those of inferior breeding. With his upright military bearing and carefully groomed moustache, he gave the impression of having stepped out of the pages of a Victorian novel, one in which he had squandered the family fortune and was described as being a cad and a scoundrel. What tends to get downplayed in stories about the missing playboy earl is that, in all likelihood, he brutally murdered the twenty-eight-year-old Sandra Rivett, and the only reason why anybody would want to find him is so that he could be held accountable for such a terrible crime.

THE PLAYBOY EARL

Richard John Bingham, Seventh Earl of Lucan, known as John to his family and Lucky to his friends, was an aristocrat through and through. He was educated at Eton and commissioned in the Coldstream Guards, then, on leaving the army, joined a merchant bank. In 1960, at the age of twenty-six, he left the bank

casino operated by Aspinall in Berkeley Square, London. Most of the members of the club were much like Lucan; they were wealthy, well-connected, and had nothing much better to do than waste their time and money playing cards for high stakes and having affairs with each other's wives.

The main problem with being a gambler is that you don't win all the time, and, in games like chemin de fer, the odds are always stacked in favor of the house. At the Clermont Club, Aspinall appears to have been fleecing his customers by

to pursue a career with working hours that probably suited his lifestyle quite a bit better. After winning £26,000 playing the card game chemin de fer, at a private party hosted by John Aspinall, he decided to quit his job in the bank and become a full-time gambler.

By 1964, he was married and had inherited his father's title and money. He had become part of the set associated with the Clermont Club, a

dishonest means and Lucan, after his initial successes, began to lose heavily. Like all compulsive gamblers, rather than quit, he increased the stakes and, in doing so, not only lost all his money, but ran up some serious debts as well. His life began to spiral out of control and, by 1974, as well as being broke, he was separated from his wife and involved in a bitter battle with her for the custody of their three children.

LUCAN'S WIFE
Lucan met his future wife, Veronica Duncan, in early 1963. They were engaged before the end of the year.

NANNY IS ATTACKED

Sandra Rivett normally had Thursday evenings off from her job as nanny to Lady Lucan's children and would often go out with her boyfriend. But on Thursday, November 7, 1974, she was at the Lucans' house because she had swapped her night off and had gone out on the Wednesday instead. Shortly before nine o'clock in the evening, she went down to the basement kitchen to make a cup of tea for Lady Lucan. There she was attacked from behind by a man wielding a piece of lead pipe. He struck her several times on the back of her head, shattering her skull and killing her almost immediately.

According to the account she would later give to the police, Lady Lucan then went down to the basement to see what had happened, having waited fifteen minutes or so for the tea. There she found her husband, who had moved out of the family home the previous year but still had a key. He attacked her with the pipe, causing her serious injury, then appeared to suddenly come to his senses and stopped, apologizing to her for what he had done. She managed to get out of the house and raised the alarm in a local pub and, by the time the police arrived a few minutes later, Lord Lucan had left. They found Rivett's dead body in a large mail bag on the kitchen floor.

Shortly afterward, Lucan made a phone call to his mother from a private number in London, which the police were unable to trace. He told her that a terrible accident had taken place at the house in Lower Belgrave Street and asked her to go over there to look after the children. The story he told, which he would repeat a number of times to different people, was that he had been outside the house and, on looking through the window, had seen a man attacking Rivett and his wife. By the time he had gotten into the house, the man had run out through the back and climbed over a wall to get away. In their investigation, the police could find no sign of the presence of another man in the kitchen or of anybody having climbed the wall. They also found that, to be able to see into the basement from

> **Sandra Rivett was attacked from behind by a man wielding a lead pipe. He struck her several times on the back of her head, shattering her skull and killing her instantly.**

the sidewalk, a person outside would have to crouch down on their knees. As the light bulb in the kitchen had been removed, it would have been almost impossible to make out anything inside anyway. They came to the obvious conclusion that Lucan had murdered Rivett, possibly mistaking her for his wife, the intended victim, in the dark.

AFTER THE MURDER

The police later reconstructed some of Lucan's movements on the night of the murder. After making the phone call to his mother in London, he drove down to East Sussex, in the south of England, in a car he had borrowed from one of his friends at the Clermont Club. There he visited the house of Ian and Susan Maxwell-Scott to make a number of phone calls and write letters. After telling Susan Maxwell-Scott the same story he had told his mother, he left the house. The car, a Ford Corsair, was found a few days later near the port of Newhaven on the south coast. There were blood stains on the front seat and a piece of lead piping, similar to the one the police had found at the murder scene, in the trunk, but no sign of Lucan.

was arrested in New Zealand. It turned out to be John Stonehouse, an MP who had faked his suicide in order to escape his debts and run away with his mistress. Stonehouse was returned to Britain and to the jailhouse, but no such resolution was achieved in the Lucan case. Years later, in 2003, excited reports emerged in the newspapers that claimed that Lord Lucan had finally been tracked down in Goa, India. They were proved false when the man in question, an aging hippie known locally as Jungly Barry, turned out to be a folk singer from Huddersfield in West Yorkshire, England.

THE MISSING EARL

The police initially thought he could have taken the ferry from Newhaven to France or committed suicide in a fit of remorse over what he had done. But their investigations turned up no solid clues regarding his fate. Of all the numerous possible sightings of him over the years, all have proved to be dead ends.

Not long after he disappeared, an English man fitting his description

WEALTHY FRIENDS

One of the most persistent rumors to have emerged from the affair is that Lucan's friends at the Clermont Club, including John Aspinall and the incredibly wealthy financier Sir James Goldsmith, helped him to get out of Britain and set him up in a new life somewhere in Africa. There was no proof to back up these rumors and Goldsmith, before his death in 1997, was famous for using every legal means available to sue anybody who made such a suggestion. In more recent years, safe in the knowledge that Goldsmith could no longer sue anybody, a few clues have emerged that suggest that there may be some truth in the rumor.

A woman who worked as Aspinall's secretary in the early 1980s has claimed that she booked flights for Lucan's children to go out to Kenya and Gabon in Africa. According to her story, the details were arranged in phone calls between Aspinall, Goldsmith, and Lucan, and the trips were organized so that Lucan could see his children. It is impossible to know if the secretary was telling the truth, even if, in interviews with the BBC, her account appeared to be reliable. George Bingham, Lucan's oldest son, certainly doesn't believe her, saying that, while he has been to Africa on a number of occasions, he has never been to Gabon in his life.

In further recent developments, a watch bearing an inscription to Lucan is said to have turned up in an antiques store in South Africa. Photographs show Lucan wearing a watch of the same model. But it would be simple enough to find one of them and to add an inscription in the hope of increasing its value, so it cannot be taken as definitive proof of Lucan's presence in the country. A more telling clue emerged in an interview given to the British tabloid

PRESUMED DEAD

In a recent twist on the Lucan mystery, in February 2016, the High Court in London issued a presumption of death certificate for the missing peer. This, in effect, enables Lucan's son George Bingham to inherit the earldom. The judge made the declaration on the basis that she was satisfied that Lucan had not been known to be alive for at least seven years. However, it was stated that the death certificate can be revoked if the peer reappears. The hearing also revealed that the police were no longer actively looking for Rivett's murderer, although the case has not been closed.

newspaper the *Daily Mirror* in 2012 by Hugh Bingham, Lucan's younger brother, who has not spoken of the disappearance before and now lives in South Africa himself. He told the newspaper that he thought Lucan had escaped to Africa and, although he had not seen or spoken to him since before the murder in Belgravia, thought he could still be alive. If Lucan were still alive he would now be in his early eighties and, if found, could still face justice for the crime he committed nearly forty years ago.

If Lucan was found to be alive, it would put an end to this sorry saga and show that, no matter how well-connected Lucan might have been, he is as responsible for his actions as the rest of us.

DID A DINGO TAKE BABY AZARIA?

August 17, 1980

Clue: A crying baby is snatched in the Australian outback

Main players: The Chamberlain family, the Australian media, and the judicial system

Outcome: It took thirty years, but justice finally prevailed

On the evening of November 17, 1980, the Chamberlain family, Mark and Lindy and their three children, Aidan, Reagan, and nine-week-old baby Azaria, were combining those two favorite Aussie pastimes of camping in the bush and having a barbecue. They had pitched their tent in a designated camping area near Uluru, or Ayers Rock, as it was still known at the time. They were with five other families, who were doing much the same thing, and were cooking dinner at the communal barbecue area no more than 80 feet (25 m) from their tent. It was just about eight o'clock. The tragic events of the following few minutes would remain with them for the rest of their lives. The ensuing legal battle would not be settled until the publication of the report by the fourth inquest held on June 12, 2012, almost thirty-two years later.

THE FATAL FEW MINUTES

Lindy Chamberlain would later describe how she carried Azaria to the tent, where four-year-old Reagan was already asleep, to put her to bed for the night and then went to the car to get a can of beans for Aidan. Shortly after she got back to the barbecue, she heard a baby crying and, as the noise was coming from the direction of the tent, she went back there to check on Azaria. Other people at the barbecue also reported hearing the baby. Then, very shortly after Lindy had gone over toward the tent, they heard her shout, "My God, a dingo has got my baby." Lindy had apparently seen a dingo disappearing into the darkness carrying Azaria in its mouth and initially tried to follow the animal in the direction she thought it had taken, before coming back to the tent to check if the baby was really gone.

Very shortly after Lindy had gone over toward the tent, they heard her shout, "My God, a dingo has got my baby." Lindy had apparently seen a dingo disappearing into the darkness carrying Azaria in its mouth.

DINGO
The dingo is a wild dog found in Australia. Attacks on children are rare but have happened on a number of occasions.

A search of the area around the camp ground and the sand dunes beyond began immediately, with park rangers and local police arriving within twenty minutes to help find the baby girl. The following day, a local man, known to be an expert tracker, found dingo prints at the rear of the Chamberlains' tent and at a number of places around the campsite. He described one set of tracks as showing that the dingo had been carrying something heavy and, in a few cases, dragging it along the ground. The trail was lost, but the tracker said that at the time he was sure that a dingo had taken the baby, a view shared by everybody else who had been present at the campground that night.

DOUBTS ARE RAISED

Despite this, doubts about the version of events given by Lindy Chamberlain began to surface not long afterward. Dingoes were not known to have behaved that way before and were thought to be incapable of carrying the weight of a baby for any distance at all. A week after Azaria went missing, her diaper, jumpsuit, and the onesie she had been wearing were found, but not the jacket Lindy had said she was wearing over the rest of her clothes. Intense speculation began in the media about the case, focusing particularly on how a dingo could have removed the baby's clothes and why the jacket was not found. The Chamberlains were members of the religious sect of Seventh-day Adventists and articles in some newspapers suggested that they had been involved in some sort of strange religious practices that involved sacrificing a baby. The name Azaria was even said to mean "sacrifice in the wilderness," which, although completely untrue, added fuel to the fire of public opinion. In addition, the behavior of Mark and Lindy Chamberlain in televised interviews was said not to be consistent with that of grieving parents.

INQUEST AND CONVICTION

The first coroner's inquest was held in December 1980 against a backdrop of media sensationalism. While it came to the conclusion that a dingo had killed Azaria, doubts remained over the baby's clothing. The coroner gave the opinion that they must have been removed by somebody, remarking that, after the baby was dead, her body "was taken from the possession of the dingo and disposed of by an unknown method, by a person or person's name unknown."

After the coroner's verdict, a forensic examination of the Chamberlains' car found stains of fetal blood, which could only have come from an infant, under the front passenger seat. Tears in Azaria's jumpsuit, according to an expert, were consistent with the cuts made by a sharp metal blade, not the teeth of a dingo. Lindy was charged with the murder of her daughter and Michael with being an accessory to murder. At the subsequent trial, the evidence obtained by the forensic investigation and the testimony of expert witnesses outweighed the witness statements of the people who

> **Forensic examination of the Chamerlains' car found stains of fetal blood, which could only have come from an infant, under the front passenger seat.**

had been at the campground at the time, and both were found guilty as charged. Lindy was sentenced to life imprisonment and Michael was given a suspended sentence.

RELEASED FROM JAIL

Questions about the validity of the forensic evidence were raised almost as soon as Lindy was sent to jail. The tests that found blood in the Chamberlains' car were shown to be wildly inaccurate, with all sorts of other liquids providing exactly the same results as blood stains. If this was not enough for the case to be reopened, the discovery of Azaria's jacket near the site of a number of dingo dens certainly was because it tended to confirm that Lindy had been telling the truth about Azaria's clothing that day. Lindy was released from jail pending an appeal, having already served almost three years of her sentence. At a hearing held in September 1988, all convictions against both her and her husband were reversed.

MEDIA SENSATIONALISM

The case has subsequently been used as an example of how an investigation and trial can be influenced by media sensationalism. Particularly striking was the uproar surrounding the Chamberlains' unconventional religious beliefs. Without the involvement of journalists, who appear to have been

THE CHAMBERLAINS
The media depicted Mark and Lindy Chamberlain as being indifferent to their daughter's death.

more interested in twisting the facts to get a better story, it now appears unlikely that charges would have been brought against the Chamberlains in the first place. The police initially accepted the statements made by witnesses at the campground as being credible and, had they stuck to this view, a miscarriage of justice could have been avoided. The subsequent forensic evidence would most likely not have been given precedence over the eyewitness statements had not both the press and public opinion been so united in accepting anything that appeared to point toward the Chamberlains' guilt.

A fourth and final inquest was held in 2012 to examine evidence of dingo attacks on children, which are not very common, but have occurred on a number of occasions, particularly in places where the dingoes have become used to humans through regular contact. In the coroner's report, published on June 12, 2012, it was made clear that Azaria Chamberlain was killed by dingoes and her death certificate was amended accordingly.

WHO WAS THE MYSTERIOUS PIANO MAN?

2005

Clue: A young man was found wandering on a beach

Main players: A piano player, the Kent police, and mental health services

Verdict: It all sorted itself out in the end

The English seaside town of Sheerness on the Isle of Sheppey is rarely mentioned in the British press, a fact that makes it a surprising setting for a story that was reported around the world. On April 7, 2005, it suddenly burst onto the stage for its fifteen minutes of fame over a relatively minor incident that nevertheless caught the attention of the public because of its strange and mysterious nature. A young man wearing a suit and tie was seen wandering on the beach. Although he obviously did not present a threat to anybody, the police were called because he appeared to be disorientated and confused. When he was approached, he was found to be soaking wet and was either unable or unwilling to respond to any of the questions he was asked. Out of concern for his safety, thinking that he had either attempted to kill himself or was contemplating suicide, the police picked him up and took him to the psychiatric unit of the Medway Maritime Hospital in Gillingham.

THE PIANO MAN

If that was all there was to the story, it would have struggled to make the front page of the *Sheerness Times Guardian* let alone getting picked up by numerous international news agencies. What set it apart was what happened next. In an effort to communicate with the young man, one of the nurses in the psychiatric unit gave him a pencil and some paper, hoping he would be able to respond in

> "But there is much more to the story than that which has so far appeared in the press—the story of a young man who wanted to see the world, but got lost on the way. It's not an uncommon story. Millions of parents have lost their children by trying to force them into lives like their own. The only thing unique this time around is the result."
>
> —From *Der Spiegel* website, August 30, 2005

writing even if he could not speak. Rather than writing a message, he drew a picture of a piano and, when he was sat in front of one, began to play. Journalists latched on to this ability, reporting that he played for hours at a time and that he could be a concert pianist who had lost his memory or had some sort of mental breakdown. The photograph published alongside the story showed a tall, thin, fair-haired young man with a lost expression on his face, described in the newspapers as being that of a sensitive and tormented artist.

Despite the photograph being widely published, both in Britain and in many countries around the world, nobody recognized the young man. He became known as the Piano Man and, in an attempt to trace his identity, the photograph was sent to orchestras and other musical groups in Europe and farther afield. Various leads were followed up; he was thought at different times to be a Czech musician, a French busker, and an Italian mime artist. A helpline was set up in an effort to deal with the public response. As well as taking calls from people who genuinely thought they knew who he was, there were also the usual array of loonies who felt the need to share their opinions on the case with anyone who would listen.

PIANIST
The young man who was found wandering on the beach couldn't speak but he did play the piano for hours, it was reported.

DIFFERENT DIAGNOSES

Expert opinion was as confused as the public over the Piano Man and came up with a range of different diagnoses to explain what was wrong with him. Some, perhaps having seen the movie *Rain Man* too many times, thought he was someone suffering from autism who had an exceptional talent in a particular field. One eminent psychiatrist suggested he had undergone a psychotic episode that had manifested itself as an inability to speak. Another thought he was nothing but a hoax, putting it all on just to draw attention to himself. If true, then the Piano Man was very good at it. Details emerged that supported this theory,

SHEERNESS
The town hit the headlines after the Piano Man was found wandering on the beach.

including the fact that, when he was first found, all the labels had been removed from the clothes he was wearing. It looked like an effort to prevent authorities from being able to track down his identity rather than the actions of a man in the middle of some sort of mental breakdown.

MYSTERY SOLVED

After four months, nobody who knew the Piano Man's identity had come forward; no members of his family, no former school or college friends, no former work colleagues. Interpreters had spoken in a variety of different languages to him and, even though he had shown some response to Norwegian, little else had been achieved. Then he woke up one morning in the middle of August and began to speak. He said his name was Andreas Grassi and that he was twenty years old and came from a village near Waldmünchen in eastern Bavaria, not far from the border with the Czech Republic. Immediately prior to his discovery on the beach, he had been working in France, but he had no idea how he had gotten to England or how he had ended up on the beach.

FLOWN HOME

Before the press became aware of these developments, the hospital contacted the German Embassy in London and, after his identity was confirmed, he was flown home. It turned out that his piano-playing ability had been exaggerated and, while he was not a bad musician, he was certainly no virtuoso. After his family had lost touch with him while he was in France, they had reported him as being missing to the French police, to be told that, as he was over eighteen, there was nothing much they could do about it. The photograph of him had been published widely in Germany, as it had across Europe, but nobody in his family had recognized him because he had changed his appearance simply by dyeing his hair.

BACKSTORY

Once the identity of the Piano Man was revealed, stories emerged about his upbringing and background. He appeared to be an unhappy young man who had grown up on a dairy farm in Bavaria. He was something of a misfit in the farming community, telling his school friends that he might be gay and dreaming of leading a more glamorous life than one that involved milking the cows twice a day. At eighteen, he had opted to work in a care home for people with mental illness rather than do military service and had hoped to pursue a career in TV. Nothing much came of his ambitions and, after finishing work in the care home, he moved to France and got another similar job.

Grassi and his family did not want to speak to the media and mostly communicated through a lawyer. According to his parents, he had no memory of what had happened to him and they vigorously denied that he had been involved in any sort of hoax. As neither Grassi nor anybody else has ever attempted to capitalize on the publicity generated in the media, it would appear that they are most probably telling the truth.

According to his parents, he had no memory of what had happened to him and they vigorously denied that he had been in any sort of a hoax.

WHY DID AIR FRANCE FLIGHT 447 CRASH?

June 1, 2009

Clue: The plane encountered a belt of severe weather

Main players: Three Air France pilots and a lot of confusion

Verdict: What should have been a minor incident got out of control

Flying is often said to be the safest method of transport and, in truth, in recent years the record of the major passenger carriers has been impressive. But when an accident happens, it tends to be a catastrophic one, as was the case with Air France Flight 447, which crashed into the Atlantic Ocean on June 1, 2009, while en route from Rio de Janeiro to Paris with the loss of all 216 passengers and twelve crew. The shock of such a terrible loss of life was made even worse by the mysterious nature of the accident. The plane, an Airbus 330-200, went missing somewhere over the Atlantic between Brazil and the African continent, beyond the reach of radar coverage and without sending a distress call. It is rare for a passenger plane to disappear so completely, and great efforts have been made to understand the circumstances of the crash in order to prevent anything similar from happening again.

THE BLACK BOXES

Despite a massive search, it took five days for any wreckage to be found. The plane had gone down in a remote and very deep part of the ocean, where depths reach 15,000 feet (4,500 m), so locating the flight recorders proved an almost impossible task. In the end, they were found in May 2011 by autonomous underwater vehicles, robots that can operate at great depth without an operator. The data recovered from these flight recorders, sometimes known as the black boxes, has finally enabled air crash investigators to get an understanding of what happened. The plane had encountered a belt of severe weather, which played a role in the crash as it affected important readings provided by

The initial problem of severe weather affecting important readings was then compounded by serious mistakes made by the pilots. These human errors caused an otherwise perfectly airworthy plane to crash.

THE PLANE
Air France A330-203 F-GZCP lands at
Paris Charles de Gaulle Airport in 2007.
The aircraft was destroyed two years later
when the plane plunged into the Atlantic.

the plane's instruments to the three pilots
of the plane. This initial problem was
then compounded by serious mistakes
made by the pilot in control of the
aircraft at the time, and also by the
failure of the other two pilots to realize
what was happening until it was too late.
These human errors caused an otherwise
perfectly airworthy plane to crash.

Under normal circumstances, pilots
would navigate around weather systems
to avoid the worst of any potential
turbulence, but in the case of AF447 it
seems that several smaller storms masked
a much more severe one, so the pilots
were unaware of it until it was too late to
avoid. At this time the senior pilot, Marc
Dubois, was taking a break and was not
in the cockpit. The least experienced of

the three pilots, Pierre-Cédric Bonin,
was flying the plane, with David Robert
sitting in the copilot's seat. Bonin may
have been the most junior of the pilots,
but he still had almost three thousand
hours' experience in passenger jets and,
between him and Robert, there really
should not have been a problem even
though they hit a tropical thunderstorm.
Over the next four minutes, the actions
taken by Bonin and the failure of Robert,
and Dubois, once he had been called
back to the cockpit, to spot what Bonin
was doing in time, was what ultimately
caused the crash.

NOSE UP
The first signs of a problem occurred
in the airspeed indicators, which went
blank, causing the autopilot to give the
control of the plane to Bonin. This is
thought to have been caused by ice
forming on the plane's pitot tubes,
pressure gauges on the outside of the
aircraft that measure air velocity.

DROPPED OUT OF THE SKY

The French air crash investigators, the Bureau d'Enquêtes et d'Analyses, blamed the crash on the pilots for continuing to climb despite stall warnings in the cockpit. By doing so, the plane lost so much speed that, in effect, it ceased to fly and dropped out of the sky.

Once Bonin had control, he should have maintained a constant airspeed by holding the plane at a set pitch and maintaining a constant thrust. Instead of doing this, he pulled back on the control stick to bring the nose of the plane up and kept it there, causing a steady drop in airspeed. Robert did not notice what Bonin was doing until a stall warning sounded, at which point he told Bonin to move down.

In modern jets, the control stick does not actually operate the plane directly, but instead uses what is known as fly-by-wire technology in which the movements of the stick made by the pilot are sent to computers that then send commands to the engine and hydraulic systems. Once Bonin had pulled back on the stick, the computers would have continued to keep the nose of the plane up until instructed to do otherwise by another movement of the stick. Even

after he had been told to descend, Bonin, apparently thinking that the plane was close to the ground when it was actually above thirty thousand feet, pulled the stick back a second time. The plane was now effectively in a stall, losing altitude more quickly than it was flying through the air. Dubois returned to the cockpit, but by the time he and Robert had realized Bonin was still flying the plane with the nose up, it was too late to do anything about it.

TOO LATE

The only course of action that could have prevented a crash was for the plane to be put into a dive so that it would pick up speed and get out of the stall. Robert took over the controls once he realized this, but they were already too close to the surface of the ocean for him to be able to dive. His last recorded words were, "Damn it, we're going to crash. This can't be happening." Unfortunately for him and for everybody else on the plane, it very much was happening and, within a matter of a few seconds, the plane hit the water.

CHANGES

The ensuing air crash investigation report, published on July 5, 2102, recommended a variety of procedural changes, which many airlines around the world had already implemented to prevent any chance of another similar accident. Airbus now uses a different

---

The plane was now effectively in a stall, losing altitude more quickly than it was flying through the air. Robert's last recorded words were, "Damn it, we're going to crash. This can't be happening."

> *"Modern airliners are not supposed to fall out of the sky. Especially if they are highly automated, fly-by-wire passenger jets such as the Airbus 330. Like the unsinkable* Titanic, *the Airbus 330 was considered an unstallable aeroplane. It was equipped with digital systems that unerringly corrected for pilot error as well as any buffeting caused by bad weather. Until one fatal night two years ago, the Airbus 330 had had an exemplary safety record. What caused the Airbus 330 used on Air France Flight 447 from Rio de Janeiro to Paris to plunge into the Atlantic, killing all 228 people on board, remains one of the biggest mysteries in aviation history."*
>
> —From an article in *The Economist* on March 25, 2011

design of pitot tubes to eliminate the risk of them icing up. These measures, together with a general awareness of the need for all the pilots of a plane to be fully aware of what the others are doing at all times, have further improved the safety of flying. But, however sophisticated the technology becomes and however advanced the safety procedures are, human error can never be eliminated completely. Life just isn't that simple.

PITOT TUBE
Ice on the plane's pitot tubes started the sequence of events that ended in disaster.

WHO WAS THE FOREST BOY OF BERLIN?

2011

Clue: A young man arrives in Berlin from the nearby forest

Main players: Ray and Robin

Verdict: It all came out in the wash

The similarities between the stories of the Forest Boy of Berlin and Kaspar Hauser (see page 106) are obvious to anybody familiar with them and go well beyond the simple fact that they both occurred in Germany. Those of a more suspicious nature, who would most probably think of Hauser as a fraud in the first place, might well have come to the conclusion that the Forest Boy had read about him and decided to give it a try himself. Why anybody would want to do so is difficult to know, particularly as Hauser's story ended tragically with his death either by murder or suicide.

Whatever the truth of the matter, those people who thought it was a hoax right from the start were proved right when, on June 16, 2012, the true identity of the Forest Boy was revealed. All it had taken to solve the mystery was for a photograph of him to be published, which was recognized by family and friends immediately, leading to the question of why this had not been done right at the start. It would have saved a whole lot of messing around.

THE STORY
On September 5, 2011, a young man turned up at the City Hall in Berlin with a rucksack and a tent claiming he had lived in the forests to the south of the city for the previous five years. He spoke in English, saying his name was Ray and that his parents, Doreen and Ryan, were both dead. Ever since his mother had died in a car accident five years previously, he had been living rough in the forest with his father. After Ray's father had also died, he buried the body and did what his father had told him to do, "walk north until you reach civilization and then ask for help." It had taken him five days to walk to Berlin and, when he got there, he had nothing on him that could identify him. The only personal possession he appeared to have was an amulet inscribed with the initials R and D,

[*"This is no joke any more. He made right fools of us."*

—**Quote from a Berlin police spokesman**]

which he wore around his neck. Other than that, he was a complete mystery.

Doubts were immediately raised about the story Ray told to the Berlin authorities. When he first arrived, he hardly looked as though he had been living rough or had spent the previous five days walking across Germany. He was clean and tidy, in much better physical condition than might be expected, and the tent he had with him looked almost brand new. Nevertheless, under the circumstances, there was little else that the authorities could do, as he was thought to be seventeen years old,

LIVING IN THE FOREST

The young man claimed he had been living rough in the forests to the south of Berlin.

A young man turned up at the City Hall in Berlin with a rucksack and a tent claiming he had lived in the forests to the south of the city for the previous five years.

than to take him into youth custody. He was sent to a social care facility for young homeless people where he was looked after while the Berlin police made inquiries in an effort to establish his identity. While this was happening, the media got hold of the story and it was reported widely in Germany and many other countries around the world. Ray was called the "Forest Boy" by the newspapers, and the circumstances of his arrival in Berlin and his appearance

INVENTED STORY

Once the hoax had been exposed and Ray's real identity as Robin van Helsum had been revealed, it turned out that he had gone on a trip to Germany with a friend from his hometown of Hengelo in the Netherlands. After a few days, the friend had decided to go home and Robin carried on and, for reasons known only to himself, traveled to Berlin with an invented story. His family back in Holland had reported him as being missing three days before he arrived at the City Hall, but, because he was over eighteen, no action was taken over the report and the connection with the Forest Boy was not made.

discussed in detail. But, despite the coverage, nobody came forward with any further information about him, so he stayed in the care home.

SEARCH FOR REAL IDENTITY

The Berlin police clearly did not believe Ray's story and made strenuous efforts to discover his real identity. Linguistic experts were brought in to listen to his voice in the hope of establishing where he was from by recognizing the slight accent in his spoken English. The consensus of opinion was that he was from the Czech Republic, which tallied with his own account of having arrived in Berlin from the south. But, as events would subsequently demonstrate, this proved to be very wide of the mark.

After several months, he was persuaded to give a DNA sample, but its analysis revealed nothing other than that he was of European origin, which had been obvious all along. His DNA profile and fingerprints were compared with details held in international databases, which simply showed that he did not have a criminal record anywhere in Europe. In fact, every avenue investigated by the police failed to find anything out about him at all, until, in a move described as a "last resort," the photograph was finally released on June 12, 2012, nine months after Ray had been taken into custody.

ROBIN VAN HELSUM

Within a few days, a number of people recognized him, including his step-mother. She contacted the police to tell them that he was Robin van Helsum, who, in reality, was twenty years old and came from the town of Hengelo in the Netherlands. When confronted by the truth, Robin owned up to the hoax, although he has yet to explain what he thought he was playing at.

SHOCKED BY THE FRAUD

As he was twenty, Robin was now in a fair amount of trouble. A spokesman for the care home described Robin as being, "a nice young man" and said everybody

Some of the German newspapers were less than sympathetic once the hoax was exposed, changing Robin's nickname from the "Forest Boy" to the "Lying Dutchman."

there had gotten along with him very well and were shocked to find out he was a fraudster. As he is a citizen of another EU country, the German authorities don't have the power to throw him out of the country.

COURT CASE

After he was evicted from his care home, he disappeared for a while, believed to be traveling around until he was found working in a Burger King in Berlin.

CITY HALL

Ray arrived at Berlin City Hall with nothing more than a rucksack and a tent.

On September 26, 2013, a court case was brought against him in Berlin. It was decided not to convict him of fraud if he agreed to 150 hours of community service. In the end he got off lightly, but no doubt he was given a strict talking to and told to go away and not do it again.

FURTHER READING

In general, the most useful single book for any earnest student of history is a good historical atlas. *The Times Atlas of World History* is probably the best. For general reference and fact checking without expense or inconvenience, the internet is a remarkable source, and Wikipedia (www. wikipedia.org) in particular is a great starting point, although its nature as an open-source encyclopedia to which almost anyone can contribute means you should pay close attention to the references and footnotes if you want to make the most of it. You will also find some excellent links and information at www.bbc. co.uk/history.

For the history of ancient civilizations, there is a wealth of information at the internet Classics Archive (http://classics.mit. edu/), which contains English translations of "441 works of classical literature by fifty-nine different authors." It is an absolute treasure trove for the works of Greek and Roman historians.

BOOKS

Aveni, Anthony. *Nasca: Eighth Wonder of the World*. London: British Museum Press, 2000.

Baigent, Michael, Richard Leigh, and Henry Lincoln. *The Holy Blood and the Holy Grail*. London: Jonathan Cape, 1982.

Barber, Richard. *The Holy Grail: The History of a Legend*. London: Allen Lane, 2004.

Beattie, Owen, and John Geiger. *Frozen in Time: The Fate of the Franklin Expedition*. London: Bloomsbury, 1987.

Begg, Paul. *Jack the Ripper: The Definitive History*. London: Longman, 2003.

Begg, Paul. *The Mary Celeste: The Greatest Mystery of the Sea*. London: Longman, 2006.

Bruce, J. Campbell. *Escape from Alcatraz*. New York: McGraw-Hill, 1963.

Bryson, John. *Evil Angels*. Victoria: Penguin Books (Australia), 1986.

Bugliosi, Vincent. *Four Days in November: The Assassination of President John F. Kennedy*. New York: W.W. Norton and Company, 2007.

Butcher, Geoffrey. *Next to a Letter from Home: Major Glenn Miller's Wartime Band*. London: Mainstream Publishing, 1986.

Carroll, Maureen. *Earthly Paradises: Ancient Gardens in History and Archaeology*. London: British Museum Press, 2003.

Castleden, Rodney. *Atlantis Destroyed*. London: Routledge, 1998.

Coe, Michael D. *The Maya* (8th edition). London: Thames and Hudson, 2011.

Diamond, Jared. *Collapse: How Societies Choose to Fail or Survive*. London: Allen Lane, 2005.

Douglas-Hamilton, James. *The Truth About Rudolf Hess*. London: Mainstream Publishing, 1993

Gill, Richardson L. *The Great Maya Droughts: Life, Water and Death*. Albuquerque University of New Mexico Press, 2001.

Graysmith, Robert. *The Zodia Unmasked: The Identity of America's Most Elusive Serial Killer.* New York: Berkeley Books, 2007.

Kitchen, Martin. *Kaspar Hauser: Europe's Child.* Basingstoke: Palgrave, 2001.

Kusche, Lawrence David. *The Bermuda Triangle Solved.* London: Prometheus Publishing, 1975.

Lovell, Mary S. *The Sound of Wings: The Biography of Amelia Earhart.* London: Hutchinson, 1989.

Marchant, Jo. *Decoding the Heavens: Solving the Mystery of the World's First Computer.* London: William Heinemann, 2008.

Mattheissen, Peter. *The Snow Leopard.* New York: Viking Press, 1978.

Meadows, Anne. *Digging Up Butch and Sundance.* Lincoln: University of Nebraska Press, 1994.

Meeks, Dmitri. "Locating Punt," *in Mysterious Lands*, ed. David O'Connor and Stephen Quirke. London: Viking, 2003.

Messner, Reinhold. *My Quest for the Yeti: Confronting the Himalayas' Deepest Mystery.* London: Pan Books, 2001.

Munro-Hay, Stuart. *The Quest for the Ark of the Covenant.* London: Tauris, 2005.

Nicholl, Charles. *Leonardo da Vinci: The Flights of the Mind.* London: Allen Lane, 2004.

Parfitt, Tudor. *The Lost Tribes of Israel: The History of a Myth.* London. Weidenfeld and Nicolson, 2002.

Parker Pearson, Mike. *Stonehenge: Explaining the Greatest Stone Age Mystery.* London: Simon and Schuster, 2012.

Patton, Phil. *Dreamland: Travels Inside the Secret World of Roswell and Area 51.* New York: Villard, 1998.

Pearson, John. *The Gamblers.* London: Century, 2005.

Pryor, Francis. *Britain AD: A Quest for Arthur, England and the Anglo-Saxons.* London: HarperCollins, 2004.

Pryor, Francis. *Britain BC: Life in Britain and Ireland Before the Romans.* London. HarperCollins, 2003.

Riggs, David. *The World of Christopher Marlowe.* London: Faber & Faber, 2004.

Roberts, Alice. *The Incredible Human Journey.* London: Bloomsbury, 2009.

Sayer, Ian, and Douglas Botting. *Nazi Gold: The Story of the World's Greatest Robbery—and its Aftermath.* London: Granada, 1984.

Shapiro, James. *Contested Will: Who Wrote Shakespeare?* London: Faber & Faber, 2010.

Shaw, Ian. *The Oxford History of Ancient Egypt.* Oxford: OUP, 2000.

Stewart, Katherine. *The Story of Loch Ness.* Edinburgh: Luath, 2005.

Stringer, Chris. *The Origin of Our Species.* London: Allen Lane, 2011.

Vermes, Geza. *The Story of the Scrolls: The Miraculous Discovery and True Significance of the Scrolls.* Harmondsworth: Penguin Books, 2010.

Wilson, Ian. *The Shroud.* London: Bantam Press, 2010.

Winters, Kathleen C. *Amelia Earhart: The Turbulent Life of an American Icon.* New York: Palgrave Macmillan, 2010.

Wynn, Thomas, and Frederick L. Coolridge. *How to Think Like a Neanderthal.* Oxford: OUP, 2012.

INDEX

PICTURE CREDITS

Key: t=top, b=bottom, l=left, r=right, c=center

All images public domain unless otherwise indicated:

Alamy: 9t Rob Walls, 67br AF archive, 125b Chronicle, 139tl Photos 12.

Dreamstime: 11t Avenikolas, 20tl Dreamshot63, 29b Rzs, 48tl Nicku, 51r Gepapix, 62t Sepavo, 69bl Alberto Tentoni, 70r Perseomedusa, 73t Jarnogz, 75b Jarnogz, 79t Vincenthanna, 81t Robert Lerich, 82tl Underworld, 87tr Thakala, 97r Edwardgerges, 100 Georgios Kollidas, 136tr Carlos Soler Martinez 141tr Meunierd, 149t Jakich, 173tr Eperceptions,175t Nyvltart, 179b Kropic, 190b Dmitri Illarionov, 203t Zcello, 207b Dimitrisurkov, 215b Vitalalp, 217 Phonak.

Getty Images: 10t Alan Thorne/epa, 16r Phas, 19t De Agostini, 31t Jason Hawkes, 51t Gepapix, 55t Aristidis Vafeiadakis/Zuma Press, 61b The Bridgeman Art Library, 65bl The Bridgeman Art Library, 90br Heritage Images, 91tl UIG, 92tl UIG, 95tl DeAgostini, 105t Robert Harding World Imagery, 111r Topical Press Agency, 113b Franco Origlia/Sygma, 129t Keystone, 140t Bettmann, 150b Keystone/Stringer, 159t Hulton-Deutsch Collection, 160t Gamma-Keystone, 163t Ullstein bild, 171t Bettmann, 181tr, Bettman, 187t Corbis, 189bl, Bettmann/Corbis, 193tl Bettmann/Corbis, 195b Bettmann/Corbis, 197t Hulton-Deutsch Collection, 198tl Central Press/Stringer, 199t Hulton-Deutsch Collection, 200t Hulton-Deutsch, 205t Bettmann.

ImageMagick: 180tl ImageMagick 5.5.6 04/01/03 Q16.

iStock: 58l ZU_09.

Library of Congress: 52c Jean Antoine Valentin Foulquier, 116t, W. H. Browne, 142tl Joseph De Young, 177bl Harris & Ewing, 180l Carol M Highsmith.

Mary Evans Picture Library: 21r Mary Evans Picture Library, 53b Mary Evans Picture Library, 108-9c Interfoto Agentur, 146l Mary Evans / John Massey Stewart Collection , 157bl Weimar Archive.

National Archives and Records Administration: 167r

Science Photo Library: 25tl Mauricio Anton, 27b Equinox Graphics.

Science Museum: 43t Science Museum/Science & Society Picture Library.

Wikimedia Commons: 7r & 33r ModWilson, 13r Olaf Tausch, 14r ModWilson, 37tl D. Denisenkov, 39r Harry Burton, 40r, qwelk, 41bl Yann Forget, 57cl Marsyas, 77r N.C. Wyeth, 78l N.C. Wyeth, 85tl Aurbina, 123r Manuel González Olaechea y Franco, 155r Joann94024, 183tl Jeff dean, 208t Clem Rutter, 211r Pawel Kierzkowski, 213r Kolossos.